SCOTTISH LITERATURE INTERNATIONAL

Taking Liberties

Scottish Literature and Expressions of Freedom

EDITED BY
IAN BROWN, DAVID CLARK AND
RUBÉN JARAZO-ÁLVAREZ

Occasional Papers: Number 21
Association for Scottish Literary Studies

Published by
Scottish Literature International
Scottish Literature
7 University Gardens
University of Glasgow
Glasgow G12 8QH

Scottish Literature International is an imprint of
the Association for Scottish Literary Studies

www.asls.org.uk

ASLS is a registered charity no. SC006535

First published 2016

Text © ASLS and the individual contributors

All rights reserved. No part of this book may be
reproduced, stored in a retrieval system, or
transmitted in any form or means, electronic,
mechanical, photocopying, recording or otherwise,
without the prior permission of the
Association for Scottish Literary Studies.

A CIP catalogue for this title
is available from the British Library

ISBN 978-1-908980-21-2

Contents

Introduction   v

I: CONCEPTS AND THEMES

One   Liberty and Scottish literature   1
Alan Riach

Two   Allan Ramsay's *A Dialogue on Taste*: a painter's call to break free from English artistic conventions   19
Marion Amblard

Three   'A Common Right of Mankind' or 'A Necessary Evil'? Hume's contextualist conception of political liberty   40
Gilles Robel

Four   Versions of freedom and the theatre in Scotland since the Union   55
Jean Berton

Five   Freeing the tongue: Scots language on stage in the twentieth century   72
Ian Brown

Six   The nature of aesthetics in the works of Mary Brunton, Hugh MacDiarmid and Alasdair Gray   93
Andrew Monnickendam

II: INDIVIDUAL WRITERS AND FREEDOM

Seven   Scotland and the literary call to freedom in Mary Brunton's fiction   111
María Jesús Lorenzo Modia

Contents (continued)

Eight	Rivers, freedom and constraint in some of Stevenson's autobiographical writing *Lesley Graham*	124
Nine	Freedom and subservience in Lewis Grassic Gibbon's *Sunset Song* *Philippe Laplace*	137
Ten	Women and freedom in Muriel Spark's fiction *Margarita Estévez-Saá*	152
Eleven	Looking at America from Edinburgh Castle: postcolonial dislocations in Alice Munro's and Ann-Marie MacDonald's Scottish fictions *Pilar Somacarrera*	167
Twelve	Scottish and Galician background in Pearse Hutchinson's poetry: freedom, identity and literary landscape *José-Miguel Alonso-Giráldez*	187
Thirteen	'Shall Gaelic Die?' Iain Crichton Smith's bilingualism: entrapment or poetic freedom? *Stéphanie Noirard*	213
Fourteen	Henry Adam's *Among Unbroken Hearts* (2000): Mankind's desperate quest for freedom *Danièle Berton-Charrière*	224

Notes on Contributors   237

Introduction

IAN BROWN, DAVID CLARK AND RUBÉN JARAZO-ÁLVAREZ

One of the overarching themes evident in Scottish literary genres since the 1707 Union has been expression of conceptions of liberty or freedom or lack of liberty or freedom, variously defined. This volume explores understandings of the ways in which Scottish writers have sought to examine and represent such conceptions. While its chapters mainly focus on Scottish literary matters, a number of chapters throw complementary light, including a study of the painter Allan Ramsay's theories and writings, consideration of David Hume's views on liberty, examination of the work of Scottish–Canadian writers and an exploration of the poetry of Pearse Hutchinson, whose Scottish roots are often forgotten in the rich profusion of his links with Ireland and Iberia. The volume's focus allows it to consider, from both general perspectives and individual writers' practices, how approaches to literary practice have in Scotland often been bound up with issues of individual and collective freedom and their converse. This focus facilitates a structure into two complementary sections. The first is entitled 'Concepts and themes'; the other 'Individual writers and freedom'.

The 'Concepts and themes' chapters begin with Alan Riach's wide-ranging consideration of the use of both the word 'freedom' and the word 'liberty' in the context not only of the long view of developments over the centuries in Scottish literature, but also in the light of carefully selected insights drawn from philosophy and the practice of writers from other cultures. Entitled 'Liberty and Scottish literature', Riach's chapter opens a wide range of perspectives on broad topics addressed in this volume. Marion Amblard offers a more specific perspective on eighteenth-century Scottish approaches to the conception of freedom in art. She addresses Allan Ramsay's *A Dialogue on Taste* and considers its implications for visions of artistic freedom through resistance to the constraints of received or institutional convention. Amblard begins her chapter by observing:

> In the second half of the eighteenth century, a distinctive Scottish style of portrait painting began to emerge. Although its development coincided with that of English portraiture, the Scottish school of portrait painting has always been markedly different from its English counterpart. Both schools developed in different conditions and in the eighteenth and nineteenth centuries they did not conform to the same artistic conventions.

She moves from a detailed consideration of what she means by such differing artistic conventions to address Ramsay not only as a painter, but as a writer on painting. She sets his ideas in the context of late eighteenth-century Scottish thought in a way that casts light on debate on issues of artistic expression that would have impact on later literary practice. In the next chapter, Gilles Robel complements Amblard's discussion with his own consideration of David Hume's conception of political liberty, particularly drawing on Hume's 1741 'Of the Liberty of the Press'. The scope of Robel's chapter is marked by his three subheadings: 'Liberty and forms of government', 'Liberty and opinion', and 'Preserving Liberty'. The first three chapters, then, offer contrasting and mutually interrelated critical and theoretical perspectives on the nature of 'freedom' in Scottish culture with special emphasis on eighteenth-century thinking about the aesthetics and politics of liberty.

The next two chapters complement the first three through their focus on theatrical genres. Jean Berton offers an overview of ways in which, since the Union, Scottish playwrights have addressed issues of freedom. He does so under three headings: 'Freedom as opposed to vassalage in an occupied land'; 'The paradox of dependence and freedom'; and 'Guilt as the worst enemy of freedom'. These allow him to offer sweeping accounts which draw out themes he finds in Scottish drama across the last three centuries and in all three major theatrical languages of Scotland. Berton observes concerns with freedom recurring from writer to writer in a way that suggests the dramatic debate he is describing continues as a feature of Scottish theatrical consideration of what 'freedom' is and can be. Berton's chapter is complemented by Ian Brown's. This follows up and develops work Brown has already produced on the ways in which the use of Scots language on stage in the twentieth century has been a vehicle for freeing the expressivity of Scots theatre and its capacity to address and explore freely and directly major aspects of the Scottish experience.

Andrew Monnickendam's chapter, following the overview approach of the authors of several of the previous chapters, concludes the opening section with another wide-ranging chapter. This, while its title identifies its core concern as being with the work of Mary Brunton, Hugh MacDiarmid and Alasdair Gray, addresses fascinating perspectives on politics, religiosity and aesthetics in the relationship of the literary and visual arts and of the local and universal. In doing this, it considers mid-twentieth century contributions to the debate by, *inter alia*, Mary Ramsay and Fionn MacColla and more recent studies by Sebastian Mitchell and Rodge Glass.

The eight chapters which constitute the second section of this volume, 'Individual writers and freedom', are set out in broadly chronological order from the beginning of the nineteenth century. The first two of these discuss key conceptions of freedom in the work of nineteenth-century authors. María Jesús Lorenzo Modia addresses what she calls 'the literary call to freedom in Mary Brunton's fiction', setting Brunton's work in the larger context of women's resistance to patriarchy and the work of other women writers of her period. Lorenzo Modia makes a powerful case for Brunton as having 'a subversive agenda in terms of both gender and nation, showing that self-control is used as a means of verbalising change and as a strategy of dutiful disobedience to old patriarchal roles'. Lesley Graham's chapter on Robert Louis Stevenson explores a selection of his essays and the ways in which he uses the imagery of rivers, their flow and their constraint to express ideas of freedom or its lack. She argues Stevenson sees freedom – including 'the freedom to move forward professionally, to travel unfettered, to explore the world' – and its constraints – including 'the feeling of being hemmed in geographically; of being locked into the logic of family heredity; of being condemned to long periods of convalescence and subject to the constraints of family life' – as equally various. Graham argues that the essay form itself was for Stevenson a means of finding freedom of expression, liberty of thought.

The next two chapters address iconic Scottish writers. In his study of Lewis Grassic Gibbon's *Sunset Song*, Philippe Laplace combines consideration of freedom 'from a personal and artistic point of view' with examination of Gibbon's characters and their confrontation with freedom and subservience. He does so through the Gramscian notion of contradictory consciousness and examining Gibbon's use of the demotic as a narratological device which articulates 'his characters' ideological dispositions'. Laplace's argument considers the ways Gibbon 'expressed the basic dichotomy freedom/subservience through the image of the Land'. Margarita Estévez-Saá then draws on her research into the work of Muriel Spark and her major 2004 interview of the author along with James Brooker to explore and interrogate the many dimensions of freedom and lack of freedom Spark presents in her fiction. Estévez-Saá perceives a dichotomy there between freedom and determinism and recognises the well-established influence of 'neverthlessness' in Spark's discourse. She sees Spark's female characters attempting to live freely, but equally frustrated in trying by 'a sort of deterministic law that prevents' their absolute liberation. Meantime, as Estévez-Saá puts it, 'At the level of narrative the protagonists' aims and prospects [...] are constantly undermined and subverted by anticipatory passages that disclose their efforts' irony and sometimes futility'.

In the next two chapters, Pilar Somacarrera and José-Miguel Alonso-Giráldez examine aspects of 'Scottish' literature through alternative lenses. Somacarrera employs aspects of postcolonial theory in discussing the work of two diasporic Scots, Alice Munro and Ann-Marie MacDonald, both Canadian women authors of Scottish descent. With particular reference to their fiction set in Scotland or drawing on Scottish themes, she explores a postcolonial 'canonic anxiety' she perceives in both writers' works in relation to the freedom both of Canadian literature from Scottish literature and of Scottish literature as an autonomous phenomenon. Alonso-Giráldez's chapter re-evaluates the place of Pearse Hutchinson, usually identified as an Irish writer, in terms of his Scottish birth and affinities. His chapter provides a detailed literary and personal appreciation of a figure often neglected in discussion of 'Scottish' literature. As Somacarrera does with the diasporic writers she discusses, Alonso-Giráldez questions and challenges definitions of 'Scottishness'. Reminding us of the extent of Hutchinson's intercultural reach and, in particular, his engagement with Iberian cultures, he highlights the ways in which Hutchinson's ability to write across cultures and – through translations – languages freed him of narrow definitions of cultural identity or of the canon to which he might belong.

The final chapters of this volume each address writers who are in one sense or another liminal and explore both the freedom and the constraint that liminality can bring. The title of Stéphanie Noirard's discussion of Iain Crichton Smith's work, in offering the formulation, 'bilingualism: entrapment or poetic freedom?', highlights her approach to the issue. Sensitive reading of Smith's poetry is supported, as necessary, by syntactical analysis of the poetic structures Smith employs when writing in English, as she suggests his use of English derives part of its impact from the transposition of Gaelic grammatical structures and linguistic conventions into his English-language verse. Smith was brought up and lived on the edges of Scotland, centring himself in the very fact of the liminality and hybridity of his locations, language and art. Noirard explores the extent to which the freedom derived from his ability to transgress borders and boundaries may also have tended at times to constrain him. Issues of freedom and constraint at the margins of Scotland are also explored in the final chapter. There, Danièle Berton-Charrière continues her exploration of the playwriting of Henry Adam, in this case focussing on his 2000 play, *Among Unbroken Hearts*. Through revelatory close readings of the play, Berton-Charrière considers the ways in which Adam explores varieties of ways in which humans can seek to escape what they see as geographic or social limitations and yet find themselves entrapped by the very limits they seek to transcend. Adam introduces and explores in his play, set in the far north of the Scottish mainland, the limits of freedom and constraint embedded in his characters' very search for liberty from constraint. Whatever they seek is somehow compromised, as was the life of their junkie friend, Christie, who sought an illusory freedom through drugs only to commit suicide: Christie's escape from the constraints of life was into the ultimate constraints of death. Berton-Charrière analyses the ways in which, in Adam's play, longing for freedom can be seen to constrain and how the apparent freedom of 'Peter Pan' men is actually imprisonment. The paradox of the play's remote location, 'a dead-end open space', leaves those who seek freedom still trapped and alienated from the ability to opt for free action.

The complexity of concepts of freedom and constraint, of their expression and underlying ambiguities in Scottish literature, are explored in this volume. It recognises, without pleading 'exceptionality', the ways the approaches of Scottish artists and thinkers to ideas and versions of freedom have been and are shaped by their specific historical and cultural circumstances.

I: CONCEPTS AND THEMES

1. Liberty and Scottish Literature

ALAN RIACH

The word 'liberty' refers to a matter of value, a quality that people might wish to sustain to have greater control over their own lives, to be free from the impositions of others. This desire is entwined among the deepest roots of Scottish history, and rarely does it blossom into fruit that can be seen, held and eaten. Other ideas implied by the word include the relationship of people in society, the social contract we might enter into freely, recognition of the state of nature in which our lives exist. Understanding is a liberation. To understand human limitations is to measure them, and maybe test them. For some, the active exercise of human rights is essential to the ideal of liberty. For some, liberty implies a relation between free will and pre-determined destiny, choice and chance, the saved and the damned, and other questions of philosophical and religious import.

The word 'freedom' is probably most widely associated throughout the film-watching world with Mel Gibson's Oscar-winning *Braveheart* (1995). 'Liberty', however, has a particular resonance for readers of Scottish literature, from the phrase of Robert Burns – 'Liberty's in every blow!' – in his song 'Scots Wha Hae', which so easily becomes a cliché in the mouths of those whom another great Scottish poet has called 'Scots Wha Ha'evers' ('Havers' being a good Scots words meaning the sheer nonsense some people speak).[1] That poet, Hugh MacDiarmid, has this cautionary – and serious – note in his 1930 poem, *To Circumjack Cencrastus*:

> Freedom is inconceivable. The word
> Betrays the cause – a habit o' the mind,
> Thinkin' continually in a certain way,
> Generation after generation ...[2]

In this formulation, 'the cause' of freedom is betrayed by the singular word and its mindless repetition. The word itself defines the idea because it insists upon form. If freedom itself signifies a liberation from constriction, a breaking away from structure or form, the cause that leads to the breaking away is betrayed by the definition conferred by the word itself. The paradox is there in the opening paragraph: liberty demands self-control and a social contract, an obligation, a recognition of form. Fruits require roots.

Yet form itself is a kind of liberation, a resistance against formlessness, an assertion of identity against the threat of a stronger identity, a structure that might be required to maintain self-determination against the encroachment of other forces. When Wordsworth talks of 'The still, sad music of humanity', that word 'sad' seems to signify grave, or solemn, or serious, while the word 'music' seems to speak of something redemptive, a kind of liberation indeed, something we make through language, but something that goes beyond language too, a form of liberty.[3] This is an impulse that takes us beyond words, but it is surely and deftly conveyed by the words of the poet.

The paradox here is profound in both philosophy and art. Arguably its most precise formulation is in point 2.0121 of the second proposition of the *Tractatus Logico-Philosophicus*, where Ludwig Wittgenstein says this: 'Just as we are quite unable to imagine spatial objects outside space or temporal objects outside time, so too there is *no* object that we can imagine excluded from the possibility of combining with others.'[4] In this understanding, 'Freedom is inconceivable' by definition.

However, proposition 2.022 is: 'It is obvious that an imagined world, however different it may be from the real one, must have *something* – a form – in common with it.'[5] The reintroduction of the notion of form here has a specific bearing on the work of art. This is made evident in the famous discussion between Jean Sibelius and Gustav Mahler, in which Sibelius said that what he most admired in a symphony was 'severity of form and the profound logic that created an inner connection between all the motives' whereas Mahler by contrast declared, 'No! The symphony must be all-embracing.'[6] For Sibelius, form meant power, but for Mahler, it meant constriction. For Sibelius, form *was* power, and the symphony was a statement as unalterable, permanent and strong as the landscapes of

Finland, whereas for Mahler the symphony was a liberation, an extending and extenuating development of themes and motives and ideas, earthed not in landscape but in self-understanding, almost endless exfoliating autobiography. The difference can be heard in their work. Yet this is the paradox: each symphony of Sibelius is also a liberation (not least in the context of Finland's struggle towards political self-determination), and each symphony of Mahler possesses form. The form of the story of his life and times informs every one of them. Both propositions have truth.

Perhaps the most famous essay on the subject is J. S. Mill, *On Liberty* (1859), a study of society and the state and relations between them. In the wake of the French and American revolutions, the era demanded such investigations, and Mill is in the company of Edmund Burke's *Reflections on the Revolution in France* (1789) and Walter Bagehot's *The English Constitution* (1867, revised 1872). In America, Abraham Lincoln, in a famous speech made towards the end of the Civil War, noted that 'liberty' is a difficult word to define. The freedom of someone to rule their own life might be contradicted by the freedom of someone else to rule the lives of others. Depending on your position, liberty can look like tyranny. Beethoven's great opera *Fidelio* (1805) is about liberty. When Florestan gets out of his dungeon and when the prisoners sing, 'O welche Lust, in freier Luft, / den Atem leicht zu haben!' ('O what joy to breathe free, in open air!'), we are moved by a sense of freedom attained. Yet when the opera was performed for Hitler's birthday in Aachen in 1938, conducted by Herbert von Karajan, the Nazi dictator was identified with Florestan, not the opera's tyrannic Pizarro. We are on dangerous ground. Even Beethoven himself has been characterised as a tyrant bully by Adrienne Rich in her poem, 'The Ninth Symphony of Beethoven Understood At Last As a Sexual Message': 'A man in terror of impotence / or infertility' whose 'climacteric / music' is 'the / beating of a bloody fist upon / a splintered table'.[7] The aristocratic idea of liberty is not the same as that of the citizen, or the emperor, or the dictator.

So much of this is therefore a matter of interpretation. The liberty from fixed systems of belief is essential to what has been called academic freedom, and more generally applies to literary understanding. There is more than one way to read a poem. Interpretations may be contradictory but more than one may be true, though you do have to prove your judgement by agreed forms of argument. Milton's Satan may be damned in the Christian cosmos, but defiance against the odds and opposition to tyranny is a perennially attractive position. The angels who go with him into hell make a choice to do so, and thus possess a kind of human dignity. Viktor Frankel says: 'the ability to choose one's attitude to a given set of circumstances' is 'the last of human freedoms.' The three descriptions of the angel's Fall in *Paradise Lost* (1.44–54, 6.856–66 and of Mulciber, 1.742–46) offer repeated reworkings of the image, 'resisting closure at the very moment when the tragic outcome of historical reality appears most inevitable', in Rachel Falconer's words. This is 'the logic of the imaginary' – what Lévi-Strauss in *Tristes Tropiques* calls 'the fantasy production of a society seeking passionately to give symbolic expression to the instituions it might have had in reality.' Falconer also refers to Richard Kearney, on the 'cathartic power of play to make what is impossible at the empirical level of existence possible at a symbolic level'.[8] This idea is crucial to the commitment of so many Scottish writers over centuries, throwing down the gauntlet for freedom to repossess national self-determination.

These philosophical notions I have just sketched are merely that – notions and sketches. To apply them to specific moments in Scottish literature and history is to recognise an important connection between historical fact and the literary imagination, to see how some of the most memorable works of Scottish literature predict or arise from, are in different ways connected to, or indeed predict or prompt, particular historical, political and religious or philosophical movements. For example, consider the idea of liberty in relation to the stories of Columba, leaving Ireland for Iona, of Wallace and Bruce and the Wars of Independence, of the Reformation, the Covenanters, the Jacobites, the industrial working-class poets collected in Tom Leonard's anthology *Radical Renfrew* (1990), or Lenin's Bolshevik consul in Glasgow, John Maclean, and the poets who have written in his memory.[9]

Liberty might seem a constant theme in the history of Scottish literature and indeed in all art and philosophy. Yet in almost every specific instance there is ambiguity. Consider the relation between Enlightenment and Romanticism in the works of Robert Burns and Walter Scott. Both are writers who embody characteristics which can legitimately be described as aspects of the ethos of both Enlightenment and Romanticism. We might think of these terms with reference to English literature in a linear historical progress, from the Enlightenment forms of classical structure and social satire in the poetry of Alexander Pope, with all its snap and crackle, to the leap of individualism and unique personal identity in the assertions of heightened perception in Wordsworth or Shelley. Yet Burns is both uniquely individualistic ('*I, Rob, am here*'[10]) and thoroughly self-embedded in an ideal of social order (even the birds in 'Now westlin winds' prefer to observe their natural location in field, mountain and woodland[11]), while Scott is clearly a man of the politically conservative Enlightenment (his commitment to progress included the instalment of gas lights at Abbotsford) yet equally, he is also the author of *The Heart of Midlothian*, whose heroine is no aristocrat or heroic knight but a 'common cow-feeder's daughter'. Jeanie Deans is as comprehensive an assertion of the value and validity of the individual representative of common humanity as Burns's Tam o' Shanter, glorious beyond the realms of kings.

The theme of liberty in Scottish literature is so persistent that the risk of cliché is self-evident. So let me continue with a reference I hope might be surprising. We are familiar enough with the perennial desire to speak clearly to others, to rejuvenate the language, to make it new, in Ezra Pound's term. It is an urge as close to Wordsworth in his time, as to Pound and William Carlos Williams in theirs, or to Tom Leonard and Liz Lochhead, or Irvine Welsh and Alan Bissett in ours. If this is a canonical certainty, what about that least canonical of Scottish writers, Alexander Trocchi? This is from *Cain's Book* (1960):

> The mind under heroin evades perception as it does ordinarily; one is aware only of contents. But that whole way of posing the question, of dividing the mind from what it's aware of, is fruitless. Nor is it that the objects of perception are intrusive in an electric way as they are under mescalin or lysergic acid, nor that things strike one with more intensity or in a more enchanted or detailed way as I have sometimes experienced under marijuana; it is that the perceiving

turns inward, the eyelids droop, the blood is aware of itself, a slow phosphorescence in all the fabric of flesh and nerve and bone; it is that the organism has a sense of being intact and unbrittle, and, above all, *inviolable*. For the attitude born of this sense of inviolability some Americans have used the word 'cool.'[12]

This, I believe, is the moment when the word 'cool' enters Scottish literature for the first time. And it has less to do with drugs than with a deep refreshment of literary style. This is what Roland Barthes might describe as 'writing degree zero'.[13] The studied neutrality of a certain form of address, a certain mentality, a receptivity that is also an act of resistance and indeed assertion. The style itself is inviolable, unwavering, steely and strong.

We may be more familiar with the idea of liberty or freedom from other sources in Scottish literature and history but isn't this exactly what Trocchi is drawing our attention to as well? Set it alongside a few canonical texts and test the hypothesis.

The ideal of 'freedom' – conceived as independence from imperial English authority in the Wars of Independence led by William Wallace and Robert the Bruce – was rapidly translated from historical event into literary artefact by John Barbour in *The Bruce* (c. 1376) and Blind Hary in *The Wallace* (c. 1488). The essential trope is the story of David and Goliath. In Scottish literature, the figuration recurs again and again. These are the most famous lines on the subject from Barbour's *Bruce*:

> A! Fredome is a noble thing
> Fredome mays man to haiff liking.
> Fredome all solace to man giffis,
> He levys at es that frely levys.
> A noble hart may haiff nane es
> Na ellys nocht that may him ples
> Gyff fredome failyhe, for fre liking
> Is yharnyt our all othir thing.
> Na he that ay hass levyt fre
> May nocht knaw weill the propyrté

> The angyr na the wrechyt dome
> That is couplyt to foule thyrldome,
> Bot gyff he had assayit it,
> Than all perquer he suld it wyt,
> And suld think fredome mar to prys,
> Than all the gold in warld that is.[14]

It is worth giving the lines translated into an English version:

> Ah, Freedom is a noble thing!
> Freedom makes people have liking.
> Freedom helps people to live.
> He lives easefully who lives freely.
> A noble heart may have no rest
> Nor anything else that might please,
> If freedom fails; for freedom to choose
> Is valued above all other things.
> No – he who has always lived free
> Does not know well the property,
> The anger, no, the wretched fate
> That is coupled to slavery
> But, if he has experienced it,
> Then he should know it for what it is
> And would consider freedom more to be prized
> Than all the gold in the world.

One of the foundational myths of Scotland here might be traced back to the 1320 Declaration of Arbroath, a piece of writing whose rhetorical brilliance justly continues to be influential hundreds of years later. But its political authority is authorised by its literary value. We should not neglect the serious, solemn, 'sad music' of its moment, and its example.

In the eighteenth century, Hamilton of Gilbertfield rewrites Hary's *Wallace* in a contemporary idiom, and Burns reads it fresh, and writes: 'the story of Wallace poured a Scottish prejudice into my veins which will boil along there, till the flood-gates of life shut in eternal rest.'[15] And he writes his own version of Bruce's address to the troops at Bannockburn, in 'Scots Wha Hae', noted above, providing an image of the defending Scots sending the invading army homeward to think again, that will reappear in the twentieth century in the Corries' famous song, 'Flower of Scotland'. But *The Wallace* of Hamilton of Gilbertfield (c. 1665–1751) neither sentimentalises the violence of warfare not trivialises the ideals being fought for:

> Now all is death and wounds; the crimson plain
> Floats round in blood, and groans beneath its slain.
> Promiscuous crowds one common ruin share,
> And death alone employs the wasteful war.
> They trembling fly by conquering Scots oppress'd,
> And the broad ranks of battle lie defac'd;
> A false usurper sinks in ev'ry foe,
> And liberty returns with every blow.[16]

Burns transforms this into his own anthem:

> By Oppression's woes and pains!
> By your Sons in servile chains!
> We will drain our dearest veins,
> But they *shall* be free!
>
> Lay the proud Usurpers low!
> Tyrants fall in every foe!
> LIBERTY's in every blow!
> Let us DO – OR DIE!!![17]

The moment is precise, both in the battle described, Bannockburn, in 1314, and in the moment Burns himself occupies, at the end of the century which began with the Treaty of Union. Yet Burns goes further in 'The Jolly Beggars, or, Love and Liberty: A Cantata':

> A fig for those by law protected!
> LIBERTY's a glorious feast!
> Courts for Cowards were erected,
> Churches built to please the PRIEST.[18]

In the stance of resistance to imposed authority, there is a political continuity that runs, however surprisingly, from the Reformers, with all their staunch Protestantism, through to the Jacobites, with their hierarchical Catholic loyalties, and then on to the Covenanters, with their extreme Protestantism once again. Pride may be the liability in this configuration, but self-determination is at its heart. The thrawn and twisted willow trees in MacDiarmid's poem, 'The Sauchs in the Reuch Heuch Hauch' are comic distortions and stand, or skewer themselves, in wayward, oblique, diagonal shapes, at the opposite end of the spectrum from the magnificent, tall, strong oak trees of the great English artist John Constable, yet they are permanent living symbols of resistance to all authority, Rome, England, the God of any religion or even the sun itself.[19]

In *The Bruce*, Barbour tells us that Freedom is a noble thing, that 'mayss man to have liking' – which I would like to read wilfully as 'may allow' people to have 'liking' – the pleasure of choosing what to enjoy in life, without harm to others.

To understand the meaning of these records of an impulse towards 'liberty', we must separate an essence from its surroundings, its accumulated carapace. This is Alexander Trocchi once again, in *Cain's Book*:

> For centuries, we in the West have been dominated by the Aristotelian impulse to classify. It is no doubt because conventional classifications become part of prevailing economic structure that all real revolt is hastily fixed like a bright butterfly on a classificatory pin; the anti-play, *Godot*, being from one point of view unanswerable, is with all speed acclaimed 'best-play-of-the-year'; anti-literature is rendered innocuous by granting it a place in conventional histories of literature. The Shakespearean industry has little to do with Shakespeare.[20]

Liberty or freedom is a foundational myth in Scotland's story but it is related, if not identical, to another, even more ancient myth: the myth of kinship. Fraternity or sorority – family connections extending across differences – is a myth that predates the Wars of Independence in Scotland. The idea of freedom may be historically anchored in those wars but the myth of kinship has equally secure historical foundations in the arrival of St Columba from Ireland in AD 563. Only by being out of sight of Ireland could he do his work in Iona. And the poem attributed to Columba, the *Altus Prosator* is in itself an evocation of a struggle for liberation. This is the last verse in Edwin Morgan's translation, 'The Maker on High':

> Zabulus burns to ashes all those adversaries
> who deny that the saviour was Son to the Father
> but we shall fly to meet him and immediately greet him
> and be with him in the dignity of all such diversity
> as our deeds make deserved and we without swerve
> shall live beyond history in the state of glory.[21]

That phrase, 'the dignity of all such diversity' is the key to this sense of liberty, an understanding that diversity is a benison ensuring human dignity. Securing such an understanding was heroic work for a warrior and it is appropriate to note that in Ciaran Carson's introduction to his translation of the Celtic epic, *The Tain*, it is suggested that Columba and the pre-Christian Celtic warrior hero Cuchulainn may be, in fact, in certain lights, the same interchangeable figure.

In the light of this correlation of spiritual and physical authority, of affinity and liberty, of hierarchical social organisation and the responsibilities of authority to protect the most vulnerable, consider William Dunbar's poem 'The Thistle and the Rose', written as a celebration of the marriage of King James IV and Margaret Tudor in 1503. The political moment might warrant extensive exegesis but here the most important point to emphasise is that even in this strictly courtly poem, in which the exigencies of political and religious power are explicitly confirmed, Dunbar imagines a scene in which 'Dame Nature' has authority over earthly things, the king of beasts, the king of birds and the king of flowers, lion, eagle and thistle, equally, and insists upon advising them on both the political efficacy and the social worth of fair justice. To the lion, she says:

> Exerce iustice with mercy and conscience,
> And lat no small beist suffir skaith na skornis
> Of greit beastis that bene of moir piscence.
> Do law elyk to aipis and vnicornis [...]

To the eagle: 'be als iust to awppis and owlis, / As vnto pacokkis, papingais or crennis, / And mak a law for wycht fowlis and for wrennis'. And to the thistle: 'In field go furth, and fend the laif; // And, sen thow art a king, be thow discreit [...] lat no nettill vyle, and full of vyce, / Hir fallow to the gudly flour delyce'. So the lion and the eagle must be even-handed in their dispensation of justice, and the thistle, while insisting upon the hierarchy of difference between weeds and delightful flowers, should defend flowers fairly.[22]

Marshall Walker identifies this vision of ideal social justice as a key theme in Scottish literature generally, with regard to the depiction of common humanity. In his essay 'The Kailyard and the Kraal', Walker says this: 'One theme on which Scottish literary history offers a series of variations is the folk, the lot of common people.'[23] This theme emphasises the value of underlying equality, humanity beyond hierarchical accident or political manoeuvring. It is mythologically fanciful perhaps, but there is no doubting its presence, and Walker cites examples from as diverse a range of authors as David Lyndsay, Francis Hutchison, David Hume, Adam Smith, Henry Mackenzie, Ramsay, Fergusson, Burns, Scott, Hogg, Galt, Robert Louis Stevenson, Charles Murray, John Davidson, J. M. Barrie and the full complement of major twentieth-century poets, from MacDiarmid on.

What appears to be emerging, then, in our consideration of liberty in Scottish literature, is, perhaps surprisingly, a sense of value that is much more than simply resistance, or a rhetorical call for freedom from abstract oppression. It is rather a deep understanding of the complementarity of form and freedom, order and liberty, an affinity of purpose across generations with regard to individual purpose and social structure. We have noted the work Alexander Trocchi already. One of the most famous confrontations in twentieth-century Scottish literature was that enacted between him and Hugh MacDiarmid at the Edinburgh Festival on 21 August 1962. At a public event, the venomous verbosity was loud, sharp and memorable. Yet closer study of the correspondence between the two writers after this public occasion reveals Trocchi's respectful acknowledgement of purpose and affinity of political and artistic ambition with MacDiarmid. On 17 May 1964, Trocchi wrote to MacDiarmid acknowledging that there are aspects of life and art upon which they cannot be in accord but adding emphatically that on certain vital issues 'we can hardly fail to be in agreement, and I, for my part, am most sorry that the particular circumstances in which we first met one another were such as to bring the former into prominence and distract our attention from the latter. Amongst this latter is our common revolt against the smug philistinism of many of our countrymen. That the good folk of the Edinburgh establishment should take pride in smothering the literary side of the festival this year is for both of us, I am sure, bloody shocking evidence of their barbarism.' Trocchi expresses his hope that MacDiarmid might join him and his colleagues in an 'unofficial conference' and take his 'rightful place at the head of our shock troops'. He goes further: 'I am not in the least anxious to continue a public sniping match with a man for whom I have always had the profoundest respect.' On 7 August 1964, Trocchi wrote to MacDiarmid trying to arrange a meeting and enclosing details of a proposal to create a network of writers of critical affinity, and on 26 August 1964, Trocchi wrote again trying to arrange a meeting with the older poet, saying, 'to meet you properly is one of the reasons I am here.'[24] It was not to be, but the correspondence adds a vital qualification to the more easily sensationalised confrontation of 1962. Both Trocchi and MacDiarmid understood the idea of liberty as being essential for political and literary resistance and commitment, and equally essential in the work that all the arts and, above all, literature does most effectively.

The American poet Adrienne Rich begins her little book *Poetry and Commitment* (2007), based on a plenary lecture in the 2006 'Poetry and Politics' conference at the University of Stirling, with these words:

'There's an invisible presence in this room, whom I want to invoke: the great Scottish Marxist bard Hugh MacDiarmid. I'll begin by reading from his exuberant, discursive manifesto called, bluntly, 'The Kind of Poetry I Want'. I'll offer a few extracts and hope you'll read the whole poem for yourselves,' and she quotes, among other passages, these lines:

> Poetry of such an integration as cannot be effected
> Until a new and conscious organisation of society
> Generates a new view
> Of the world as a whole ...
>
> – A learned poetry wholly free
> Of the brutal love of ignorance;
> And the poetry of a poet with no use
> For any of the simpler forms of personal success.

Rich described the poem as

> A manifesto of desire for 'a new and conscious organisation of society' and a poetic view to match it. A manifesto that acknowledges the scope, tensions, and contradictions of the poet's undertaking. Let's bear in mind the phrases 'difficult knowledge', 'the concentrated strength of all our being', the poem as 'wide-angled', but also the image of the poet as nurse in the operating theatre: 'fearfully alert'.[25]

The values that Rich endorses in MacDiarmid are manifest. So with reference to them, we might consider the central opposition between the effort of culture and the restrictions of political and poetic form which MacDiarmid describes in his poem addressed to the Fascist South African poet Roy Campbell, supporter of Franco in the Spanish Civil War in the 1930s. MacDiarmid imagines the typical reader of Campbell's poems:

> A stout man, walking with a waddle, with a face
> Creased and puffed into a score

> Of unhealthy rolls and crevices
> And a red and bulbous nose;
> A rich man who fawns his way through life,
> With a thick husky voice, naturally coarse,
> Through which with grotesque insistence runs a tone
> Of mock culture – a man whose fat finger
> Ticks off the feet in Campbell's lines
> 'Left, right! Left, right!' and whose aesthetic sense
> Delights to hear the recurrent crack
> Of the hippopotamus hide whip or to note
> The sibilance as of rubber truncheons every here and there.[26]

Against this horrific, George Grosz-like caricature, MacDiarmid proposes a definition of culture and what the cultivation of the arts might bring:

> The effort of culture is towards greater differentiation
> Of perceptions and desires and values and ends,
> Holding them from moment to moment
> In a perpetually changing but stable equilibrium.[27]

This is poetry as disclosure of what liberty might mean. It is not the negative definition offered by Robert Frost, T. S. Eliot or Wallace Stevens. For Frost, a poem provides 'a momentary stay against confusion'; for T. S. Eliot in 'East Coker', IV, 'the whole earth is our hospital'; and for Wallace Stevens 'reality is a cliché from which we escape by metaphor'. As Marshall Walker says, 'Confusion, hospital, escape – a doleful trio.'[28] What MacDiarmid is proposing is a joyful engagement with contradiction and a faith in the unpredictable kinship we might feel across differences.

This is the question at the centre of Liz Lochhead's poem 'Something I'm Not', where the title runs on into the first line, or rather, becomes the first line, as it contradicts its own certainty: 'Something I'm not // familiar with, the tune / of their talking / comes tumbling before me [...]' Describing her neighbour and her neighbour's child, she acknowledges their difference and at the core of the poem, asks: 'how does she feel?' – at which point, the sympathy and humanity, the freedom 'to have liking', begins to infuse the words.[29] All art is the sensitisation of the world.

Let this chapter draw to a conclusion with a story that opens the theme out from Scottish literature to a much wider context. The American scholar and writer Kim Stafford tells us that when Dick Cheney was Secretary of Defence, he came to Portland, Oregon, to give a keynote address for an organisation called the World Affairs Council, at a ceremony where it had been decided to present an award to two citizens from Portland: Phil Knight, CEO of Nike (for his contributions to world understanding through international business), and Stafford himself, for his contributions to world understanding through teaching. Stafford found himself at the awards-banquet head table, realising, as the plates were being swept away, that he was effectively about to give a speech to Dick Cheney. Stafford describes the moment:

> Secretary Cheney chose as his keynote theme, 'The Assets of Security', which turned out to include an array of innovative weaponry: catastrophic submarines, smart weapons operated from remote points, and other terrors. As I listened, another list began to form in my mind, what might be called 'the assets of peace' – beginning with childhood, music, food, personal letters, compassion, parenting at home and across boundaries, the urge to dance, and poetry. [...]
> When I rose to accept the award, my words came forth like this:
> 'We live in a world where a few people could destroy us all. But a few people could not save us. The math doesn't work that way. The only way we can be saved is for many people, and finally all people, to recognise and live by interdependence on earth. Even though they are not funded as such, education, language study, the arts and cultural exchanges among the divided populations of the world are the highest priority of our time. These are the assets of peace.'[30]

Liberty to acquire, deploy and exercise such assets of peace can never be passively realised. We might enjoy it freely in a given context but there are always others out there who would willingly colonise us and close that liberty down. Understanding what is at stake is only the first requirement in the struggle to bring such liberty into a greater provenance. Supposing an independent Scotland, the arts will have no less urgent work to keep our critical sensibilities sharp.

In 'Two Notes on Wallace Stevens', in his book of essays *The Hunter Gracchus* (1996), Guy Davenport says: 'All of twentieth-century art participated in a navigational correction. It was the sense of our greatest creative minds that we had gone off course. Wittgenstein changed the direction of philosophy: we had, he said, wandered away from real philosophy. Picasso, Pound, Joyce, Gertrude Stein – all were resetters of courses.'[31] In Scotland, we could immediately add MacDiarmid and Lewis Grassic Gibbon to that list. Later, in an essay on the drawings of Paul Cadmus, Davenport writes: 'Despite every attempt of satire to keep us sane, we [in the United States] have put Dwight Eisenhower, Richard Nixon, Ronald Reagan, and George Bush in the White House. It is not so much that we betrayed ourselves in putting them there (we began doing that when the ink was still wet on the Declaration of Independence) but that we betrayed the critical sense, which satire exists to educate, that would have kept us from electing the wrongest people to the executive chair of the republic.'[32]

Apply this now to Scotland.

The critical sense is precisely what all our best writers and artists help us not to betray. That is the liberty Scottish literature – like any other literature – insists upon and exemplifies. Its work is never done.

Notes

1. Hugh MacDiarmid, *Lucky Poet: A Self-Study in Literature and Political Ideas*, ed. Alan Riach (Manchester: Carcanet, 1994), pp. 148–49.
2. Hugh MacDiarmid, *The Complete Poems*, ed. Grieve and Aitken, vol. 1 (Manchester: Carcanet, 1993), pp. 185–86.
3. William Wordsworth, 'Tintern Abbey', in *Selected Poems*, ed. Roger Shattuck (London: Heinemann, 1981), pp. 52–57 (p. 55).
4. Ludwig Wittgenstein, *Tractatus Logico-Philosophicus*, trans. by D. F. Pears and B. F. McGuiness with an introduction by Bertrand Russell (London: Routledge & Kegan Paul, 1977), p. 6.
5. Ibid., p. 7.

6   Cited in Marshall Walker, *Dear Sibelius: Letter from a Junky* (Glasgow: Kennedy & Boyd, 2008), pp. 52–53.
7   lime-tree.blogspot.co.uk/2007/08/adrienne-rich-ninth-symphony-of.html [accessed 25 January 2015]
8   Viktor E. Frankel, *Man's Search for Meaning: An Introduction to Logotherapy* (New York, 1962); Claude Lévi-Strauss, *Tristes Tropiques* (New York, 1971) and Richard Kearney, *The Wake of Imagination* (Minneapolis, 1988); all quoted in Rachel Falconer, 'Is There Freedom Afterwards? A Dialogue between *Paradise Lost* and DeLillo's *Falling Man*', *Milton Studies*, vol. 52 (Duquesne University Press, 2012).
9   See Tom Leonard (ed.), *Radical Renfrew* (Edinburgh: Polygon, 1990); and T. S. Law and Thurso Berwick, eds, *Homage to John Maclean* (Larkhall: The John Maclean Society, 1973).
10 Robert Burns, 'To the Same' ['Second Epistle to James Lapraik'], *Poems and Songs*, ed. by Kinsley (London: Oxford University Press, 1969), pp. 69–72 (p. 71).
11 Ibid., 'Song, composed in August' ['Now Westlin' Winds'], pp. 2–3.
12 Alexander Trocchi, *Cain's Book* (London: Quartet Books, 1973), p. 2.
13 Roland Barthes, *Writing Degree Zero*, trans. by Annette Lavers and Colin Smith (London: Jonathan Cape, 1967).
14 John Barbour, *The Bruce*, ed. by A. A. M. Duncan (Edinburgh: Canongate, 1997), p. 57.
15 Robert Burns, *The Letters*, ed. by J. Logie Robertson (London: Walter Scott, 1887), p. 68.
16 William Hamilton of Gilbertfield, *Blind Harry's Wallace* (Edinburgh: Luath Press, 1998), p. 75; see also Lesley Duncan and Elspeth King, eds, *The Wallace Muse: Poems and artworks inspired by the life and legend of William Wallace* (Edinburgh: Luath Press, 2005), pp. 28–31 (p. 31).
17 Robert Burns, 'Robert Bruce's March to Bannockburn – ' ['Scots Wha Ha'e'], in *Poems and Songs*, pp. 561–62 (562).
18 Ibid., 'Love and Liberty: A Cantata' ['The Jolly Beggars'], in *Poems and Songs*, pp. 157–69 (p. 168).
19 Hugh MacDiarmid, 'The Sauchs in the Reuch Heuch Hauch', in op. cit., p. 18.
20 Alexander Trocchi, op. cit., p. 34.
21 Edwin Morgan, 'The Maker on High', in *Collected Translations* (Manchester: Carcanet, 1996), pp. 389–93 (p. 393).
22 William Dunbar, '52' ['The Thistle and the Rose'], in *The Poems*, ed. by Bawcutt, vol. 1 (Glasgow: Association for Scottish Literary Studies, 1998), pp. 163–68 (pp. 166, 167).
23 Marshall Walker, 'The Kailyard and the Kraal', in *Comrades and Vexations: Some Objects in a Life* (Glasgow: Kennedy & Boyd, 2013), pp. 261–74 (p. 267).
24 *Dear Grieve: Letters to Hugh MacDiarmid (C. M. Grieve)*, ed. by John Manson (Glasgow: Kennedy & Boyd, 2011), pp. 468–69, 469, 470–72.
25 Adrienne Rich, *Poetry & Commitment* with an Afterword by Mark Doty (London & New York: W. W. Norton, 2007), p. 3.
26 Hugh MacDiarmid, 'England's Double Knavery', *The Complete Poems*, ed. by Grieve and Aitken, vol. 2 (Manchester: Carcanet, 1994), pp. 1133–38 (pp. 1137–38).
27 Ibid., p. 1138.
28 Marshall Walker, *Scottish Literature Since 1707* (Harlow: Longman, 1996), p. 304.
29 Liz Lochhead, 'Something I'm Not', in *Dreaming Frankenstein & Collected Poems* (Edinburgh: Polygon, 1984), pp. 138–39.

30 Kim Stafford, 'Afterword: Learning from Strangers', in *The Muses Among Us: Eloquent Listening and Other Pleasures of the Writer's Craft* (Athens and London: The University of Georgia Press, 2003), pp. 122–33 (pp. 131–32).
31 Guy Davenport, 'Two Notes on Wallace Stevens', in *The Hunter Gracchus and Other Papers on Literature and Art* (Washington: Counterpoint, 1996), pp. 154–58 (p. 156).
32 Ibid., 'The Drawings of Paul Cadmus', pp. 279–86 (p. 286).

2. Allan Ramsay's *A Dialogue on Taste*: a painter's call to break free from English artistic conventions

MARION AMBLARD

In the second half of the eighteenth century, a distinctive Scottish style of portrait painting began to emerge. Although its development coincided with that of English portraiture, the Scottish school of portrait painting has always been markedly different from its English counterpart. Both schools developed in different conditions and in the eighteenth and nineteenth centuries they did not conform to the same artistic conventions.[1]

England had long attracted eminent foreign painters; back in the sixteenth century, Hans Holbein (c. 1497–1543) had painted for King Henry VIII (1491–1547) and in the seventeenth century Rubens (1577–1640) and Van Dyck (1599–1641) worked for James VI of Scotland and I of England (1566–1625) and for his son King Charles I (1600–1649); the Dutch portraitist Peter Lely (1618–80) was the most popular artist at the court of Charles II (1630–1685) and was appointed Principal Painter to the King in 1661; at Lely's death, German-born Godfrey Kneller (1623–1723) became the dominant court painter and worked successively for James VII and II (1633–1701), Mary II (1662–1694) and William III (1650–1702), Queen Anne (1665–1714) and King George I (1660–1727) who made him a baronet in 1715. The country was not devoid of native painters but until the end of the 1730s they generally imitated the foreign artists working at the court and were unable to develop a native style. Among others, in the seventeenth century, William Dobson (1611–1646) and John Riley (1646–1691), who both worked at the court, executed portraits in a manner reminiscent of Van Dyck's style and at the beginning of the eighteenth century Jonathan Richardson (1667–1745), who had been a pupil of Riley, was indebted to Lely and Kneller.

In Scotland, political and economic conditions only began to be favourable to the development of pictorial art from the second half of the eighteenth century. Unlike England, Scotland attracted few foreign painters and the majority of Scottish artists left their native country as after the Reformation and the Union of the Crowns in 1603 painters were deprived of their two main patrons, the Catholic Church and the monarch. At the end of the seventeenth century, the Dutch painter Jacob De Wet (1641–1697) lived a few years in Edinburgh where he painted several canvases and decorative paintings for his Scottish patrons' mansions.[2] At the same period, John Baptist de Medina (1659–1710), an artist of Flemish–Spanish origin left London to open his studio in Scotland where he became the most popular portraitist and he was knighted by the Scottish Parliament in 1706.[3] By the 1750s, William Delacour (c. 1700–1767), a French painter, also came to work in Edinburgh where he became the first teacher of the newly-opened Trustees' Academy.

If few painters worked in Scotland in the seventeenth and eighteenth centuries it was mainly because the request for paintings was very limited until the beginning of the nineteenth century. In fact, the number of patrons was so restricted that, apart from Sir Henry Raeburn (1756–1823), artists could not make a living from their paintings only: they had to diversify their activities by executing engravings, decorative paintings or teaching drawing.[4] Moreover, before 1798, when the Trustees' Academy opened its first classes devoted to the teaching of the fine arts, young people aspiring to an artistic career could only get rudimentary training by enrolling as an apprentice to a craftsman working as a coach painter, a house painter or as a goldsmith.[5] Thus most eighteenth-century painters decided to leave Scotland to settle in London, which was the main artistic centre in Great Britain. Some also opened their studio in Italy, as was the case with Jacob More (1740–1790) and Gavin Hamilton (1723–1798) who worked as a landscape painter and a history painter in Rome and two painters, John Smibert (1688–1751) and Cosmo Alexander (1724–1772), also went to work in the British North American colonies.[6]

Most eighteenth-century Scottish painters trained in London where they could study with a renowned painter or in one of the fine art academies which had opened at the beginning of the century. They also usually spent several years in Italy to complete their training and they returned to London where they opened their studio.[7] As they worked in England, Scottish portraitists had to conform to the dominant English artistic conventions, yet they rapidly developed their own style with disregard for these artistic principles to paint portraits characterised by realism, sobriety and simplicity. Allan Ramsay (1713–1784),[8] who was one of the eighteenth-century Scottish painters who trained and lived in London, was the first portraitist to break free from English artistic conventions. He opened his studio in the English capital in 1738 and he began painting portraits following the precepts he had been taught. With his pictures, he quickly became one of the most fashionable portraitists in London.[9] However from the mid-1750s he did not hesitate to adopt a new style of painting rejecting the prevailing aesthetic theories in England.

This chapter examines Ramsay's aesthetic essay, *A Dialogue on Taste*, whose publication in 1755 marked a watershed in the portraitist's career since it coincided with the adoption of his new style; it will also stress the importance of this treatise in the history of Scottish art as it laid the foundations of the Scottish school of portrait painting. We will briefly reconsider the established artistic conventions of eighteenth-century English portraiture focusing mainly on Jonathan Richardson's *Essay on the Theory of Painting* (1715) which, until the publication of the discourses delivered by Sir Joshua Reynolds (1723–1792) at the Royal Academy, defined the most influential aesthetic theories in England. We will also examine a few portraits painted by Ramsay to notice that for almost two decades he tried to conform to the main English portrait conventions but as some of his pictures show he was at odds with these principles. Then with an analysis of *A Dialogue on Taste* we will understand what the main characteristics of his new style were and how he drew on contemporary Scottish thinkers' theories to define a set of artistic conventions which contributed to the development of the Scottish school of portraiture.

*

In eighteenth-century Britain and Continental Europe, painting was highly codified. In fine art academies and in the various treatises on painting, young artists were taught that there was a hierarchy of genres and that history painting was considered as the noblest form of art. This hierarchy had been set up by André Félibien (1619–1695) who stated in the foreword of his *Conférences de l'Académie Royale de Peinture et de Sculpture pendant l'Année 1667*:

> Celuy qui fait parfaitement des païsages est au dessus d'un autre qui ne fait que des fruits, des fleurs ou des coquilles. Celuy qui peint des animaux vivans est plus estimable que ceux qui ne représentent que des choses mortes & sans mouvement ; Et comme la figure de l'homme est le plus parfait ouvrage de Dieu sur la terre, il est certain aussi que celuy qui se rend l'imitateur de Dieu en peignant des figures humaines, est beaucoup plus excellent que tous les autres. […] Néanmoins un Peintre qui ne fait que des portraits, n'a pas encore atteint cette haute perfection de l'Art, & ne peut prétendre à l'honneur que reçoivent les plus sçavans. Il faut pour cela passer d'une seule figure à la représentation de plusieurs ensemble ; il faut traiter l'histoire & la fable; il faut représenter de grandes actions comme les Historiens ou des sujets agréables comme les Poëtes ; Et montant encore plus haut, il faut par des compositions allégoriques, sçavoir couvrir sous le voile de la fable les vertus des grands hommes, & les mystères les plus relevez. L'on appelle un grand Peintre celuy qui s'acquite bien de semblables entreprises. C'est en quoi consiste la force, la noblesse & la grandeur de cet Art.[10]

(The artist who does perfect landscapes is superior to another who paints only fruit, flowers and shells. The artist who paints living animals deserves more respect than those who represent only still, lifeless subjects. And as the human figure is God's most perfect work on earth, it is certainly the case that the artist who imitates God by painting human figures, is more outstanding by far than all the others. […] However, although it is a real achievement to make human figure appear alive, and to give the appearance of movement to something which cannot move; it is still the case that an artist who paints only portraits has not yet achieved the greatest perfection of art and cannot aspire to the honour bestowed on the most learned of his colleagues. To achieve this, it is necessary to move on from the representation of a single figure to that of a group; to deal with historical and legendary subjects and to represent the great actions recounted by historians or the pleasing subjects treated by poets. And, in order to scale even greater heights, an artist must know how to conceal the virtues of great men and the most elevated mysteries beneath the veil of legendary tales and allegorical compositions. A great painter is successful in ventures of this kind. Herein lies the force, nobility and greatness of his art.)

To gain recognition, painters had to respect certain artistic principles which were different for each genre and which differed from one country to another and evolved in accordance with the prevailing artistic style. In England, the main conventions followed by the first generation of painters of the English school of portraiture were defined by Jonathan Richardson in *An Essay on the Theory of Painting*, published in 1715. Richardson was first and foremost a portraitist,[11] but he is now best remembered for his writings. In total, he published three treatises on art: *An Essay on the Theory of Painting* was followed in 1719 by *An Essay on the Whole Art of Criticism as it Relates to Painting and an Argument in Behalf of the Science of the Connoisseur* and in 1722, based on his son's account of his travel to Italy, he wrote *An Account of Some of the Statues, Bas-Reliefs, Drawings, and Pictures in Italy*, which became a reference work for the aristocrats who went on the Grand Tour. Although most of *An Essay on the Theory of Painting* is devoted to history painting, this treatise led to a reappraisal of portraiture in England.[12] Without challenging the hierarchy of pictorial genres, Richardson argued that history paintings as well as portraits were a source of aesthetic pleasure and instilled moral values:

> Supposing two men perfectly equal in all other respects, only [that] one is conversant with the works of the best masters [...] and the other not; the former shall necessarily gain the ascendant and have noble ideas, more love to his country, more moral virtue, more faith, more piety and devotion than the other; he shall be a more ingenious and a better man.[13]

Regarding portraits, he asserted they were not just pleasant ornaments as he believed that 'the Picture of an absent Relation, or Friend, helps to keep up those sentiments which frequently languish by Absence and may be instrumental to maintain, and sometimes to augment Friendship, and Paternal, Filial, and Conjugual Love, and Duty'.[14] It is also in this essay that Richardson formulated the main principle of eighteenth-century English portraiture when he claimed that portraitists should not aim at painting a truthful likeness of the sitter, on the contrary, they should improve the sitter's physical appearance and create an idealised image as he wrote:

> Common Nature is no more fit for a Picture than plain Narration is for a Poem: a Painter must raise his Ideas beyond what he sees, and form a Model of Perfection in his Own Mind which is not to be found in Reality; but yet Such a one as is Probable, and Rational. Particularly with respect to Mankind, he must as it were raise the whole Species, and give them all imaginable Beauty, and Grace, Dignity, and Perfection; Every several Character, whether it be Good, or Bad, Amiable, or Detestable, must be stronger, and more Perfect.[15]

In his essay, he gave artists many rules to follow to become successful portraitists and paint portraits comparable to those of the greatest masters: for instance, he explained how light and shade should be disposed and which range of colours should be used; he also mentioned the type of dresses and accessories which should be represented to dignify the sitter.[16] Besides, throughout his treatise, Richardson repeatedly emphasised the necessity to study carefully and to copy the works of the greatest Renaissance painters and the best antique marbles; to portraitists, he also recommended imitating the pictures of Van Dyck, a baroque artist who, according to him, was one of the best portraitists of all time as he wrote that Van Dyck 'generally kept to Nature, chosen in its best Moments, and something Rais'd, and Improv'd; for which reason he is [...] the best Model for Portrait-Painting'.[17] Richardson's theories were in accordance with the tenets of the baroque style, which was the dominant artistic trend in British painting before the advent of neoclassicism in the late eighteenth century. Baroque portraits generally conveyed a glorifying image of the person depicted by representing in lavish surroundings a sitter wearing elegant clothes and adopting a theatrical pose.

Most eighteenth-century English portraitists conformed to Richardson's principles: the influence of his theories is particularly noticeable in the portraits of his son-in-law, Thomas Hudson (1701–1779), as well as in the paintings and writings of Joshua Reynolds, who had trained under Hudson. According to Richard Wendorf, Richardson's theories also had an impact on William Hogarth (1697–1764).[18] For the portrait of Lady Lucy Manners, Duchess of Montrose, by Hudson and the portraits of Master Thomas Lister and of William Frederick, 2nd Duke of Gloucester, by Reynolds, both portraitists drew their inspiration from Van Dyck; for the three-quarter-length portrait of the Duchess of Montrose, Hudson imitated more precisely the décolleté black dress and the wide black hat with white ostrich plumes represented in the portrait of Susanna Lunden,[19] a picture which was then thought to be by Van Dyck but which had actually been painted by Rubens. Because of their dress and their pose, the young boys in the full-length portraits executed by Reynolds are reminiscent of Prince Charles – later King Charles II – as depicted by Van Dyck in the portrait of the five children of Charles I.[20] A study of the portraits Ramsay painted before the mid-1750s shows that he complied with Richardson's theories. For instance, when he executed the portraits of Norman Macleod and of Master John Prideaux Basset[21] he followed Richardson's recommendations by representing the sitters in the same pose as the Apollo Belvedere, which was at the time one of the most famous antique statues.[22] Indeed in his *Essay on the Theory of Painting* Richardson explained to young painters that they should copy the pose of a renowned work of art as it imparts dignity to their sitter:

> [artists should not] be ashamed to be sometimes plagiary, 'tis what the greatest Painters, and Poets have allow'd themselves in. *Rafaëlle* has borrow'd many Figures, and Groups of Figures from the Antique. [...] The Painter that can take a Hint, or insert a Figure, or Groupes

of Figures from another Man, and mix these with his Own, so as to make a good Composition, will thereby establish such a Reputation to himself, as to be above fearing to suffer by the share those to whom he is beholden will have in it.[23]

For the portrait of Master John Prideaux Basset painted in 1747, Ramsay did not draw his inspiration only from the celebrated classical statue, as the sitter's clothes are almost identical to the dress worn by Prince Charles in the portrait of Charles I's five children painted by Van Dyck.

The portrait of Norman Macleod dated 1748 can be considered as one of the last major pictures Ramsay painted following English portrait conventions as well as the baroque tradition he had been taught during his training with Hans Hysing (1678–c. 1753) in London and with Francesco Solimena (1657–1747) and Francesco Imperiali (1679–1740) in Italy. From 1754, he no longer painted pictures conforming to these conventions apart from the official portraits of King George III (1738–1820) and of the royal family. Some of his works painted before 1754 already showed that Ramsay was not at ease with these principles. In the portrait of Lady Margaret Hall of Dunglass,[24] dated 1752, there is a discrepancy between the magnificent setting and the soberly dressed woman whose physical appearance is uncompromisingly rendered by the artist. As a result the overall effect of the painting is not harmonious: the frail old lady wearing a plain black dress contrasts with the elaborate background, including two traditional baroque trappings, a crimson curtain and column.

Ramsay's decision to break free from English portrait conventions and from baroque principles coincided with two important events in his life: in 1752, he eloped with Margaret Lindsay who became his second wife[25] and two years later he visited Italy for the second time. Ramsay's adoption of a new style may also be linked to the fact that Joshua Reynolds opened his studio in London in 1752 and with his full-length portrait of Captain Augustus Keppel[26] which is based on Ramsay's *Norman Macleod*, Reynolds was immediately successful and was a serious rival for Ramsay. His new style is also the application of the artistic theories he formulated in 1755 in his aesthetic essay *A Dialogue on Taste*.

Nowadays in Scotland, Ramsay is celebrated for his portraits; in his lifetime he was also a renowned and prolific writer who published twelve essays and a collection of poems. After an accident in 1773 in which he injured his right arm, Ramsay was unable to paint and devoted his time to his literary pursuits and when he died an obituary published in the *Gentleman's Magazine* on 10 August 1784 celebrated his literary talents rather than his artistic career:

> Died at Dover on his return from the continent in his 71st year, Allan Ramsay Esq., Principal Portrait Painter to their Majesties. By his death, the polite and the literary world have sustained an irreparable loss, as few men have excelled him in correctness of taste, brilliancy of wit, or soundness of understanding. His publications are numerous and various; several of them are on political subjects in which he displayed much useful knowledge of the constitution of his country, for which he was a strenuous and disinterested advocate.[27]

Son of the celebrated poet Allan Ramsay (1684–1758), Ramsay the painter started writing poems at a young age[28] and longed for literary fame.[29] Throughout his career he was able to meet some of the most eminent European writers and philosophers: in 1765, he met Diderot (1713–1784) in Paris and, the year after, David Hume (1711–1776) introduced him to Jean-Jacques Rousseau (1712–1778) who was in exile in London. Ramsay also corresponded with Voltaire (1694–1778) and visited him twice in 1765 and in 1773. However, he was more closely connected with Hume who was one of his close friends.[30] With the help of Hume and Adam Smith (1723–1790), Ramsay set up in Edinburgh the Select Society in 1754 which was a debating society including many prominent figures such Lord Kames (1696–1782), James Adam (1732–1794) and his brother Robert (1728–1792), William Robertson (1721–1793) and Adam Ferguson (1723–1815). Hume thought highly of Ramsay's talents as a painter and sat for two portraits executed in 1754 and in 1766; he also asked Ramsay's opinion concerning the manuscript of his first volume of *History of England* (1754) and following the portraitist's advice he modified several passages in his book. As for him, Ramsay was deeply influenced by Hume's theories when he wrote his aesthetic essay *A Dialogue on Taste*. If Ramsay's poems were severely criticised by his contemporaries,[31] his essays which mainly dealt with economic and political issues got a better reception. His pamphlet on one of the most important judicial cases of 1753 *A Letter to the Right Honourable the Earl of – Concerning the Affair of Elizabeth Canning, by a Clergyman* (1753) was a major success and was mentioned by Voltaire in his essay entitled *Histoire d'Elizabeth Canning, et Jean Calas* (1762).[32] *A Dialogue on Taste*, which was mainly written during a stay in Edinburgh in 1753, is the only essay in which Ramsay presented his artistic theories and is the first aesthetic treatise written by a Scottish painter. If this work was not as critically acclaimed as the essay concerning the affair of Elizabeth Canning, Hume wrote to Ramsay who was in Italy when it was published to inform him that 'it has met with a very good reception from the wits and critics'.[33]

A Dialogue on Taste takes the form of a dialogue between two characters, Lord Modish and Colonel Freeman who are in the company of Lady Modish and Lady Harriot. The concepts of taste and beauty are the main topics of the conversation. As his name indicates, Lord Modish defends contemporary taste and generally accepted ideas of beauty; Freeman represents Ramsay's point of view and is not afraid of showing his preferences even if they run counter to the prevailing taste. The essay begins with Lord Modish disapproving of the colonel who has just told him that champagne is not his favourite drink and that he prefers Samuel Butler's writings to those of Virgil. According to Lord Modish these two examples reveal the colonel's bad taste as it does not conform to current taste: Virgil was then considered as one of the greatest writers and champagne was the most prestigious alcoholic beverage. This discussion leads the two characters to wonder whether taste and beauty are determined by universal rules. Lord Modish believes that there are such standards and that a man whose taste conforms to that of the majority of people is a man of refinement and good taste. As for him, Colonel Freeman does not believe in such universal rules or standards and demonstrates that there is no such thing as good or bad taste as taste is subjective:

> The proper objects of taste, or feeling, are such as are relative to the person only who is actuated by them, who is the sole judge whether those feelings be agreeable, or otherwise; and being informed of this simple fact from himself, no farther consequence can be drawn from it, neither does it admit of any dispute.[34]

According to Freeman, judgments, unlike taste, are determined by standards common to all men and it is thanks to these standards that we can say whether a statement is true or false or an action is right or wrong. As there is no standard of taste, everyone is free to like whatever they want and one cannot disapprove of their taste. The same opinion is also defended by Hume in *Of the Standard of Taste* (1757) who wrote: 'the proverb has justly determined it to be fruitless to dispute concerning taste. It is very natural, and even quite necessary, to extend this axiom to mental, as well as bodily taste'.[35]

Then the colonel discusses the concept of beauty, talking first of all about feminine beauty. As Hume who considered that 'beauty is no quality in things themselves: it exists merely in the mind which contemplates them; and each mind perceives a different beauty',[36] Freeman argues that beauty is subjective and this has always been a problem for artists, as he explains:

> No sooner were the arts of painting and sculpture brought to some degree of excellence, but the artists, in representing Venus, and Helen, or any other personage, from whom beauty was expected, must have found all their endeavours to please rendered ineffectual by the variety of sentiments which different men, by various structure of their nerves and organs, have of beauty: so that the painter's mistress however beautiful she might appear to him, and however justly he might portray her, would have little chance of charming the spectators.[37]

However if it is impossible for painters and sculptors to represent a woman whose beauty will be unanimously recognised, it is possible for them to sculpt or depict a woman who will not be unpleasant to anyone. Freeman states that ugliness is determined by criteria common to all men. A face with irregular features, for example, is never pleasant. He claims that it was the reason why ancient artists gave their sitters' symmetrical and regular facial features:

> The painter's business was [...] to give his goddess neither a high nor a low, but a straight nose, with cheeks that was neither fat nor lean, preserving the same mediocrity in all the proportions of her face. Upon such a principle as this we may suppose it was that Polycletus formed his Venus, which Pliny says called the canon or standard; and that he actually did so, still farther appears by all the antique statues now remaining.[38]

According to Freeman, the goddesses represented by ancient sculptors and painters are not unpleasant but they are not beautiful either. The artists Freeman met in Rome told him that at first they had been disappointed with antique works. However, the more they studied them the more they got used to them and admired them. The colonel takes up a theory formulated by Hume in *A Treatise of Human Nature* (1739–1740) and then defended by Adam Smith in *The Theory of Moral Sentiments* (1759) which claimed that out of habit we get to like things which were unpleasant at first. Indeed according to Hume,

> Nothing has a greater effect both to encrease and diminish our passions, to convert [...] pain into pleasure, than customs and repetition [...] [they] will sometimes be so powerful as even to convert pain into pleasure, and give us a relish in time for what at first was most harsh and disagreeable.[39]

This view is echoed by Freeman when he explains that

> This after-admiration of [antique statues] is far from being a proof of their having anything remarkably beautiful in themselves; and is

nothing more than the common effect of habit, which is itself not only in things of indifferent nature, such as cookery, dress, and furniture, but also in things that are at first extremely nauseous and disagreeable, such as tobacco, coffee, and other drugs.[40]

This statement runs counter to the opinion of Ramsay's contemporaries who greatly admired antique artefacts after the discovery of Herculaneum and Pompeii in 1738 and 1748. Ramsay's point of view may also seem paradoxical as he had always been highly interested in ancient civilisations: in 1739, he translated and published two letters written by his friend Camillo Paderni, in charge of excavations at Herculaneum, who gave him a detailed account of the findings. Furthermore, at the end of his life, Ramsay undertook excavations at Licenza to find the villa of the Roman poet Horace and planned to publish his essay entitled *An Inquiry into the Situation and Circumstances of Horace's Sabine Villa Written during Travels through Italy in the Years 1775, 1776, and 1777*.[41] Nevertheless, the pictorial style he adopted from 1754 was perfectly consistent with Freeman's point of view on ancient art as he did not generalise his sitters' features. On the contrary, in the portraits he painted from this period, he aimed at capturing a realistic likeness of the sitter. Ramsay's opinion and new style departed from the theories of Jonathan Richardson and Joshua Reynolds, keen admirers of ancient art.

In his seventh discourse delivered at the Royal Academy in 1776, Reynolds presented his theory on taste and beauty and refuted the theories of his Scottish rival. According to him, taste was determined by standards common to all men; thus, like judgments, taste was not subjective, even if

> They both, in the popular opinion, pretend to an entire exemption from the restraint of rules. It is supposed that their powers are intuitive; that under the name [...] of taste an exact judgment is given, without our knowing why, and without our being under the least obligation to reason, precept, or experience. One can scarce state these opinions without exposing their absurdity; yet they are constantly in the mouths of men, and particularly of artists.[42]

Moreover, Reynolds claimed that there undoubtedly existed a universal and unchangeable standard of taste as several generations had admired the same works of art. However, he believed that only artists and gentlemen who had studied the fine arts were able to understand and appreciate paintings. Like Richardson, he argued that nature was not perfect and that painters had to improve it and idealise their sitters as he stated that 'beauty [...] does not consist in taking what lies immediately before you'.[43] In his fourth discourse he explained that

> If a portrait painter is desirous to raise and improve his subject, he has no other means than by approaching it to a general idea. He leaves out all the minute breaks and peculiarities in the face, and changes the dress from a temporary fashion to one more permanent, which has annexed to it no ideas of meanness from its being familiar to us. But if an exact resemblance of an individual be considered as the sole object to be aimed at, the portrait painter will be apt to lose more than he gains by the acquired dignity taken from general nature. It is very difficult to ennoble the character of a countenance but at the expense of the likeness, which is what is most generally required by such as sit to the painter.[44]

Even if in his discourses he did not mention Ramsay, Reynolds had a low opinion of his rival's portraits and once declared that '[Ramsay was] a man of remarkable good sense, yet not a good painter'.[45] It is true that the aesthetic theories of the two portraitists were opposed as Reynolds followed Richardson's principles whereas Ramsay claimed that painters should represent nature and men as faithfully as possible, according to him 'the agreeable [...] cannot be separated from the exact'.[46]

Ramsay believed that artists had to respect certain principles to paint pleasant pictures. He thought, like Reynolds, that the appreciation of paintings depended on judgment and not on taste. Nevertheless, unlike Reynolds, he argued that these standards were universal: even if they had not studied art, all men were able to judge whether a painting was pleasant. In order to demonstrate this point to Modish, Freeman proposes the following experiment:

> Bring one of your tenant's daughters, and I venture to lay a wager that she shall be struck with your picture by La Tour, and no less with the view of your seat by Lambert and shall, fifty to one express her approbation by saying, they are *vastly natural*. When she has said this, she has shewn that she knew the proper standard, by which her approbation was to be directed, as much, at least, as she would have done, if she had got Aristotle by heart and all his commentators [...].[47]

According to Ramsay, artists had to respect two principles: they had to paint mimetic representations and draw their inspiration from everyday life, because men seemed to have a preference for what was familiar to them. The second rule is reminiscent of Hume's theories when he wrote that

> Contiguous objects must have an influence much superior to the distant and remote. Accordingly we find in common life, that men are principally concerned about those objects, which are not much removed either in space or time, enjoying the present, and leaving what is afar off to the care of chance and fortune.[48]

Ramsay's artistic theories were redolent of those of Hume, and when he asserted that the beauty of a painting consisted in a mimetic representation of nature, he also repeated the theories of another Scottish philosopher, Francis Hutcheson (1694–1746), who claimed in *An Enquiry into the Original Ideas of Beauty and Virtue* (1725) that

> An exact Imitation shall still be *beautiful*, tho the Original were entirely void of it: Thus the *Deformitys* of old Age in a Picture, the *rudest Rocks* or *Mountains* in a *Landskip*, if well represented, shall have abundant *Beauty* [...].[49]

To conclude, the portraits painted by Ramsay after the publication of *A Dialogue on Taste* show that he applied his theories to his own artistic practice. Indeed, he entirely broke free from English portrait conventions to paint works characterised by an accurate portrayal of facial features as well as by the sobriety of the settings and the informality of the sitter's pose. Paintings such as the bust-length portrait of Lady Hervey[50] in which the sitter's double chin is visible and the portrait of the Duchess of Argyll contrast with the idealised images presented in the portraits of Joshua Reynolds, who was the leader of the English school of portraiture.[51] Although Reynolds became the most popular painter in London, Ramsay continued to have a successful career until 1773 and was the first Scottish artist to be appointed Painter in Ordinary to the King in 1767. He had an important influence on the Scottish portraitists of the second half of the eighteenth century: his success encouraged young artists to imitate his style and David Martin (1737-1797) and Alexander Nasmyth (1758-1840), who both trained with Ramsay and returned to Edinburgh to open their studio, absorbed and handed down their master's style to the following generation of portraitists.[52] Thus with his paintings and his aesthetic essays clearly influenced by the theories of contemporary Scottish thinkers, Ramsay defined a set of artistic conventions which contributed to the development of an identifiable Scottish style of portraiture.

Notes

1. The development of painting in Great Britain has been studied in detail by Waterhouse. See Ellis Kirkham Waterhouse, *Painting in Britain 1530 to 1790* (Harmondsworth: Pelican History of Art, 1994). For a comprehensive survey of the history of Scottish art see Duncan Macmillan, *Scottish Art 1460-2000*, 2nd edn. (Edinburgh: Mainstream Publishing, 2000). See also Murdo Macdonald, *Scottish Art* (London: Thames and Hudson, 2000).
2. For example, De Wet painted the ceiling of the Vine Room in Kellie Castle. See Julia Lloyd Williams, 'The Import of Art: the Taste for Northern European Goods in Scotland in the Seventeenth Century', in *The North Sea and Culture (1550-1800)*, ed. by Juliette Roding and Lex Heerma Van Voss (Hilversum: Verloren Publishers, 1996), pp. 301-02.
3. For more specific information on de Medina, see Rosalind K. Marshall, *John de Medina, 1659-1710*, Scottish Masters Series 7 (Edinburgh: National Galleries of Scotland, 1988).

4   Patrons commissioned few paintings and until the beginning of the nineteenth century they almost exclusively bought portraits.
5   Alexander Nasmyth (1758–1840) was apprenticed to a coach painter and David Roberts (1796–1864) trained with a house painter; as for Raeburn, he worked as an apprentice to a goldsmith. The Trustees' Academy was founded in 1760 to train young people who wanted to work in the textile industry. The advertisement published in *The Edinburgh Evening Courant* to announce the opening of the academy stated that: 'The commissioners and Trustees for improving fisheries and manufactures in Scotland, do hereby advertise, that by an agreement with Mr. De la Cour painter, he has opened a school in this city for persons of both sexes that shall be presented to him by the trustees, whom he is to teach gratis, the ART of DRAWING for the use of manufactures, especially the drawing of PATTERNS for the LINEN and WOOLLEN MANUFACTURES.' *Edinburgh Evening Courant*, 27 June 1760, n. p.

   For the history of the Trustees' Academy see Patricia Brookes, '*The Trustees' Academy, Edinburgh, 1760–1801: the Patronage of Art and Design in the Scottish Enlight-enment*' (unpublished doctoral thesis, University of Syracuse, 1989). Two fine art schools had been created in Scotland but they were short-lived: the Saint Luke Academy was opened in Edinburgh from 1729 to 1731; the Foulis Academy was set up in Glasgow in 1753 and closed in 1775.
6   As for her, Katherine Read (1723–1778) spent several years working in the British colonies in India. The life and career of Jacob More and Gavin Hamilton in Rome have been studied in Marion Amblard, 'La carrière de Jacob More et de Gavin Hamilton en Italie : L'impact de ces deux peintres sur l'art pictural écossais au XVIIIe siècle', in *L'Écosse et ses doubles. Ancien monde – nouveau monde. Old World – New World. Scotland and Its Doubles*, ed. by Morag Landi (Paris: L'Harmattan, 2010), pp. 89–106. For more specific information on Jacob More see Patricia. R. Andrew, 'Jacob More 1740–1793', 2 vols (unpublished doctoral thesis, Edinburgh University, 1981). On Gavin Hamilton see also David Irwin, 'Gavin Hamilton: Archaeologist, Painter, and Dealer', *The Art Bulletin* (June 1962), 87–102. Julia Lloyd Williams, *Gavin Hamilton 1723–1798*, Scottish Masters Series 18 (Edinburgh: National Galleries of Scotland, 1994). Brendan Cassidy, *The Life and Letters of Gavin Hamilton (1723–1798): Artist & Art Dealer in Eighteenth-Century Rome*, 2 vols (London: Harvey Miller, 2012).

   Smibert settled in Boston in 1728 where he remained until his death in 1751. Cosmo Alexander lived in the American colonies from 1766 to 1771. On the career of John Smibert see Richard Saunders, *John Smibert. Colonial America's First Painter* (New Haven and London: Yale University Press, 1995). On the life and art of Cosmo Alexander see James Holloway, *Patrons and Painters: Art in Scotland 1650–1760* (Edinburgh: National Galleries of Scotland, 1989), pp. 85–103.
7   On eighteenth-century Scottish painters' training in Italy see Marion Amblard, 'The Scottish Painters' Exile in Italy in the Eighteenth Century', in *Études Écossaises* 13 (Grenoble: Ellug, 2010), pp. 59–77.
8   The life and art of Allan Ramsay have been studied in detail by Alastair Smart: Alastair Smart, *The Life and Art of Allan Ramsay* (London: Routledge and Kegan Paul, 1952); Alistair Smart, *Allan Ramsay 1713–1784* (Edinburgh: Scottish National Portrait Gallery, 1992). See also Mungo Campbell, *Allan Ramsay: Portraits of the Enlightenment* (Munich: Prestel, 2013).

9   A few months after settling in London, Ramsay wrote to his friend Alexander Cunyngham that he had already 'put all your *Vanlois* and *Soldis* and *Rosios* to flight and now play the first fiddle [himself]'. Quoted in *Allan Ramsay 1713-1784*, p. 45.
10 André Félibien, *Conférences de l'Académie Royale de Peinture et de Sculpture pendant l'Année 1667* (Paris: Frédéric Léonard, 1669), n. pag.
11 Richardson was a pupil of John Riley; after Kneller's death he was one of the most successful native-born portraitists in London. Among others he painted the portrait of Prime Minister Sir Robert Walpole (1676-1745) and the famous portrait of Alexander Pope (1688-1744) which is now on display at the National Portrait Gallery in London.
12 This also partly contributed to the growing number of requests for portraits. Until the first decades of the eighteenth century, only the patrons belonging to the upper social classes could afford portraits. The Earl of Fife strongly disapproved of that new trend and wrote: 'Very few people presented themselves to a painter except those who were of great families, or remarkable for their actions in the service of their country, or for some other extraordinary circumstances, so that the field for enquiry was not extended, as lately, when everybody almost who can afford twenty pounds, has the portraits of himself, wife and children painted. Those, therefore, who collect next century, even with the aid of the annual Exhibition, will hardly be able to find out the numerous bad painters, and the uninteresting obscure persons so represented'. Quoted in Marcia Pointon, *Hanging the Head: Portraiture and Social Formation in Eighteenth-Century England* (New Haven: Yale University Press, 1993), p. 2.
13 Jonathan Richardson, *An Essay on the Theory of Painting* (London: n.p., 1725), p. 13.
14 Richardson, p. 13.
15 Ibid., pp. 172-73.
16 Thus Richardson explained about colours: 'Perfect Black, and White are disagreeable; for which reason a Painter should break those Extreams of Colours that there may be a Warmth, and Mellowness in his Work: Let him (in Flesh especially) remember to avoid the Chalk, the Brick, and the Charcoal, and think of the Pearl, and a ripe Peach' (ibid., p. 159). Moreover, he gave recommendations about how fabrics should be represented: 'a piece of silk, or Cloth hung, or laid flat, has not the Beauty tho' the Colour of it be pleasing, as when flung into Folds; nay a piece of Silk that has little Beauty in it self shall be much improv'd only by being Pink'd, Water'd, or Quilted; the Reason is, in these Cases there arises a Variety produced by Lights, Shades, and Reflections' (Ibid., pp. 158-59). He also explained: 'the Draperies must have broad Masses of Light, and Shadow, and noble large Folds to give a Greatness; and These artfully subdivided, add Grace' (ibid., p. 193). Richardson devoted several pages of his essay to the type of clothes painters should represent in their paintings (ibid., pp. 193-99).
17 Ibid., p. 207.
18 Richard Wendorf, *The Elements of Life. Biography and Portrait-Painting in Stuart and Georgian England* (Oxford: Clarendon Press, 1990), p. 137.
19 Thomas Hudson, *Lady Lucy Manners, Duchess of Montrose*, c. 1740, oil on canvas, National Trust Collections, Calke Abbey, Derbyshire.
    Joshua Reynolds, *Thomas Lister, the Brown Boy*, 1752-1764, oil on canvas, Cartwright Hall Art Gallery, Bradford; *William Frederick, 2nd Duke of Gloucester*, 1780, oil on canvas, Trinity College, University of Cambridge, Cambridge; Peter P. Rubens, *Susanna Lunden, 'Le Chapeau de Paille'*, c. 1622-1625, oil on canvas, National Gallery, London.

20 Anthony Van Dyck, *The Five Children of King Charles I*, 1637, oil on canvas, The Royal Collection.
21 Allan Ramsay, *Norman Macleod, 22nd Chief of Macleod*, 1748, oil on canvas. Dunvegan Castle, Skye; *Master John Prideaux Basset*, c. 1747, oil on canvas, private collection.
22 Professor Duncan Macmillan has also noticed that for the portrait of Lady Mary Coke, Ramsay reproduced the pose of the statue of the Roman goddess Minerva which is in the collection of the Vatican museums. Macmillan, p. 107.
23 Richardson, pp. 86–87.
24 Allan Ramsay, *Lady Margaret Hall of Dunglass*, 1752, oil on canvas, Tate Britain, London.
25 Ramsay first got married in 1739 to Ann Ramsay with whom he had three children. Two of these children did not survive to adulthood and his wife passed away in 1743 giving birth to their third child. In 1752, he married Margaret Lindsay, daughter of Sir Alexander Lindsay of Evelick.
26 Joshua Reynolds, *Captain the Honourable Augustus Keppel*, 1752, oil on canvas, National Maritime Museum, London.
27 *Gentleman's Magazine and His Historical Chronicle*, 10 August 1784, p. 638.
28 On Ramsay's literary career see Iain Gordon Brown, *Poet and Painter. Allan Ramsay Father and Son, 1684–1784* (Edinburgh: National Library of Scotland, 1984).
29 According to his first biographer, Allan Cunningham, Ramsay 'was accused of being more anxious to be thought an accomplished scholar, and a man of understanding and taste, than a good painter, – a profession for which he was said to have but a cold regard', in *The Lives of the Most Eminent British Painters, Sculptors and Architects*, 6 vols. (London: John Murray, 1832), v, p. 36.
30 On the friendship between Ramsay and Hume and the links between Ramsay's portraits and Hume's theories see Robert Mankin, 'De proche en loin : Allan Ramsay peint la philosophie', in *Bulletin de la société d'études anglo-américaines des XVIIe et XVIIIe siècles* 52 (2001), pp. 155–72.
31 In 1771, Scottish writer Henry Mackenzie sent a letter in which he explained: 'Since I am on the subject of poetry I will enclose one given me lately, written by a man whom everyone allows to be a painter, and who is himself very desirous of being thought an Author of some consequence, to wit Allan Ramsay. […] The idea is good enough, and the versification polish'd into a laudable smoothness.' Henry Mackenzie, 'Letter to Mrs Rose', 1771, Edinburgh, National Library of Scotland, MS 647, fols 19–20.

Horace Walpole shared Mackenzie's opinion and wrote: 'I do not mean that I wonder at his being a bad poet; I didn't know he was one at all […] but an old dotard! To be sporting and playing at leap frog with brats!'. Quoted in Iain Gordon Brown, 'The Pamphlets of Allan Ramsay the Younger', *The Book Collector* 37 (1988), p. 60.
32 Voltaire mentioned *A Letter to the Right Honourable the Earl of – Concerning the Affair of Elizabeth Canning, by a Clergyman* and wrote that it was written by 'un philosophe nommé Mr. Ramsay'. Voltaire. 'Histoire d'Elizabeth Canning, et Jean Calas', in *Mélanges de Philosophie, de Morale, et de Politique par Mr. De Voltaire*, (London: 1772), viii, p. 249.
33 John Young Thomson Greig (ed.), *The Letters of David Hume*, 2 vols (Oxford: Oxford University Press, 1932), I, p. 221
34 Allan Ramsay, 'On Taste', in *The Investigator. Containing the Following the Tract: I. On Ridicule, II. On Elizabeth Canning, III. On Naturalization, IV. On Taste* (1755), (London: n. pub., 1762), pp. 9–10.

35 David Hume, *Four Dissertations, I. The Natural History of Religion, II. Of the Passions, III. Of Tragedy, IV. Of the Standard of Taste* (London: A. Millar, 1757), p. 209.
36 Hume, *Four Dissertations*, pp. 208-09.
37 Ramsay, 'On Taste', p. 21.
38 Ramsay, 'On Taste', p. 24.
39 David Hume, *A Treatise of Human Nature*, (1739-40), 2 vols (London: Thomas and Joseph Allman, 1817), II, pp. 115-16. Adam Smith took up a similar idea in *The Theory of Moral Sentiments* when he wrote:'There are other principles besides those already enumerated, which have a considerable influence upon the moral sentiments of mankind. [...] These principles are customs and fashion, principles which extend their dominion over our judgments concerning beauty of every kind.' in *The Theory of Moral Sentiments*, (1759), ed. by Knud Haakonssen (Cambridge: Cambridge University Press, 2002), p. 227.
40 Ramsay, 'On Taste', p. 25.
41 The manuscript can be consulted at the National Library of Scotland, Edinburgh. A. Ramsay, 'An Inquiry into the Situation and Circumstances of Horace's Sabine Villa Written during Travels through Italy in the Years 1775,1776, and 1777', 1777, Edinburgh, National Library of Scotland, MS 730. For more specific information on this essay see Bernard D. Frischer and Iain G. Brown (eds), *Allan Ramsay and the Search for Horace's Villa* (Aldershot: Ashgate, 2001).
42 Joshua Reynolds, *The Discourses of Sir Joshua Reynolds* (London: James Carpenter, 1842), p. 116. Reynolds also criticised Hume's theory as he wrote 'the common saying that tastes are not to be disputed, owes its influence, and its general reception, to the same error which leads us to imagine this faculty of too high an original too submit to the authority of an earthly' (p. 121).
43 Ibid., p. 122.
44 Ibid., p. 71.
45 Smart, *Allan Ramsay: Painter, Essayist and Man of the Enlightenment*, p. 106.
46 Ramsay, 'On Ridicule', p. 63. On the contrary, Reynolds wrote: 'the likeness, consists more in taking the general air, than in observing the exact similitude of every feature.' (p. 55).
47 Ramsay, 'On Taste', p. 57. This is also one Hume's theories in 'Of the Standard of Taste', but he stated that only a few men knew about these standards.
48 David Hume, *Four Dissertations, I. The Natural History of Religion, II. Of the Passions, III. Of Tragedy, IV. Of the Standard of Taste* (London: A. Millar, 1757), p. 167.
49 Francis Hutcheson, 'An Enquiry into the Original Ideas of Beauty and Virtue', (1725), in *Collected Works of Francis Hutcheson*, 4 vols (Hildesheim: Georg Olms Verlagsbuchhandlung, 1971), I, pp. 35-36.
50 Allan Ramsay, *Mary Lepel, Lady Hervey*, c. 1762, oil on canvas, National Trust, Suffolk; *Elizabeth Gunning, Duchess of Argyll*, 1760, oil on canvas, Scottish National Portrait Gallery, Edinburgh.
51 In 1760, Reynolds painted a full-length portrait of the Duchess of Argyll (The Lady Lever Art Gallery, Liverpool); the dress and the pose of the sitter gave her the air of an antique statue.
52 Martin was in contact with Henry Raeburn (1756-1823) who was the leading portraitist in the opening decades of the nineteenth century and the most influential artist on

nineteenth-century Scottish portraiture. Although Raeburn did not train with him, Martin's influence his noticeable in Raeburn's early portraits.

Raeburn and Ramsay's technique and style are different, but both painters aimed at painting a truthful likeness of their sitters and their portraits are also characterised by the sobriety and simplicity of the composition.

3. 'A Common Right of Mankind' or 'A Necessary Evil'? Hume's contextualist conception of political liberty

GILLES ROBEL

This chapter will focus on one specific form of political liberty examined in one of Hume's essays, 'Of the Liberty of the Press' (1741), but its contention is that this essay opens a window into the main features and complexities of Hume's conception of political liberty. 'Of the Liberty of the Press' is one of Hume's very first essays published after what he regarded as the 'failure' of the *Treatise of Human Nature*. Drawing his inspiration from Addison, Hume chose a journalistic genre more susceptible to enabling him to develop a form of commerce between the 'dominions of knowledge' and those of 'conversation'.[1] Hume corrected and amended his essays over the years and 'Of the Liberty of the Press' is the essay which received the most extensive alterations, making his approach of the question quite puzzling to the modern reader, perhaps more familiar with John Stuart Mill's discussion of the subject in chapter two of *On Liberty*.[2] One of the main characteristics and difficulties of Hume's empirical approach is his reluctance to conceptualise political liberty. For Hume liberty is a notion which cannot be examined *in abstracto* but only as part of an analysis of its development and contribution to a specific political and social setting. Such reluctance has often been misinterpreted, but we will try to show that it is philosophically grounded and that it enables Hume to develop on original approach, far removed from the dominant beliefs of the time.

'Of the Liberty of the Press' has tended to attract more attention for what was removed from it than for what Hume left in it. In the original version of the essays, Hume raises two questions: first 'how it happens that Great Britain alone enjoys this peculiar privilege' of allowing people to communicate their thoughts freely, and second 'whether such a liberty be advantageous or prejudicial'. In the first version of the essay, i.e. from 1741 to 1768, Hume's point of view seems fairly similar to that of anyone who regarded the constitutional settlement of 1688 as a 'perfect system of liberty'. The birth of the liberty of the press can indeed be traced back to the abolition of the Imprimatur with the lapse of the Licensing Order in 1694.[3] Hume explains that the liberty of press in Britain is caused by its mixed form of government: in a regime 'which is neither wholly monarchical, nor wholly republican the spirit of the people must frequently be rouzed, in order to curb the ambition of the court'. Hume describes the press as a kind of fourth estate, a watchdog designed to stop any attempts of the crown to encroach on Parliamentary power. And the press was useful to control the power of the government as well: after the replacement of the Triennial Act by the Septennial Act in 1716, which consolidated Robert Walpole's power and that of a Whig oligarchy, a large number of newspapers and pamphlets, such as Bolingbroke's *Craftsman* were published for that purpose.

As regards the question of the benefits of the liberty of the press, Hume explains that grievances should be vented freely, that a whisper is more dangerous than a pamphlet and that the press helps to promote a plurality of interests. It is therefore an essential component of the culture of politeness.[4] In the original version of the essay, Hume concludes that: 'this liberty is attended with so few inconveniencies, that it may be claimed as the common right of mankind, and ought to be indulged almost in every government.'[5] However, from the 1770 edition onwards, the second question and its long development is replaced by a rather abrupt concluding paragraph: 'It must however be allowed, that the unbounded liberty of the press, though it be difficult, perhaps impossible, to propose a suitable remedy for it, is one of the evils, attending those mixt forms of government.'[6] So from being a 'common right of mankind' the freedom of the press had become a 'necessary evil' in a mixed form of government.

The most obvious reason for the change are the famous Wilkesite disturbances triggered by the English journalist and politician John Wilkes after the publication of the *North Briton* number 45; they affected England between 1762 and 1771. Privately Hume reacted very strongly to those events, and his reaction is all the more so interesting since these are the only major political troubles he experienced in his lifetime with the exception of the 1745 Jacobite Rising, which he did not even witness. It is hard to recognise the 'man of mild disposition, of command of temper' – as Hume describes himself in his autobiography – in the letters he sends at the time, in which he calls the rioters 'Barbarians on the Thames' or 'scum of London'.[7] After 1768, Hume revises all his writings related to political liberty to stress the importance of order and authority, removing 'happy' from his description of the British government, or changing a passage stating that *habeas corpus* '*is essentially requisite* for the protection of liberty' to '*seems necessary* for the protection of liberty' [author's emphases] in his *History*.[8] Commentator Duncan Forbes sees the change in his essay on the press as 'the most striking example of a retreat in the later Hume from a liberal to a less liberal position', stopping short of calling it 'reactionary conservatism'.[9] According to David Miller, it shows that for Hume 'liberty is the jam, security the bread', and for that 'he must ultimately side with the Conservatives'.[10] So Hume corrected his essay in the light of contemporary events. Does the contextualisation of his writings affect the consistency of this thought? And is this some sort of Burkeian overreaction?

    A close analysis of the essay shows that Hume's position has not changed that much and that the second version of the essay is in any case far more consistent with his overall philosophy. As regards the liberty of the press, Hume had expressed some distrust in the 1741 version of the essay ('it has not as yet produced any pernicious effect'), but it was then toned down. His optimism is founded on the fact that the press can educate people, and the hope that the British people have reached a sufficient degree of maturity and civilisation not to be seduced by demagogues: 'it is to be hoped, that men, being every day more accustomed to the free discussion of public affairs, will improve in the judgment of them, and be with greater difficulty seduced by every idle rumour and popular clamour'.[11] In the light of the Wilkes affair, Hume realised that that time had not arrived yet, and that a bigoted and jingoistic newspaper such as the *North Briton* could pose a serious threat. Hume's assessment of the dangers of an unbounded liberty therefore changed after 1768.[12]

Liberty and forms of government

The contextualisation of liberty in Hume goes further than taking account of political events: for him the question of the liberty of the press is inextricably linked to forms of government. In his answer to the first question, Hume extends his analysis from the British government to various political regimes, and from the freedom of the press to political liberty in general, and its relationship to authority. And in so doing he questions the prevailing beliefs of the time. The difficulty is that Hume's terminology is sometimes ambiguous and needs to be clarified.

In his political and historical writings, Hume makes an implicit distinction between three forms of liberty which correspond to specific social and political settings. The first one is a form of individual liberty which results from a lack of external constraints, the freedom for an individual to do as he pleases, which Hume occasionally calls 'natural liberty' or 'licentiousness': 'The heart of man delights in liberty: the very image of constraint is grievous to it: when you would confine it by violence, or what would otherwise have been its choice, the inclination immediately changes, and desire is turned into aversion' ('Of Polygamy and Divorces').[13] In his *History of England*, Hume criticises the so-called Whig interpretation of history – also shared by many Tories – according to which there was in England an 'ancient' or 'timeless constitution' which had preserved liberty down the ages.[14] He shows that in Saxon times it was merely that form of 'natural liberty' which prevailed:

> On the whole, notwithstanding the seeming liberty or rather licentiousness of the Anglo-Saxons, the great body even of the free citizens, in those ages, really enjoyed much less true liberty, than where the execution of laws is the most severe, and where subjects are reduced to the strictest subordination and dependence on the civil magistrate.[15]

So for Hume this form of liberty is a threat to the stability of society and is mainly an illusion.

The second form of liberty is what he calls 'civil liberty', i.e. the possibility for members of society to enjoy the rights which are granted to them as members of civil society. Civil liberty results from the lack of arbitrary constraints. For Hume, any form of government which respects the rule of law is a regime where civil liberty can prevail. This is a radical departure from the Whig contractualist view and Republican discourse, whereby there is a logical and necessary connection between civil liberty and free representative regimes. Hume attacks the 'fashionable system' – which he calls 'religious' or vulgar Whiggism[16] loosely based on Locke's theories which is used to show the superiority of English liberty over French slavery: in the *Second Treatise* Locke argued that absolute monarchy is 'inconsistent with civil society, and so can be no form of government at all'.[17] For Hume, civil liberty is guaranteed by the security brought by the existence of rules and laws which can be anticipated, and therefore a modern absolute monarchy such as the French monarchy – which he calls a civilised monarchy – is a form of government which is perfectly compatible with civil liberty: 'It may now be affirmed of civilized monarchies, what was formerly said in praise of republics alone, that they are a government of Laws, not of Men' ('Of Civil Liberty').[18]

Finally there is a third form of liberty, which can be called 'political liberty', and refers to the right for each citizen or subject to take a direct or indirect part in the government or political life of the country. This type of liberty requires the existence of strict constitutional safeguards and can only really exist in what Hume calls 'free governments'. A free government being defined as a government which 'admits of a partition of power among several members, whose united authority is no less, or is commonly greater, than that of any monarch, but who [...] must act by general and equal laws, that are previously known to all the members, and to all their subjects.'[19] In Hume's lifetime, the only governments which fit the description are republics such as Holland, or a limited monarchy like Britain. Political liberty can take different forms, such as *habeas corpus*, the freedom of the press or religious freedom, and can only exist if there are no arbitrary constraints at all, not even the royal prerogative. At least this is what Hume seems to imply in the definition he gives of a law voted under James I to restrict the power of monopolies:

It was there supposed, that every subject of England had entire power to dispose of his own actions, provided he did no injury to any of his fellow-subjects; and that *no prerogative of the king, no power of any magistrate, nothing but the authority alone of laws* [author's emphasis], could restrain that unlimited freedom. The full prosecution of this noble principle into all its natural consequences, has at last, through many contests, produced that singular and happy government, which we enjoy at present.[20]

Hume thinks that the political liberty brought by the 1688 settlement is the 'perfection of civil society', and that no country in the world has reached such a level of freedom, especially in matters of freedom of speech: 'Nothing is more apt to surprize a foreigner, than the extreme liberty, which we enjoy in this country, of communicating whatever we please to the public, and of openly censuring every measure, entered into by the king or his ministers'.[21]

Liberty and opinion

What is interesting to notice in this typology is the connection Hume makes between liberty and various stages of development. It is an implicit criticism of the perception of liberty as a universal right and of the 'vulgar' Whig doctrine which uses the same term – liberty – to encapsulate the lack of constraints, the transition from barbarism to civilisation and the emergence of a free constitution.[22]

But what precisely is the articulation between the different forms of liberty? Is it right to consider, as David Miller does, that for Hume liberty is essentially a luxury? The answer lies in the relationship between liberty and authority. As Hume writes in his last essay, 'Of the Origin of Government', 'In all governments, there is a perpetual intestine struggle, open or secret, between authority and liberty; and neither of them can ever absolutely prevail in the contest'.[23] There is in fact for Hume a dialectical relationship between authority and liberty, the one being the condition of the existence and development of the other: 'Liberty is the perfection of civil society; but still authority must be acknowledged essential to its very existence: and in those contests, which so often take place between the one and the other, the latter may, on that account, challenge the preference'.²⁴ So civil liberty is not in itself dispensable and Hume refuses to say if authority is preferable to liberty *in abstracto*: it all depends on the political and social context of the time. The authority of government is not founded on any extra-historical notion, be it a hypothetical state of nature, a timeless constitution or an 'original contract' – it rests on the opinion of its subjects:

> Nothing is more surprizing [...] than the easiness with which the many are governed by the few [...]. When we enquire by what means this wonder is effected, we shall find, that as force is always on the side of the governed, the governors have nothing to support them but opinion. It is therefore on opinion only that government is founded.²⁵

In each historical period and each regime, opinion has a different awareness of the limits which can be set to the actions of the sovereign or the subjects, and on this awareness depends the legitimacy of resistance to the government.²⁶

The relationship between the authority of a government and the level of liberty allowed to its subjects is therefore quite complex. In his attempts to explain why Great Britain enjoyed so much liberty of the press, Hume underlines a paradox which marks a clear departure from prevalent ideas: free governments are not necessarily the regimes where liberty is the most secure. In a civilised monarchy the strength and security of the position of the magistrate means that he has no reason to distrust his subjects and therefore he can grant them large liberties.²⁷ Whereas in a republican regime, liberties are more at risk because the law is stronger, reducing the liberty of each individual:

> In a government such as that of France, which is absolute, and where law, custom and religion concur [...] to make people fully satisfied with their condition, the monarch cannot entertain any jealousy against his subjects, and therefore is apt to indulge them in great liberties both of speech and action. In a government altogether

> republican, such as that of Holland [...] there is no danger in entrusting the magistrates with large discretionary powers which lay a considerable restraint on men's actions and make every private citizen pay a great respect to the government'.[28]

In a mixed constitution such a liberty helps keep the balance between the discretionary powers of the king and the powers of Parliament. The liberty of the press is both an instrument for the protection of civil liberties and a manifestation of such a liberty. But Hume provides an essentially utilitarian rationale for that liberty: it is only good insofar as it does not challenge the existence of liberty itself.

In order to understand Hume's conception of liberty, it is important to stress that he considers society as a system of conventions. Laws get more refined, civilisation improves and liberty increases as men gradually experience the advantages they bring to them. The difference between a barbarian and a civilised man is therefore mainly a difference of degree, not of nature, the latter being able to adjust the conventions in order finely to tune the balance between authority and liberty, whereas the former is entirely submitted to conventions: 'Can we expect, that a government will be well modelled by a people, who know not how to make a spinning-wheel, or to employ a loom to advantage? Not to mention, that all ignorant ages are infested with superstition, which throws government off its bias [...]'.[29] The history of civilisation is the story of the gradual development of the rule of law, but such progress is not linear: 'Law [...] is the slow product of order and liberty'.[30] The contextual and historical nature of liberty leads to a paradox: as men become more civilised, they learn to enjoy the benefits of the rule of law but their rights get defined more explicitly and precisely, and they become more jealous of them, hence more able and willing to resist authority which conditions its development: 'Liberty, in a country of the highest liberty, is left entirely to its own defence, without any countenance or protection. The wild state of nature is renewed in one of the most civilized societies of mankind [...]' ('Of Some Remarkable Customs').[31] (The expression 'wild state of nature' does not refer to a Hobbesian pre-social state of war but to the triumph of natural liberty over other forms of liberty.) Liberty, therefore, contains the seeds of its own destruction, and this paradox is at the heart of the British system of government, hence Hume's reaction to the Wilkesite disturbances.

Preserving Liberty

Burke's reaction to the French Revolution was a reaction of fear caused by a new phenomenon which could question ancient traditions. Hume's reaction to Wilkes twenty years earlier is different: he does not think that he is faced with a new phenomenon, but is afraid that history might be repeating itself.

The vocabulary used by Hume in his letters on Wilkes and the disturbances is in fact very similar to the one he uses in his *History* about the Republican leaders at the time of the 'Civil War' (War of the Three Nations) in the seventeenth century. While he approves of the measures taken by the Commons to reduce Charles I's prerogative, he shows that an immoderate zeal in favour of an abstract conception of liberty is dangerous for liberty itself.[32] He shows that Republican leaders suppressed liberties in the name of liberty itself, and that the people were quite surprisingly willing to obey them: 'Never, in this island, was known a more severe and arbitrary government, than was generally exercised, by the patrons of liberty'.[33] Hume also writes about 'the madness of the people', 'the furies of fanaticism' under Cromwell.

He emphasises the fact that at the time of the War of the Three Nations, such a type of political and religious fanaticism was new and the people or the mob could easily be deluded:

> The veneration for parliament was at this time extreme throughout the nation [...]. Few or no instances of their encroaching ambition or selfish claims had hitherto been observed. Men considered the House of Commons in no other light than as representatives of their nation [...] who were the eternal guardians of law and liberty.[34]

But one century later the context had changed and Hume hoped that a certain number of lessons had been drawn. There is probably in Hume's attitude at the time some disappointment at the realisation that in spite of the development of commerce, civilisation had not progressed as fast as he had hoped, and the passion he had cultivated in his youth for the English culture and literary scene had converted into *Schadenfreude*: 'It has been my Misfortune to write in the Language of the most stupid and factious Barbarians in the World; and it is long since I have renounced all desire of their Approbation' (25 October 1769).[35] In an answer to a letter from Turgot, who was congratulating him on the progress of liberty with the Wilkesite disturbances, Hume explains very clearly that there is nothing to rejoice about, and deplores 'the usual return of Barbarism and Ignorance'. In short, the English are proving not to be civilised enough to enjoy extensive political liberties:

> Our governement has become a Chimera; and is too perfect in the point of Liberty, for so vile a beast as an Englishman, who is a Man, a bad Animal too, corrupted by above a Century of Licentiousness. The Misfortune is, that this Liberty can scarcely be retrench'd without the Danger of being entirely lost [...].[36]

Hume's reaction can therefore be explained by the fact that he sees three different sets of danger. The first danger is constitutional. The Wilkesite disturbances show the fragility of the 1688 settlement and the inability of the government to react to the troubles is particularly worrying, when what is at stake is a conflict between 'the mob and the Constitution': as the City of London has just given the King 'A Remonstrance and Petition praying for the Dissolution of Parliament and the Removal of Evil Ministers' which was instantly published in the press, Hume writes to his London publisher:

> To punish it as it deserves woud certainly produce a Fray; but what signifies a Fray, in comparison of losing all Authority to Government. There must necessarily be a Struggle between the Mob and the Constitution [...]. I wish therefore [...] that vigorous Measures will be taken; an impeachment immediately voted of the Mayor [...] and the Habeas Corpus suspended till next meeting of Parliament. Good God! What abandon'd Madmen there are in England![37]

This is why Hume calls for radical steps such as the suspension of *habeas corpus*, which is one of the political liberties only the most civilised societies can enjoy. The excessive liberty means that the balance of the mixed government is now increasingly tilting towards a republic. Yet as Hume explains in one of his letters to his nephew, 'any attempt towards it can in our [country] only produce Anarchy, which is the immediate Forerunner of Despotism' (8 Dec. 1775).[38] In other words the transformation of Britain into a republic would entail the suppression of all liberties: an absolute monarchy would in Hume's eyes be a far more gentle death for Britain's mixed government than a republic.[39]

The second danger is economic. The jingoisim and xenophobia stirred up by John Wilkes encouraged a belligerent policy, and this helped Prime Minister William Pitt the Elder to consolidate his power at the time of the Seven Years War. This resulted in an expensive war policy which increased the national debt and in Hume's eyes weakened the government, with the danger that a more authoritarian government might be established which would endanger liberties: 'The Kingdom may be thriving [...] but all this is nothing in comparison of the continual Encrease of our Debts, in every idle War, into which, it seems, the Mob of London are to rush every Minister' (11 March 1771).[40]

Hume uses particularly harsh terms against 'the mob' or 'the rabble' in his correspondence. There is undeniably an element of fear of the uneducated common people in Hume as in most Enlightened writers, but his attacks are mainly focused at their leaders and members of the 'middling ranks' who have benefited from the stability of the government. As he writes in 1763: 'the present Madness [is] encourag'd by Lyes, Calumnies, Imposture and every infamous Art usual among popular Leaders'.[41] Such a denunciation of the rabble and its leaders clearly echoes Hume's pages on the Civil War and stems from the last danger, which is a philosophical danger.

Unlike Burke, Hume does not consider that the Wilkes and Liberty riots are a positive development which will give an opportunity to enlarge the representativeness of Parliament. He draws parallels with the War of the Three Nations because he feels that the same mechanisms are at work, namely the intrusion of metaphysics into politics: where there was religious enthusiasm in the seventeenth century, he now sees political enthusiasm. In his philosophical writings, Hume tries to reform philosophy by invalidating any system of thought which judges reality with standards which do not derive from it, or which is independent from the prejudices of common life.[42] Such a philosophy, which he calls 'false philosophy', leads either to the kind of ataraxia described at the end of the first book of the *Treatise*, or to a form of alienation which has serious political consequences, leading to violence and instability. They appeared at the time of the War of the Three Nations with the development of 'parties from principles' such as religious sects but also Puritan movements: 'Parties from principle, especially abstract speculative principles, are conceptually absurd, and perhaps the most extraordinary and unaccountable phenomenon that has yet appeared in human affairs'.[43] As he explains at the end of the second *Enquiry*, false philosophy 'bends every branch of knowledge to its own purpose, without much regard to the phenomena of nature, or to the unbiased sentiments of the mind, hence reasoning, and even language, have been warped from their natural course'.[44]

This is precisely what happens to the concept of liberty at the time of the Wilkesite disturbances. On several instances Hume insists on the fact that this rebellion is without grounds:

> Here is a People thrown into Disorders [...] merely from the Abuse of Liberty, chiefly the Liberty of the Press; without any Grievance, I do not say, real, but even imaginary; and without any of them being able to tell one Circumstance of Government which they wish to have corrected (16 June 1768).[45]

But he is careful to make a distinction between the slogan and the concept:

> I wish, that People do not take a Disgust at Liberty: a word, that has been so much profan'd by these polluted Mouths, that men of Sense are sick at the very mention of it. I hope a new term will be invented to express so valuable and good a thing'. (26 October 1772).[46]

So in the case of his essay on the liberty of the press, Hume's reaction may seem out of proportion to the modern reader if one does not take into account the philosophical grounds of his corrections. The 'fashionable system of liberty' does not just induce a constitutional imbalance: it can prevent people from understanding liberty, it can alienate the British from the liberty they actually enjoy, and by demanding even more liberty, they risk losing it altogether. From Hume's point of view, the mob shouting 'Wilkes and Liberty!' is not oppressed, and their quest for an ideal liberty leads them to ignore their actual freedom. Hume is one of the first thinkers to identify a process he calls 'philosophical chymistry' whereby concepts are 'twisted and moulded' by ideologies and lose their meaning.[47] This phenomenon induces a Manichean vision whereby those who do not venerate liberty are necessarily its enemies, and such a vision is at the heart of the Whig interpretation of history: one of its main proponents, Catherine Macaulay, wrote in the preface to her *History of England* that since her childhood 'liberty had become the objects of a secondary worship in [her] delighted imagination'.[48]

As Bernard Bailyn wrote: 'It would be difficult to exaggerate the keenness of Eighteenth-century Britons's sense of their multifarious accomplishments and world eminence and their distinctiveness in the achievement of liberty'.[49] In his political philosophy, and by developing a contextualist conception of liberty, Hume tries to reform contemporary English political discourse and practices. By showing that liberty is a historical and gradual concept, he shows that it is not purely an English (or even Scottish) phenomenon, but the result of a civilising process which affects most of Europe with the development of commerce. The true revolution is not so much 1688 and its 'matchless constitution' but the transition from a feudal to a commercial civilisation. In so doing, he finds himself at large with the proponents of the Whig ideology based on Lockean theories, with the classical Republican discourse, and with the dogmatic approach of many of his fellow *Philosophes*. But what is important to see is that his attacks against the dogma of liberty are not attacks against liberty itself: it is order to preserve liberty conceived as a contextual phenomenon.

Notes

1. David Hume, *Essays Moral, Political and Literary,* ed. by E. F. Miller, 2nd edn (Indianapolis: Liberty Classics, 1987), p. 535.
2. John Stuart Mill, 'On Liberty', *Texts and Commentaries,* ed. by Alan Ryan (London: Norton, 1997), pp. 52–84.
3. The 1662 Printing Act was not renewed by Parliament in 1694. This marked the end of pre-publication censorship for books but other forms of legal control developed in the 18th Century with the Licensing act of 1737 on drama, and judicial and parliamentary control of the press through libel laws.
4. Marc Hanvelt, 'Politeness, a Plurality of Interests, and the Public Realm: Hume on the Liberty of the Press', *History of Political Thought,* 33.4 (2012), pp. 627–46 (p. 637).
5. David Hume, *Essays,* p. 604.
6. Ibid., p. 13.
7. David Hume, *The Letters of David Hume.,* ed. by J. Y. T. Greig, 2 vols (Oxford: Clarendon, 1932) II, p. 209, 215, 210. *Further Letters of David Hume,* ed. by F. Waldmann (Edinburgh: Edinburgh Bibliographical Society, 2014) p. 81.
8. David Hume, *Letters,* II, p. 261. David Hume, *The History of England,* pref. W. B. Todd, 6 vols (Indianapolis: Liberty Classics, 1983) VI, p. 367.
9. Duncan Forbes, *Hume's Philosophical Politics* (Cambridge: Cambridge University Press, 1975), pp. 184, 191.
10. David Miller, *Philosophy and Ideology in Hume's Political Thought* (Cambridge: Cambridge University Press, 1981), p. 195.
11. David Hume, *Essays,* pp. 604–05.
12. John B. Stewart, *Opinion and Reform in Hume's Political Philosophy* (Princeton: Princeton University Press, 1992), p. 307.
13. David Hume, *Essays,* p. 87
14. After 1720 and the eviction of the Tories from power, the 1688 settlement is supported by both parties and the dominant ideology – 'vulgar Whiggism' – consists in a strong belief in the notions of toleration and liberty. Whigs and Tories believe in the existence of an 'ancient constitution' dating back from the Saxons, which has always limited the power of the king and secured the 'old spirit of liberty' in Britain.
15. David Hume, *History,* I, pp. 168–169.
16. The distinction between 'religious Whigs' i.e. dogmatic Whigs and 'political Whigs' is made in his 1745 pamphlet *A True Account of the Behaviour and Conduct of Archibald Stewart.*
17. John Locke, *Two Treatises of Government,* ed. by P. Laslett (Cambridge: Cambridge University Press, 1988), p. 326.
18. David Hume, *Essays,* p. 94.
19. Ibid., p. 40–41.
20. David Hume, *History,* V, p. 114.
21. David Hume, *Essays,* p. 9.
22. Nicholas Capaldi and Donald W. Livingston (eds), *Liberty in Hume's History of England* (Dordrecht Kluwer, 1990), p. 197.
23. David Hume, *Essays,* p. 40.
24. Ibid., p. 41.
25. Ibid., p. 32.

26 Ibid., p. 40.
27 P. Pettit, 'Republican Theory and Political Trust', in *Trust and Governance,* ed. by M. Levi and V. Braithwaite (New York: Russell Sage Foundation, 1998) pp. 295–314 (p. 297).
28 David Hume, *Essays*, p. 10.
29 Ibid., *Essays*, p. 273.
30 Ibid., p. 124.
31 Ibid., p. 375–76.
32 E. F. Miller, 'Hume on Liberty in the Successive English Constitutions', in *Liberty in Hume's History of England,* ed. by N. Capaldi and D. W. Livingston (Dordrecht: Kluwer, 1990) pp. 53–103 (p. 91).
33 David Hume, *History,* V, p. 528.
34 Ibid., p. 388–89.
35 David Hume, *Letters*, II, p. 209.
36 Ibid., p. 216.
37 Ibid., p. 217–18.
38 Ibid., p. 306.
39 David Hume, *Essays,* p. 53.
40 David Hume, *Letters*, II, p. 237.
41 Ibid., p. 215, 385.
42 Donald W. Livingston, *Hume's Philosophy of Common Life* (Chicago: University of Chicago Press, 1984), chap 10.
43 David Hume, *Essays,* p. 60.
44 David Hume, *An Enquiry concerning the Principles of Morals,* ed. by Tom Beauchamp (Oxford: Clarendon, 1998), appendix 4, p. 108.
45 David Hume, *Letters,* II, p. 180.
46 David Hume, *New Letters of David Hume,* ed. by R. Klibanski and E. C. Mossner (Oxford: Clarendon, 1954), p. 196.
47 David Hume, *Enquiry,* pp. 91, 108.
48 Catherine Macaulay, *The History of England from the Accession of James I to the Revolution,* 8 vols. (London: J. Nourse, 1763-1771), I, p. xi.
49 Bernard Bailyn, *The Ideological Origins of the American Revolution,* 2nd edn. (London: Belknap Press of Harvard University Press, 1992), pp. 17–18.

4. Versions of freedom and the theatre in Scotland since the Union

JEAN BERTON

In his twelfth essay on Civil Liberty, David Hume wrote: 'It has been observed by the ancients, that all the arts and sciences arose among free nations'.[1] Whether the Scots felt free or not in the Athens of the North within the union with England is an issue open for debate. Nevertheless, the object of this chapter is to consider how a wide variety and range of conceptions of 'freedom' are found in Scottish drama since Hume's time as themes emerge and re-emerge from the eighteenth to the twenty-first century.

After contrasting the definitions of freedom in the *Oxford English Dictionary*[2] and the *Scottish National Dictionary*,[3] I dwell neither on the obvious meaning of 'exemption or release from slavery' nor on that of 'exemption from despotic or arbitrary or autocratic control', except when viewed in a modified, warped, or somewhat ironic usage. I will deal with the notion of freedom under three headings: freedom as opposed to vassalage in an occupied land; the paradox of dependence and freedom, in cases of addiction and marriage; and guilt as the worst enemy of freedom.

Freedom as opposed to vassalage in an occupied land

The popular tragedy, *Campbell of Kilmhor*,[4] by J. A. Ferguson, staged during the 1914 Glasgow Repertory Spring Season, outlines Scottish rebels' freedom of action hindered by the action of Scottish supporters of Anglo–British law. The play develops the opposition of two contrasting views of freedom, that of Scotland with England within Great Britain and that of Scotland without England, or against Hanoverian Great Britain. The underlying element in Ferguson's drama is a pervading sense of guilt brought about by treason and greed. The tragedy openly discusses Scotland's own responsibility in handling her freedom. By contrast, John McGrath's *The Cheviot, the Stag and the Black, Black Oil* (1973), a pre-1979-referendum play, boosts a sense of political independence, with a view to giving back the Scots the freedom of use of their lands[5] that lie in the hands of lairds and multinationals and of their territorial waters belonging to the Crown. McGrath's play can be contrasted with Tim Price's pre-2014-referendum play *I'm with the Band*,[6] performed at the Traverse during the 2013 Edinburgh Festival. In this four-character play, the band leader, Damien, standing for England, has admitted that he has sacked their company manager for failing to pay VAT for the last twelve years: 'And now the taxman wants something like **** [mumbled figure] million pound!' (*IWB* 6). Barry, standing for Scotland, decides to leave the band for good:

> BARRY: *(speaking to Aaron, the Irish)* The real reason is, mate, the band, which I was getting tired of anyway, is fucked. Do you understand that? It's over. It's fucked. And I cannot be arsed trying to make something work, that I can't be arsed with any more anyway. I'm forty-two. (*IWB* 13)

This treason of the manager, amplified by the action of Damien, implies that the four players will have to pay the debt, while the manager can avoid being sued. The audience is left to interpret the metaphor freely.

Barry voices his long-standing plan to break free:

> BARRY: It's the fucking Damo-show anyway, it's always been th[at], and I'm out of it now anyway. I don't care, even if we didn't have massive – this afternoon making music my own in my pants has been the most fun I've had in, ever. / I've been thinking about leaving for ages and just didn't have the guts. There's the real reason. I got sick of being a coward. (*IWB* 14)

Barry embodies Scotland's flaw – lack of resolution. All of which is a cover for the nation's political weaknesses, i.e. internecine feuding. Such a failing is at the core of John Wood's 1883 tragedy, *Rothesay*,[7] for the villain, Albany, according to the Duchess, is ambition's slave:

> Desist !
> Else will I curse you in your flesh and blood,
> Your family and store, till evil fortune,
> Like to a bloodhound, hunts you to the doom,
> And forces you to wail at God's decrees.
> What! know I not you are ambition's slave ?
> That Rothesay stands in your ambition's way? (*Rothesay* 53)

The Duchess of Rothesay is trying to free her husband both from the Duke of Albany's greed and ambition, and from his jail. Lack of common ambition for the country is similarly at the core of Walter Scott's 1822 historical tragedy, *Halidon Hill*,[8] a satire on the events developing around the looming defeat of 19 July 1333. Scott not only presents the Scottish elite blindly fighting for Scotland's freedom but also their inability to overcome their want of common interest, discipline, and wisdom, all of which would, once again, lead to loss of freedom. This is ironically highlighted by two opposing characters, exemplifying quarrelling clans, from within the Scottish side:

> VIPONT: Since thou dost weep, [your sons'] death is unavenged?
> SWINTON: Templar, what think'st thou me ? – See yonder rock,
> From which the fountain gushes – is it less
> Compact of adamant, though waters flow from it?
> Firm hearts have moister eyes. – They *are* avenged;
> I wept not till they were – till the proud Gordon
> Had with his life-blood dyed my father's sword,
> In guerdon that he thinn'd my father's lineage,
> And then I wept my sons; and, as the Gordon
> Lay at my feet, there was a tear for him,
> Which mingled with the rest. We had been friends,
> Had shared the banquet and the chase together,
> Fought side by side, – and our first cause of strife,
> Woe to the pride of both, was but a light one!
> VIPONT: You are at feud, then, with the mighty Gordon?

SWINTON: At deadly feud. Here in this Border-land,
Where the sire's quarrels descend upon the son,
As due a part of his inheritance,
As the strong castle and the ancient blazon,
Where private Vengeance holds the scales of justice,
Weighing each drop of blood as scrupulously
As Jews or Lombards balance silver pence,
Not in this land, 'twixt Solway and Saint Abb's,
Rages a bitterer feud than mine and theirs,
The Swinton and the Gordon. (*HH* 219a)

Yet, Scott shows a way through, whatever fate might seem to demand, turning the commonplace feud into a brotherly agreement: the old Swinton and the young Gordon manage to do away with their deep-rooted antagonism to create a father-son relationship. Swinton knights young Gordon before the Regent, and both soldiers will soon be rewarded with glorious death on the battlefield. If those characters lose their lives while trying to secure their country's freedom, they are doing so after freeing themselves from the chains of hatred.

Directly implicated in Scotland's knotty union agreed with England in 1707, there lay the two-century-long crisis about the ownership of the land of Scotland when John Brandane wrote and the Scottish National Players staged his popular comedy, *The Glen is Mine*,[9] in 1924. The play's main topic concerns a crofter, Angus, at odds with his new young laird who, finding himself bankrupt after some catastrophic money investments, wants to expel him to exploit his land. Brandane clearly refers to the Crofters Holding Act passed in 1886, protecting the interests of tenants and owners, thus guaranteeing their freedom; however, in this play the crofter is championing the integrity of his native island, or, by implication nation, against an 'alien' form of greed introduced from England after the Union. What is more, in Brandane's play, another notion of freedom emerges under the guise of a definition particular to Scottish customs, according to which a 'freedom' is a piece of common land allotted to a free-man.

The paradox of dependence and freedom

This paradox can be viewed particularly in cases of addiction and matrimony. Brandane's comedy *The Glen is Mine*, gave the Scottish National Players the opportunity to explore the real dangers of losing one's freedom when facing such 'a specific burden' as alcohol-dependence. Angus's addiction to whisky equates with the danger of losing his freedom as a crofter: the would-be developers say, 'We'll buy him out all right. [...] Plenty of drams is all he wants!' (*TGIM* 38). What is more, as a widower, he is shown as quite dependent on his daughter who is about to be married and to move out of Eilean Aros to 'Faolinnvore, in Lochcarron' (*TGIM* 102). Independence from addiction of any sort as well as from male or female domination in matrimony is a common enough theme. A modern manifestation of it, freedom from male chauvinism, can be found in Harry Gibson's 1994 dramatic version of Irvine Welsh's *Trainspotting*. In this section, appropriately titled 'Libera me', Alison and Lizzie are telling off two workers on a scaffolding who have whistled at them, and they are approved by one of two 'auld wifies': 'It's guid tae see lassies stickin up fir thirsels. Wish it happened in ma day. Aye [...] ah wish ah wis your age again, hen, ah'd dae it aw different, ah kin tell ye'.[10]

In *Sgeir nan Ròn* (2002, *The Skerry of the Seals*),[11] Donald Smith's three-act Gaelic-language play, we can find a much more realistic approach to alcoholism. The heroine, Cora, is trying to free herself from the burden of frequent intoxication, 'Bha 'n òl air cus grèim fhaighinn orm. Bha e air a dhol nam fhuil. Bha mi nam "alchoholic".' ('Drinking got hold of me. It had gone into my blood. I was an "alcoholic"', *SnR* 6). She quickly admits : 'Dè eile bh' ann ach murt. Mhurt mi e. Bha mi leis an deoch.' ('What else could it have been than suicide? I was dead. I was away with alcohol', *SnR* 7). She is feeling lonely in her small Hebridean island, to which she exiled herself after being released from prison where she was sent for drink-driving with her baby boy in the back of the car. All of this led to the end of her marriage. Paradoxically enough, her time in jail freed her from addiction, but, now out of prison, recovering in a distant island makes her experience loneliness: 'Uill, mar a thuirt thu, tha mise nam aonar an seo, is tha mi aonaranach. Ach, bha uair nach b' ann mar sin a bha mi idir.' ('Well, as you're saying, I'm all by myself here. I'm a hermit. But, some time ago, I wasn't alone at all', *SnR* 5). Feeling like a hermit, 'aonaranach', is at odds with benefiting from freedom, for her attachment to her child and husband is overwhelming.

Addiction to money may be thought a particular and calamitous threat to the Gaels' culture pervading Scotland. We find a champion of freedom from money-addiction in the character of Iain Crichton Smith's Murdo in *Lazybed* (1997).[12] Murdo, who openly hates bankers and insurance brokers, appeared on stage when the new word 'workaholic' was used as a joke before it gradually labelled a symptom preceding a burn-out crisis. Smith trusted his iconic character to stage a sensible fight for freedom from 'workaholism'. Murdo refuses to work but will speak his mind to his audiences: to him, it has become vital to free himself from the contingency of working, especially as work is linked to money, and consequently to the power of money. For Murdo, freedom of speech related to outspokenness is another aspect of being able to act without hindrance or restraint. However, the rebelling hero of *Lazybed* willingly loses his state of free man, if free means a single and unmarried man, since he is going to marry fair Judith.

Marriage seen as a form of bondage is offered in a large selection of plays from comedy to tragedy. Paul MacInnes's *Peant gu Mahomet* (*Painting for Mahomet*, 2000)[13] is a one-act comedy that reminds the audience of the phrase, 'the monstrous regimen of women', a reference to John Knox's 1558 pamphlet 'The first blast of the trumpet against the monstrous regimen of women'. Alec and Sandra start the show, painting a room of the house they are going to live in after they are married; then Niall, Alec's friend, drops in and offers to go to the pub: 'NIALL: Bha mi smaoineachadh nach cuireadh tu cùl ri steallag. Chan eil teansa, tha mi cinnteach, gu faigh thu bhàrr na teadhrach a-nochd tuilleadh?' ('NIALL: I was wondering whether you'd object to a wee dram. There's no chance, I'm sure, that you can get free from the tether, tonight either?' *PgM* 9). With the help of the metaphorical joke of the tether, on offering a drink to his friend Alec while the wife-to-be is away, Niall equates marriage with loss of freedom.

Sandra is definitely against her fiancé going for a drink to the pub. Then her parents arrive and a ceilidh is eventually put on in the house against the will of Sandra and the recriminations of mother-in-law. But the boys receive the support of Donald, Sandra's father, who declares that he's definitely against the domination of women:

DOMHNALL: Gu sealladh orm Ailig, gu dè seàrsa taigh a tha seo agad? Bheil 'barricades' sa h-uile h-àite? [...]
ALAIG: Haoi, haoi, na seas a' sin on chunna tu riamh, 's gun cùrtairean air an uinneig! Thalla null a' siud, no chithear thu. (*PgM* 13)

(DOMHNALL: From what I can see, Alec, what sort of a house is that? Are there 'barricades' all over the house? [...]
ALAIG: What you've seen will last until we have hung curtains at the windows. Go over there, or else you'll be seen.)

The 'barricades' all about the house implies that the house of a married man is a fortress protecting the husband from his friends coming in for a ceilidh. And the curtains, generally chosen by the wife, symbolise enclosure; hence a sense of loss of freedom for the husband. Later on Sandra comes back in and makes a fuss on seeing that Alec has stopped working: 'SANDRA: O gu sealladh sealbh orm! Gu dè air thalamh th' air tighinn oirbh? Dè an dol air adhart tha seo?' ('SANDRA: What's that? What on earth are you doing? What's going on here?' *PgM* 18). The wife's angry attitude suggests a married man is no longer free in his house, a position hinting at unexamined – somewhat misogynistic – underlying attitudes in this play.

We find analogous behaviour in Alan Cochrane's *The Campbells are comin'* (1978).[14] Rab's sister-in-law teases: 'LIZZIE: I dinnae understand you Rab. You're no gyte a the gether, yet abody kens whae wears the breeks in your hoose' (*CAC* 14). And by way of illustration Phem, Rab's wife, blames her man because he was away from the scene when his mare peed over the minister's trousers: 'PHEM (*to* RAB *as she dabs her eyes*) – It's a' your faut. I blame naebody else' (*CAC* 15). Nonetheless, this comedy ends with a form of reconciliation that may not please every member of the audience:

PHEM: […] Aye I've been a bad tempered, naggin' schemin' wumman and waur. I've been a bad wife tae you, Rab.
RAB: I lo'e you, Phemie. Wi' a' ma hert. I've learned tae live wi' your fauts but I dae hope you'll change your weys. (*CAC* 68)

Such another dubious sexist implication can be found in John Wood's *Rothesay*, when the Duchess makes the following promise to the Duke of Albany who is detaining the Duke of Rothesay:

> Release my husband, give him to mine arms,
> And I will bless you while I live. Remember,
> The King his father, and myself, his wife,
> Have influence with him. Gladly will we
> Advise him to renounce th' uneasy craft
> Of government to you, […] (*Rothesay* 53)

Without feeling obliged to think that the Duke is about to slip from the frying pan into the fire, the audience is led to wonder whether matrimony is a better state than death.

Lastly, another example can be found in Alan Cochrane's 1979 play, *Scots wha hae*, where Robert Burns's poem 'Scots wha hae' – and all the implied references to the wars of independence from England – is conjured up.[15] Although this play, written in Lowland Scots is set in Lintonlea (near Peebles) in 1314, on the day before the Battle of Bannockburn, it must be labelled as a domestic comedy set in the Borders under the occupation by English troops. As it is, this play offers illustrations to most definitions of the word 'freedom': the laird who was rescued from the battlefield through a quid pro quo, is strongly advised, for the sake of immediate security, to don a monk's robe (*SWH* 48), which makes him feel embarrassed. Then, with a view to escaping from the English enemy that have been occupying his castle, he has to dress up as a woman, (*SWH* 60), a farcical paradox that forces him to experience a different, if not disturbing, view of married life. Nonetheless, this domestic comedy works as a warped show of bondage in matrimony challenging man's freedom and its implication can be extended to bondage lying in the oath of allegiance to the (English?) British crown.

Guilt as the worst enemy of freedom

Guilt is a particular burden that has arguably lain on the heads of the Scots for generations. Since, in the Scottish National Dictionary, 'guiltless' is introduced as a synonym for 'free', guilt, or at least a sense of it, may be understood as freedom's worst enemy. Broadly speaking, a sense of guilt has been cultivated by the Christian religion – originating from the fall from the Garden of Eden – and usually elaborated for unchristian purposes. In its own way, Calvinism has amplified a pervading atmosphere sense of guilt, and the faithful have always found it difficult and painful to escape from such a choking sense of doom.

This notion is ironically described in Ian Brown's 1989 one-woman play *Beatrice*[16] where the heroine has just been set free from the Inquisition's jail in Southern France, and feels the urgent need, laid on her by the Church's orthodox Catholic demands, to repent and explain and justify her life to her neighbours. Here is the beginning of her long monologue:

> They used to confiscate the home in cases like mine, still do, but they said in the circumstances of my case, my age, the long time ago. They say others, released, their neighbours drove them away. You won't do that, will you? I must tell you, explain, talk to you, and then, if you forgive, do not drive me away, I may stay here. My home, my ostal. How to begin? How to tell?
>
> Montaillou was my village, my home in the mountains, until I came down here. They came to it from the Lowlands, the orthodox Catholics, from the centre, from the King in Paris wherever that may be, from his Pope in Avignon who brought the Inquisition, the holy examination and punishment to the Cathars. (*Beatrice* 258)

This historical drama examines the background of rebellious, heterodox Cathars that can be spontaneously transferred, *mutatis mutandis*, to the Highlands of Scotland. Before ending her monologue, Beatrice, whom some might be tempted to compare with Mary Queen of Scots, states:

> The shock of light when I was brought up to my lowland Inquisition was pain to my eyes. And I told all. I told about Pierre. Not in rancour of hate. In fear, yes, but calmly. I was confessing my life, simply unburdening my soul. Telling them my beliefs. I told of my mountain life, my daughters, my father, my grandchildren, my charms, my love-making, my husbands, Barthelemy, Pierre [her lovers]. […]
>
> I have tried now to make an order, make a pattern in my confession, but it is not my pattern, I am not in this order. Every ordering has caused suffering and left another form of disorder. I must wear these crosses of my confusion. They have let me go from their prison, but they say I may not live here in my own house if you want to drive me away. That would tidy me away for you. But would it be right? Would it give you peace? I have done what I have done and felt what I have felt and pray that you will not drive me away. (*Beatrice* 279–80)

In her concluding words, Beatrice voices her guilt-free existentialism and calls for pardon and compassion.

Brown's female character is poles apart from Iain Crichton Smith's Murdo. Smith published many texts on the topic of freedom, and his play *Lazybed* stages a male character endowed with 'the power of self-determination attributed to the will',[17] that is to say, free from all constraints: for example, he quickly turns the minister, who is coming to preach him out of his bed, out the door. Indeed, Murdo is totally free from the highly potent pervading sense of guilt that has stifled all the members of the community. Yet, ironically enough, the most powerful notion connected with the Kirk, since its sixteenth-century foundation, is that of freedom: the meaning of 'free', in this particular case, has involved variations deserving a study much longer than the limits of this chapter can deal with.

Within a Judeo-Christian context, guilt is necessarily contrasted with the notion of forgiveness, somehow drawn from a boldness of conception of life: Walter Scott, in the tragedy of *Halidon Hill*, stages forgiveness by a leading Gordon to put an end to a family feud and a series of unnecessary killing:

> SWINTON: (*interrupting him*) Youth, since you crave me
> To be your sire in chivalry, I remind you
> War has its duties, Office has its reverence;
> Who governs in the Sovereign's name is Sovereign –
> Crave the Lord Regent's pardon.
> GORDON: You task me justly, and I crave his pardon,
> (*bows to the Regent*)
> His and these noble Lords'; and pray them all
> Bear witness to my words. – Ye noble presence,
> Here I remit unto the Knight of Swinton
> All bitter memory of my father's slaughter,
> All thoughts of malice, hatred, and revenge;
> By no base fear or composition moved,
> But by the thought, that in our country's battle
> All hearts should be as one. I do forgive him
> As freely as I pray to be forgiven,
> And once more kneel to him to sue for knighthood.
> SWINTON: (*affected, and drawing his sword*)
> Alas! brave youth, 'tis I should kneel to you,
> And, tendering thee the hilt of the fell sword
> That made thee fatherless, bid thee use the point.
> (*HH*, 227b)

Forgiveness, then, leads here to dramatically sincere love in a cleansed soul, whereas in *Auchindrane* (1830),[18] Scott uses the supernatural, with the help of a walking corpse, to denounce his murderer and have him executed.

Donald Smith's 2000 tragicomedy in Gaelic, *Cò Shaoileadh e!* (*Would you believe it?*),[19] develops a variation on Shakespeare's *Romeo and Juliet*:

two feuding families in a village on Lewis eventually lose their respective son and daughter, Niall and Màiri, who manage to run away from the stifling atmosphere in their homes, which are full of grudges, to Glasgow where they marry before sailing to Canada among other emigrants. The play builds up to the reading of the parting letter, producing a heart-rending effect, opening a violent and durable sense of guilt:

IAIN:	Eist ri seo: (*Leughaidh e*)
	"P.P.S.
	An gnothach deatamach a bh' agam ri dhèanamh an Glaschu 's e pòsadh! Phòs mi fhìn is Màiri Dhomhnaill Chaluim Choinnich feasgar Dihaoine.
	Le gaol,
	Bhuam fhìn is bho Mhàiri."
BEATHAG:	Dè rinn iad! (*Cò Shaoileadh e!*, 24)
(IAIN:	Listen to this: (*He reads*)
	"P.P.S.
	The crucial thing I had to do in Glasgow was to get married! Màiri Dhòmhnaill Chaluim Choinnich and I got married on Friday afternoon.
	With love,
	From myself and Màiri."
BEATHAG:	What have they done!)

The parents are stunned by the piece of news ('They did it!', Beathag concludes), and we cannot fail to note that no forgiveness is voiced.

Adaptations for the stage of major Scottish novels also explore issues of guilt versus freedom. David Edgar's 1992 stage version of Robert Louis Stevenson's *Dr Jekyll and Mr Hyde*[20] offers a more elaborate narrative for the stage than Stevenson's original. Edgar's protagonist, Utterson, appears as a freeman, free from passion. And he serves as a foil to Dr Jekyll who will eventually commit suicide because what has been done cannot be undone, even through pardon: 'ANNIE (*reads his letter*): You showed me that a man cannot escape his past misdeeds' (*DJMH* 76). Jekyll is guilty of rape and murder, not unlike his friend and colleague, Dr Lanyon. Jekyll says: 'Oh, Lanyon. Let me tell you. There's no escape. Try as you might, you'll always fear to sleep, for fear of waking to the moment you remember it was not a dream' (*DJMH* 70). Jekyll cannot dismiss Hyde, and must remain a prisoner of the duality of good and evil. In his dramatic version, David Edgar introduces the character of Katherine, Jekyll's sister, and makes her say: 'I'm told that everybody has a kind of – shadow in the mirror. Another self, which our conscious minds refuse to recognise' (*DJMH* 11). This 'shadow in the mirror' is a double preventing us from ever feeling free.

Reason may not suffice to assuage the overpowering sense of guilt in the mirror of passion. And support for this view can be found in the works of new Scots: indeed, Raman Mundair, in *The Algebra of Freedom* (2007),[21] propounds the idea that freedom comes as the result of forgiveness, a fundamental notion in the Muslim religion. Mundair introduces Tony who is tormented by a relentless sense of guilt about the wrong man killed by the 'firearms squad', because he had mistaken him as a terrorist. Tony's companion, Jack, is a Scottish character who feels no guilt about it.

JACK: It's late. Got to get in early – finish that damn incident report. Get it off my back.
TONY (*to* JACK): How do you sleep at night?
JACK: Fuck off, Tony.
TONY: No, I'm serious ... How do you get it all so fucking neat and tidy inside your head? Cos I've been trying and shit and I don't know how ...
JACK: The job's the job. Homelife is homelife. Plain and simple. (*AF*, 41)

Tony refuses to sign and approve the report by Jack, who then harasses Tony, repeatedly banging on the door to his flat (*AF*, 55). This may remind the spectator of insane Lady Macbeth who hears in her mind a 'knocking at the gate' (*Macbeth*, V, 1, 62). Tony, instead, is torn between the truth and his loyalty: 'JACK (*off*): That's one of the first things I taught you, Tone. It's one of the fundamentals – loyalty' (*AF* 57).

As if the author has found a way out of this stifling sense of guilt, Tony is made to meet a friendly and supportive character, Parvez, the taxi driver who helps him voice the effect of guilt:

TONY:	You ever done something you regret?
PARVEZ:	Probably.
TONY:	Run it through your head over and over. Wishing you could change it. Make it right.
PARVEZ:	But you can't.
TONY:	What?
PARVEZ:	What's done is done, right? You can't go back in time. You can't change that.
[…]	
TONY:	When you've got it wrong, when you're wrong, you know … the feeling comes, finds you, hunts you down.
PARVEZ:	And then your life isn't in your hands. It doesn't belong to you anymore …
TONY:	It takes away your sleep.
PARVEZ:	It takes away your sight…
TONY:	Taste
PARVEZ:	Touch
TONY:	Smell
PARVEZ:	Everything …
TONY:	… and nothing can bring you pleasure … peace.
PARVEZ:	You belong to it.
TONY:	You're a slave to it. You're never free, because … wherever you go, however far you go, it always turns up, you're always there … (*beat*) I'm always there. (*AF* 63–64)

Tony's painful experience of guilt can be seen as another reference to *Macbeth*, and also to Robert Wringhim, the central character of James Hogg's *Private*

Memoirs and Confessions of a Justified Sinner. (Mark Thomson adapted a version of Hogg's novel for the stage in 2009.[22] In this script we find three references to freedom: when the Reverend Wringhim tells the Laird of Dalcastle that he is a prisoner to pleasure – 'Your freedom to do what?' (*CJS* 39); when Robert relaxes, thinking he's 'free of him.' i.e. the Devil / Gil-Martin (*CJS* 52); and when Gil-Martin informs Robert: 'You are free of your words and promises' (*CJS* 36)). Tony, the guilt-ridden British character in *The Algebra of Freedom*, hears Parvez, the Moslem Asian character, say: 'Forgiveness. That's the hardest thing mate. […]' And the following stage direction runs: '*Tony stands dazed. The idea of forgiveness is an epiphany and echoes inside his head*' (*AF* 66).

Still, Mundair's message is far from purely sentimental. She voices sardonic criticism through the character of Fatima: 'Parvez. You're a hackney-cab driver. You're driving around this land of hope and glory, this land of freedom, and you're lost' (*AF* 41). Mundair is challenging Great Britain's enchanting anthem, 'Britannia, rule the waves', to make room for ex-colonised non-WASP people settling in Britain and enable them to feel free. In her Scoto-British play, Mundair introduces an Asian character, Waheed, to question the feeling of freedom in both Scotland and Britain: '"suspected insurgents" … to be suspected means that you are, in the eyes of the one who suspects, *imagined* to be guilty. […] Insurgents – someone who rises in opposition to lawful authority' (*AF* 32–33). Later Waheed carries on:

> That's the thing – they don't want to talk to us, they don't want to listen. They don't think that we are the same as them. They think they're more human than us. That their wounds are more painful – that we don't feel like they do.
>
> And you know what Parvez? It's because they think they're free. Free. And their freedom is an equation measured in oil, guns and the colour of skin. They're not interested in talking to us. Their freedom makes them deaf. Their freedom, their emptiness makes it so nothing means anything … Do you see what this is? (*AF* 35)

Waheed concludes: 'Their freedom kills. In their freedom, our voices mean nothing. Words have no impact. We have to talk in a language they understand.' (*AF* 35) Thus, the notion of freedom is reversed. Mundair, in *The Algebra of Freedom*, fitfully turns what was readily taken as an absolute notion into a relative value: for 'Dieu et mon droit' to herald an absolute notion then sounds as highly debatable as it was for David Hume.

Notes
1. David Hume, *Essays*, 'Of Civil liberty'. 1742 Part I. Essay XII. § 4.
2. *The Shorter Oxford English Dictionary* (Oxford: Clarendon Press, 1973). Abbreviated as *SOED*.
3. *The Scottish National Dictionary* (Edinburgh, Scottish National Dictionary Association Ltd, 1956). Abbreviated as *SND*.
4. J. A. Ferguson, *Campbell of Kilmhor* (London & Glasgow: Gowans & Gray Ltd, 1915).
5. *SND*, pp. 181–82.
6. Tim Price, *I'm with the band* (London: Bloomsbury Methuen Drama, 2013). Further references to this edition – abbreviated as *IWB* – are given after quotations in the text.
7. John Wood, *Rothesay* (Edinburgh: George Dryden, 1883).
8. Walter Scott, 'Halidon Hill', in *The poems and plays of sir Walter Scott*, ed. by Ernest Rhys (London: J. M. Dent & sons, 1911), pp. 216–38. Further references to this edition – abbreviated as *HH* – are given after quotations in the text.
9. John Brandane, *The Glen is Mine* (London: Constable & Company, 1925). Further references to this edition – abbreviated as *TGIM* – are given after quotations in the text.
10. Harry Gibson, *Trainspotting* (London: Vintage, 2001), p. 60.
11. Donald Smith, *Sgeir nan Ròn* (Glasgow: Gaelic Drama Association, 2002). Further references to this edition – abbreviated as *SnR* – are given after quotations in the text.
12. Iain Crichton Smith, *Lazybed* (Edinburgh: The Traverse Theatre, 1997).
13. Paul MacInnes, *Peant gu Mahomet* (Glasgow: Dràma Ghàidhlig Ghlaschu, 2000). *Peant gu Mahomet*, or literally 'painting coming to Mahomet', is only a private joke indicating a reversal of action. Further references to this edition – abbreviated as *PgR* – are given after quotations in the text.
14. Alan Cochrane, *The Campbells are comin'* (Glasgow: Brown, Son & Ferguson, 1978). Further references to this edition – abbreviated as *CAC* – are given after quotations in the text.
15. Alan Cochrane, *Scots wha hae* (Glasgow: Brown, Son & Ferguson, 1979). Further references to this edition – abbreviated as *SWH* – are given after quotations in the text.
16. *Beatrice* was first performed by Monstrous Regiment in 1989 and first published in *Coup de Theatre*, ed. by Jean Berton *Le transfert vers le texte théâtral - Coup de theatre*, 27 (RADAC, 2013), pp. 255–81.
17. *SOED*, p. 5.

18 Walter Scott, 'Auchindrane', in *The poems and plays of Sir Walter Scott*, ed. by Ernest Rhys (London: J. M. Dent & Sons, 1911), pp. 285–318.
19 Donald Smith, *Cò Shaoileadh e!* (Glasgow: Gaelic Drama Association, 2000).
20 David Edgar, *Dr Jekyll & Mr Hyde* (London: Nick Hern Books, 1996). Further references to this edition – abbreviated as *DJMH* – are given after quotations in the text.
21 Raman Mundair, *The Algebra of Freedom* (Twickenham: Aurora Metro Publication, 2007). Further references to this edition – abbreviated as *AF* – are given after quotations in the text.
22 Mark Thomson, *Confessions of a Justified Sinner* (unpublished typescript): page references are to this edition. Further references to this edition – abbreviated as *CJS* – are given after quotations in the text.

5. Freeing the tongue: Scots language on stage in the twentieth century[1]

IAN BROWN

This chapter considers a range of attitudes to the use of Scots language on stage throughout the twentieth century. It draws attention to early attempts to use Scots for significant topics before the First World War, before addressing the experiments of the Scottish National Players and Joe Corrie in the years between the wars. It addresses the development of the repertory theatre system in Scotland in the middle of the century and, in particular, the importance of the foundation of the Glasgow Unity Theatre in 1941, Glasgow Citizens' Theatre Company in 1943 and Edinburgh Gateway Theatre Company in 1953 for the future development of free use of Scots as a stage language. It reviews the situation of Scots-language theatre writing by the end of the 1960s, when Clive Perry, then Director of the Royal Lyceum Theatre, Edinburgh, (in)famously intervened, doubting the viability of Scots as a language of the stage for the future. It considers the reaction of to Perry's intervention and his reaction to that reaction, outlining the ways in which playwrights by the end of the century were using Scots freely as a vibrant part of new Scottish writing for the stage.

In 1909, Alfred Wareing, with several prominent Glaswegians, founded the Glasgow Repertory Theatre.[2] Its aims, as described in *The Glasgow Herald* of 19 March 1909, included

> the encouragement of the initiation and development of purely Scottish drama by providing a stage and acting company which will be peculiarly adapted for the production of plays national in character, written by Scottish men and women of letters.

Often this is taken to be the first attempt to establish a theatre company focused on Scottish drama in the twentieth century. Yet, in the previous year, the actor-playwright Graham Moffat whose work is discussed later in this chapter set up a company based around himself and his wife Maggie. This was launched on 26 March 1908 at the Athenaeum Hall in Glasgow. In the short pamphlet produced for this occasion Moffat calls his company the Scottish National Players (not be confused with the later company under the same name founded in 1921, also discussed later in this chapter). Through this company, Moffat asserts

> [...] an effort is being made to follow the example of the Irish National Players at the Abbey Theatre, Dublin, and to provide something similar for Scotland. [...] In 'Annie Laurie' and 'Till the Bells Ring' [two of his short plays presented on this occasion], the circumstances giving rise to the situations are Scottish, and all the characters speak the Lowland 'Braid Scots'.[3]

The next day the *Glasgow Herald* says of Moffat, 'On the whole, Mr Graham Moffat's venture as a writer of plays in "braid Scots" is to be commended'.[4] In fact Moffat's 'Scottish National Players' were soon distracted from a specifically Scottish remit by London West End success. Meantime, the Glasgow Repertory Theatre struggled through the five years until the start of the First World War, at which point it folded. Yet in those years, clearly influenced by the example of the Abbey Theatre in Dublin, as Moffat also was, it set out a model of Scottish repertory that might later in the century be returned to. David Hutchison summarises its achievements:

> a third of all the plays presented were entirely new to the stage, a remarkably high proportion. The company scored a few notable coups, in particular with the presentation in 1909 of *The Seagull*, the first production of a Chekhov play in Britain. Encouragement was given to Scottish authors and, although no masterpieces were produced and there was no upsurge comparable to the Irish one, a start was made to building a native modern dramatic tradition. Crucially, the context in which new Scottish work appeared – an eclectic mix of quality contemporary plays – was the one most suited

to stimulating indigenous writers to be ambitious. Among the Scots who wrote for the Glasgow Repertory Company were Neil Munro, best known as the author of the Para Handy stories; J. J. Bell, the creator of Wee MacGreegor; Anthony Rowley and G. J. Hamlen, who tackled contemporary themes; and Donald Colquhoun and J. S. Ferguson. The two best Scottish plays produced were Colquhoun's *Jean* and Ferguson's *Campbell of Kilmohr*.[5]

Both of the latter plays are written in Scots. The first was performed in 1910 and deals with resistance to repressive rural moral codes regarding illegitimacy. The second was produced in 1914, deals with the aftermath of the 1745 Jacobite Rising, and represents Highlanders as having a higher order of moral code than Lowlanders. Neither of these plays achieved lasting stature, but what they mark is an attempt to address both historical and contemporary material in the Scots language, although neither does so in terms of urban or industrial life. Nevertheless, while the latter certainly perpetuates the stereotype of the Highlander as noble, even Ossianic, embodiment of honour, both seek to address serious matters for a Scottish audience in the Scots language, without pandering to any tendency to treat Scots as a language for comedy alone, a diaglossic use that appeared for a time later in the century – for example, in some of the plays of James Bridie – particularly between the 1920s and the 1960s.

At the same time, one of the great Scottish theatrical successes before the First World War was Moffat's first major West End success, *Bunty Pulls the Strings* in 1911. This ran from 1911 for over six hundred performances and opened in parallel later in the same year on Broadway. His plays were mostly set in the middle of the nineteenth century – *Bunty* in about 1860 – and may broadly be seen to play to small town kailyard sympathies. *The New York Times* review (11 October 1911) of *Bunty* on its Broadway opening is explicit: 'The village of Lintiehaugh stands but a few miles distant from Thrums'.[6] The play was a hit on Broadway and toured North America at once and was thereafter from time to time revived and toured internationally over the next two decades. The play involves the complications that arise when a local elder Tammas Biggar, two years a widower, a role first played by Moffat himself, finds himself beholden to a local woman, Susie Simpson. We meet Biggar chiding his son Rab, who wants to make a career for himself in Glasgow, for failing to learn his catechism and whistling on a Sunday (even if he is whistling psalms), a breach of Sabbath decorum. We see Presbyterian sabbatarianism and sanctimony embodied in Biggar. The play develops around the means by which Biggar's daughter, Bunty, manages, through a series of clever manipulations, to rescue him from his entanglement with Susie Simpson. The play is rather slight, but one aspect of it remains of interest and that is the way Moffat used language. Later he was to report a conversation with his friend Harry Lauder, whose strategy he claimed to emulate:

> 'Harry,' I said, 'I know the secret of your phenomenal London success [...] you use the English language without even the usual Scottish abbreviations such as hae for have. You get the necessary Scottish flavour by your natural Lanarkshire accent and you speak slowly and deliberately.'
> 'Ye're right, Moffat,' said Harry, 'That's it.'[7]

Moffat asserted in the memoirs from which this anecdote is taken that he wrote not in Scots, but in Scots-accented English with a few Scots words dropped in for local colour. In talking about *Bunty*, for example, he claims to use only three Scots words – 'yella-yite', 'smeddum' and 'peelie-wallie':

> One braid Scots word purposely placed in each act, as we put a touch of mustard on a steak to help the flavour![8]

In fact – oddly given Moffat's claim – in the published text,[9] more Scots words appear than that. In Act Two, we find 'blate' (p. 46) and 'gomeril' (p. 47); in Act Three 'waggity-wa'' (p. 53), 'taupie' (p. 56), 'fashed' and 'strunts' (p. 57) and 'ben parlour' (p. 65). In a recent article in *Scottish Language* (2014),[10] I outline the evidence that Moffat actually wrote his play entirely in Scots and only later translated it largely into English for publication by the theatrical publishers Samuel French in 1932. It is striking that a successful

Scottish playwright should later rationalise his practice on publication by suggesting that he had written only in Scots-inflected English when, in fact, he had originally written the play entirely in Scots, in accordance with his manifesto of 1908 and in that form the play had been highly successful on both sides of the Atlantic. There is certainly a sense in Moffat's rewriting of his own history that he seemed to feel that to write in Scots might not ultimately be commercially successful. Yet, his playwriting in the early part of the twentieth century is as fully in Scots as that of the dramatists writing for the Glasgow Repertory Theatre. While they remained confident and free in their practice, it seems Moffat came to feel obliged somehow to deny his original creative use of the Scots language, as if he felt later constrained to claim to have written firstly in English, as if somehow Scots were not appropriate for publication of his play's text.

After the War, two initiatives the Scottish National Players (1921) – a quite separate company from Moffat's earlier company with the same name – and the Scottish Community Drama Association (1926) emerged, again with the ideas of developing Scottish drama. A key author for the former was John Brandane whose *The Glen is Mine* (1923), discussed in Jean Berton's chapter, accords very well with David Hutchison's description of the repertoire of the Scottish National Players:

> As many of the [company's] plays [...] are naturalistic in form and set in areas where dialect was still spoken at the time of writing, it was possible to use the Scots of the particular area, and this may be another reason why dramatists preferred rural settings: they were able to use Scots without producing the uneasy situation where contemporary characters speak in archaic language. The rural setting, because dialect could be employed, possibly seemed to them to be that much more Scottish than the urban one, although there was nothing to prevent a writer from rendering the Glasgow dialect on the stage, as Unity's writers were later to do.[11]

In fact in *The Glen is Mine*, Scots dialogue is reserved for lower-class characters who are figures of fun, pathos or, in the case of two young lovers, romance. Scots is here effectively ghettoised, in the diaglossic way already referred to, for romance, history or comedy. Another of Brandane's plays, *The Lifting*, reflects what Hutchison says in a particular way. Set just after the 1745 Jacobite Rising, its plot involves feuding between clans and the Hanoverian government army, mistaken identity and issues of just retribution as a Highlander is falsely convicted and about to die for killing a government soldier who was of another clan. The topic is clearly historically retrospective and the plot melodramatic. The innocent accused is freed – 'lifted' – while the real killer dies protecting him. Brandane represents the Highland characters in stereotypes rather as he did in *The Glen is Mine*. The dialogue represents, for example, the supposed quarrelsomeness of the Highlander:

> DONNACHA: Callum would quarrel with his own shinbones, look you!
> FLORA: They're the angry ones, I can see.[12]

It is clear here that Brandane seeks to reflect the English dialect of Highlanders whose English is closely influenced by Gaelic grammar and vocabulary. The dialogue of the play is sprinkled with Gaelic tags like 'Oidche mhath' ('Goodnight'), 'Mo thruaighe' ('My woe') and 'Mo chridhe' ('My heart' or 'Darling'), while, as in the passage already quoted, Gaelic syntactical idiom is regularly employed. An even clearer example is found in the following passage spoken by Callum:

> But was not I the happy one yonder, even in the dark and the rain, and me knowing that light was coming from a star wi' the name of Seonaid to it?[13]

Again, Brandane implies Gaelic idiom and employs Gaelic grammatical structures when he has Callum say 'And still-and-on, you're not for believing me'.[14] Clearly in *The Lifting* Brandane conceived of a Scottish identity that includes the linguistic habits, at least as translated, of Gaelic-speakers. Language was for Brandane and the Scottish National Players a means of freely asserting individual Scottish social and cultural identities.

The issue that emerges here, as in other plays presented by the Scottish National Players, however, is just what constitutes 'Scottish', or, for that matter, what constitutes, to quote the company's objectives, Scottish 'life and character'. In the two Brandane plays we have addressed, what emerges is that 'character' appears often as caricature or stereotype. The 'stage' Scotsman or Scotswoman is represented rather than any attempt being made to address the actual life of people in the urban communities of Scotland. Even when Scotland is defined as 'Highland', as it is in both the Brandane plays examined, we are presented with a version of rural conservatism which accepts the social status quo. *The Glen is Mine* does not examine the political and economic forces that led to the social leaders being army officers, who speak English, while their tenants are subservient and speak Scots, often Gaelic-inflected. *The Lifting* goes back in time in a melodramatic version of events following Bonnie Prince Charlie's 1745 adventure. In both plays' versions of a Scotland absorbed into a United Kingdom, British army officers, whatever their descent, own the land and are committed to a unified military, that is to say also political, structure. While there are clear attempts to record Scots or Gaelic-inflected English in dialogue, these attempts are in almost all cases at the service of a regressive and sentimental view of what Scottish life and character are, though it must be said that at least they sometimes escape the charge of using Scots only in comic dialogue. On the question of the identification of 'national' or 'nation' in their work, the theatre historian, and playwright/translator, Bill Findlay remarks of the Scottish National Players and companies that followed their path:

> despite their 'national' aspirations, held with sincerity and integrity, the companies tended to have a limited sense of 'national' when it comes to work in a Scots idiom, in that the playwrights avert their gaze from the contemporary industrial and urban reality of Scotland, and therefore from the associated linguistic reality, too. Hence work in Scots typically has country or historical settings; settings where the Scots employed could be a traditional, conservative, country-inflected Scots, or a re-imagined Lallans.[15]

In the early years of the Scottish National Players from 1921 on, however, a radical alternative, though also generally depending on amateur companies, often of great skill, appeared for a time to provide Scots-language drama that directly addressed the realities of current working life in Scotland. Joe Corrie is now mainly remembered, rightly, for his powerful drama of the impact of workplace conflict, *In Time o Strife* (1927), but already, writing in the Scots dialect of his native Fife, he had written in 1923 *Dawn*. This, as Alasdair Cameron has observed, '[was] banned [by the censor] at the start of the Second World War'.[16] Corrie's radical choices of topic in the 1920s were complemented by his lively use of Scots-language dialogue as he wrote on industrial, social and political issues at the beginning of his career, including, of course, the effects of the 1926 General Strike. His own company the Bowhill Players premièred *In Time o Strife* and presented and toured his work. It is telling, however, that the Scottish National Players presented only two plays by Corrie, one the one-act *The Shillin A Week Man* (1927), which has his heroine Mrs Paterson trying to avoid the eponymous figure to whom she owes money. As David Hutchison observes,

> There is in the piece a sense of poverty, brought out in small things such as the borrowing of tea, and in larger matters such as redundancy, strikes and the shillin' a week system itself.[17]

There is a strand of humour in Corrie's work that gradually began to take over the scope of his playwriting. Much of his later work became focused on lighter one-act plays for the Scottish Community Drama Association market, although his pioneering attempts to deal with contemporary industrial and social issues remain significant.

In fact, the major successor to Corrie's radical 1920s drama and its use of Scots in dialogue was not his own work for the SCDA of the 1930s and later, but that of Glasgow Unity Theatre formed in 1941 by an amalgamation of the Glasgow Clarion Players, the Workers' Theatre Group, the Transport Players, the Glasgow (formerly Scottish Labour College) Players and the Jewish Institute Players. As David Hutchison observes,

> These organisations had stood rather apart from the mainstream of the amateur movement and had presented material which was

aesthetically and politically more challenging than the norm. The members of Unity, for their part, sought a more socially involved theatre than existed at the time, and aimed to attract working-class audiences.[18]

Their focus was left-wing, with a focus on Scottish linguistic identity. Yet, while Corrie's and their commitment was socialist, it is hard to see in their work a view of Scotland or Scottish identity in a UK context. The themes of their early plays are quite clearly class-based without considering the place of Scotland in the Union. For them union issues are always lower case.

Until 1945, the company presented an average of three productions a year. Then, when the war ended, following the example of London Unity, Glasgow Unity formed a professional company chiefly under the direction of Robert Mitchell, formerly of the Clarion Players, and an amateur company mainly directed by Donald McBean, formerly of the Transport Players. The professional company's debut performance in April 1946 was Sean O'Casey's *Purple Dust*, and it very quickly began to produce similarly radical work on Scottish themes, beginning to explore a 'Scotland' significantly different from the kind envisaged by the Scottish National Players or much of the output for the SCDA. These plays included such work in Scots as Ena Lamont Stewart's *Men Should Weep* (1947), George Munro's *Gold in his Boots* (1947) dealing with the corruption of football business and Robert McLeish's *The Gorbals Story* (1948) about homelessness. These plays were directly concerned with a Scotland defined in terms of poverty and unemployment, urban and industrialised. It should not be thought, however, that these plays constituted the whole range of the Unity repertoire. At one point for example they presented an adaptation of J. J. Bell's *Wee MacGreegor*, a sentimental view of working-class life in Glasgow. In seeking to make the company financially viable they appear to have been prepared to aim for more commercial plays. Yet Unity's representation of Scottish life in Scots language performances did break new ground not only in their famous radical plays of working life, but also in their programming of overseas radical texts including Robert Mitchell's Scots-language version of Gorki's *The Lower Depths* and in their championing of Scots-language drama of a more traditional kind.

The company's programme at the first Edinburgh Festival Fringe in 1947 comprised *The Lower Depths* and Robert McLellan's *Torwatletie*, a Scots-language comedy set in Jacobite times that might almost have been presented by the Scottish National Players. What is more, Unity had premiered *Torwatletie* at the Queen's Theatre, Glasgow, in 1946, presumably in the hope of a popular success that would bring in income, but also marking an inclusive commitment to Scots-language drama, McLellan being at that time a leading experimenter with Scots on stage. Indeed, the company's commitment to him is marked by the fact that it premièred his *The Flouers o Edinburgh* at the King's Edinburgh during the 1948 Edinburgh Festival. The radical version of Scottish life that Unity is usually credited with was, then, not the only version of that life they presented; it is an oversimplification to suppose otherwise. What one can say, though, about their policy of producing such work as McLellan's is that they were not simply adopting a complaisant stance to the kind of sentimental drama often produced by the Scottish National Players. While *Torwatletie* does not take the themes of a retrogressive historical view of Scotland forward very far, *The Flouers o Edinburgh* is full of complex argument about the nature of Scots language, the Enlightenment, imperialism and cultural identity. In a sense, its very nature embeds Scots at its heart, so that the play itself becomes an expression of the power and variety of the Scots language and the conflicted nature of Scottish identity after the 1707 Union as the anglicisation process I have called elsewhere the (Rule) Britannia Project[19] took effect – and, by implication, in the period in which the play was written. McLellan's play is not socialist in theme as many Unity scripts are conventionally thought to be, but, rather, offers a radical interrogation of what Scottish identity or identities might be, albeit in the context of a historical drama set in the eighteenth century. And when McLellan came to publish his scripts, he did so in Scots, his position a very long way from the kind of linguistic compromise on publication that Moffat had earlier felt it necessary to make.

Unity was not, of course, the first company to support McLellan's use of

Scots dialogue. The Little Theatre movement had led to the founding of number of venues in Glasgow including the Curtain where it presented McLellan's first play, *Jeddart Justice* (1933). It premièred several other of McLellan's plays, including *Toom Byres* (1936) and *Jamie the Saxt* (1937), both at the Lyric Theatre. The development of such a repertoire may be seen against the developing repertory movement in Scotland. It can also be seen to offer a fresh expression and interrogation of what being Scots may be. Although the Glasgow Rep with its commitment in principle to a Scottish repertoire was the first recognisably modern repertory company in Scotland, succeeding repertory companies did not necessarily follow through this commitment. From 1928 to 1933, The Masque Theatre had alternated its programme between Glasgow and Edinburgh though plans for a permanent repertory theatre building in Edinburgh fell through in 1932. The Brandon-Thomas Players replaced this company. This company came to Edinburgh in 1933 where it was a success, as it was in Glasgow. After providing repertory seasons in both cities the company moved to London in 1937 where it failed to be successful. Meantime in 1935 Marjorie Dence had become the owner of Perth Theatre where, with her own building, she established a repertory company and in 1939 Dundee Rep was founded. In 1933 in St Andrews A. B. Paterson had founded a little theatre in a cowshed, to make the Byre Theatre which became professional during the war. In 1941 Wilson Barrett, who had acted with the Brandon-Thomas Company, settled to provide rep in Edinburgh, which it did in Howard and Wyndham theatres until 1955. These reps all – with the exception of the Byre, which, however, focused on a summer-holidaying audience by and large – concentrated on a general repertoire, being in effect outreach arms of the rep movement in England without a specific commitment to Scottish work.[20]

The first major shift in this process came with James Bridie's establishment of the Glasgow Citizens' Theatre Company, firstly in 1943 in the Athenaeum on Buchanan Street and, from 1945, in its present building in the Gorbals. Bridie sought to develop a repertoire that included, beside his own work, other new Scottish writing. In 1953 in Edinburgh a parallel company was formed at the Gateway Theatre by the playwright Robert Kemp and the actors Lennox Milne and Tom Fleming. All three had a commitment to developing a modern Scottish repertoire within an international programme. Although it is difficult to discern a single explicit view of the place of Scotland in the British context in their work, what is clear is that, as with the National Drama in the nineteenth century, this body of artists, whatever their personal politics, were creating a clear vision of a distinct, non-English, but actually also implicitly non-Unionist/British, theatre in terms of repertoire, management and, very often, language.

Unity Theatre ceased to be a going concern in 1951. By the time it did collapse, the environment for Scottish drama was becoming, as we have seen, increasingly varied. Part of this was that Robert McLellan had become by the late 1940s a key figure in developing Scots-language drama. His themes were still historical, but he was engaging through them with issues of contemporary relevance. His use of language was also significant. Although an older contemporary like MacDiarmid was working with a synthetic form of Scots, drawing on the work of medieval makars and the vocabulary of Jamieson's dictionary, as Hutchison notes,

> The Scots [McLellan] uses in his plays is based on spoken language and is not a synthetic construct. After the controversy which arose out of MacDiarmid's use of Jamieson's dictionary to cull words with which the poet himself was not familiar, McLellan resolved that he, as a playwright, would never resort to this device. In fact, he has said that he has found himself on occasion using words which cannot be found in Jamieson, but which he is nonetheless sure he has heard used in the past.[21]

McLellan's experiments coincided with a new opening of Scottish theatre after the Second World War. Not only was the modern Scottish repertory framework under development but the Edinburgh Festival was launched. In fact one of the earliest impacts of the Festival was on Robert Kemp, later to co-found the Gateway Company. Fluent in French, he had seen, after peace was declared, the first-ever visit to Edinburgh in 1945 of the Comédie-Française, which brought productions of Molière's *Tartuffe* and *L'Impromptu de Versailles* (as well as *Phèdre* and *Le Barbier de Seville*). Two years later, the Parisian Compagnie Jouvet du Théâtre de l'Athénée appeared in the programme of the first Edinburgh Festival. Of the two plays Jouvet's company presented, one was Molière's *L'École des femmes*. By the next February, Kemp had premièred his Scots-language version of this classic, *Let Wives Tak Tent*, in the Gateway Theatre before it was produced later in the same year at the Citizens'. Such an immediate impact, arguably the beginning of what is now a strong tradition of translation of European classics into Scots, was matched in the next Festival programme. Then, Kemp's edited version of David Lindsay's sixteenth-century masterpiece stunned audiences, Cairns Craig and Randall Stevenson observe:

> That early Festival production of *Ane Satyre of the Thrie Estaitis* established proximities between stage and audience which were not only physical, but above all linguistic, reminding its audiences – and a generation of writers, actors and directors – of the continuing vitality of Scots as a dramatic medium. Guthrie's production helped consolidate for the drama particular powers of writing in Scots which authors of the Scottish Renaissance movement had developed in other ways for poetry and the novel in the 1920s, and to establish in the theatre a kind of unique and naturally political performative space for Scots language and identity. In the theatre, the Scottish voice could be heard, live and direct, and not silent on the page as in poetry, or interpreted and masked by the 'standard' speech of a narrator. [...] From the 1920s to the 1940s, in a period of profound economic and political crisis, it was in drama that the experiences of the working classes and the urban world of industrial Scotland – barely registered in fiction at the time – were most directly captured with the liberating voice of the stage symbolically enacting a kind of freedom characters were so often denied in their lives.[22]

Beside McLellan and Kemp's Scots-language dramatic experiments of the 1940s we find two plays by Alexander Reid emerging in the early 1950s, *The Lass wi the Muckle Mou* (1950) and *The Warld's Wonder* (1953), the latter almost what we would now call magical realist. Again, these plays are set in the past, as Kemp's translation of Molière inevitably is. Katja Lenz has observed that a motivation for this type of historical drama 'may lie in its usability as a vehicle for asserting the national culture, for marking it off from the English or the joint British one, by demonstrating the existence of a separate history'.[23] Murray Pittock has argued that this identification of Scots language with Scottish identity has a long history:

> This association of Scots language with the 'true' and 'traditional' nation can also be found in the arguments of sixteenth-century Catholic apologists like Ninian Winzet: there were some Jacobites as late as 1745 who liked to keep alive the speech of Court Scots [...][24]

Alexander Reid may be seen to be conscious of this tradition when he makes his famous statement about Scots language and the stage and foresees the stage use of contemporary urban Scots:

> The return to Scots is a return to meaning and sincerity. We can only grow from our own roots and our roots are not English [...] If we are to fulfil our hope that Scotland may some day make a contribution to World Drama [...] we can only do so by cherishing, not repressing our national peculiarities (including our language), though whether a Scottish national drama, if it comes to birth, will be written in Braid Scots or the speech, redeemed for literary purposes, of Argyle Street, Glasgow, or the Kirkgate, Leith, is anyone's guess.[25]

Here, a playwright whose own work followed the historicist path appears to recognise the possible force of the contemporary demotic, something already seen, but not yet widely followed, in the work of Corrie and Lamont Stewart, *inter alia*, as they wrote important alternatives to historical and romantic drama in modern Scots dialects. What Reid particularly identifies here, however, is 'a Scottish national drama', one with its own linguistic registers and distinct from a centralised monolingual West End commercial or London-centric repertory system. In using this term, he also echoes the nineteenth-century Scottish 'National Drama' that asserted Scottish theatrical difference, basing itself largely on staging versions of Walter Scott's novels. On a personal note, I did not know this quotation when I began to write plays myself in the late 1960s. I did, however, have the feeling of which Katja Lenz has reminded us, that the decision to use the Scots language for the stage was certainly an artistic decision, but it was also a matter of socio-cultural identities. In that perspective, what Reid says about meaning and sincerity and roots makes sense, and not perhaps just in the dialectal terms he sets out.

One path, then, was that of McLellan, Kemp and Reid, who tended to work on historical topics, often with important resonances for the present, but yet with a backward-looking eye. Kemp's fine translations, or versions, of Molière, *Let Wives Tak Tent* (1948) and *L'Avare* (*The Miser*) entitled *The Laird o Grippy* (1955), are where his major Scots-language drama is to be found. While these plays continue to be produced on the contemporary stage, they by the very definition of their French original are set, like McLellan's and Reid's, in a by-gone time. This strand of theatre seemed by the end of the 1950s to be a dying genre. The second pathway involved a strong tradition, partly derived from Corrie's example in his more serious plays, of substantial drama in Scots. That included, of course, the repertoire of the Glasgow Unity including such plays as Lamont Stewart's *Men Should Weep* and McLeish's *The Gorbals Story*. But after Unity's demise this strand also seemed to fall away. Certainly, Unity's use of Scots language and commitment to radical themes had an influence on Roddy McMillan's *All in Good Faith*, presented at the Citizens' Theatre in 1954 and written not just in the Unity style, but with a cast including Unity actors like Marjorie Thomson, Andrew Keir and McMillan himself. However, the reaction to the play discouraged McMillan and he was not to write in this way again for two decades. Meantime, the sentimental-comic SCDA school, if it can be called that, continued and was not taken seriously, perceived as an amateur ghetto.

By the late 1960s, then, there were theatre directors in Scotland who thought that Scots had grown dramatically unusable in the forms in which it had been preserved. In 1968, as mentioned at the beginning of this chapter, the then Artistic Director of the Royal Lyceum Theatre in Edinburgh, Clive Perry, who had come to the company in 1966, said in an interview in the

Scotsman that Scots was a language that was essentially passé and would not work on the stage any more. The future of new drama in Scotland, he argued, was to be written in English: he claimed audiences were not

> willing to sit through a play whose vocabulary they don't understand. As regards the future of Scottish theatre, it may be that there is no such thing as a totally individual Scots language left. National drama with a tongue of its own is not for the future. Plays about contemporary Scotland will be in English with only a slight accent.[26]

Indeed, Perry's assistant at the time, Richard Eyre, told me as late as 1990 that he did not believe that Scots was a language with its own integrity, but was rather a working-class dialect. Given both Perry and Eyre, like many theatre directors in Britain then and now, were Oxbridge graduates, it is easy to see their attitudes as shaped by a centralised – perhaps unconsciously cultural-imperialist British, implicitly unionist – agenda. Certainly, with regard to Eyre and his later role as Director of the National Theatre on London's South Bank, it is possible to see the ideology of his theatrical career trajectory determined in this way. Perry's is a more complex case, however.

Reid had written what he did in 1958, a decade before Perry's famous statement. Yet despite Perry's doubts about the possibility of the fulfilment of Reid's vision, within three years of his expressing these doubts, he presented Stewart Conn's *The Burning* (1971) at the Royal Lyceum, arguably the dawning of the renewed and still continuing modern interest in contemporary Scots-language drama. As I will address in a moment, *The Burning* is about historical incidents, but uses contemporary demotic. And, having appointed Bill Bryden as assistant director in 1971, in 1972, the year after *The Burning*, Perry presented, to an enthusiastic reception, Bryden's *Willie Rough*, not in the language perhaps of 'Argyle Street, Glasgow, or the Kirkgate, Leith', but certainly in the language, as Bryden understood it, of his native Greenock. Scots for the stage might yet draw on the rural and the folk tradition, but its modern demotic varieties were now clearly viable as stage languages capable of dealing with a wide range of experience, including the urban and industrial. This development gives rise to an interesting question. Given he felt able to produce such plays as *The Burning* and *Willie Rough*, and, indeed, in 1973 my own *Carnegie*, set mainly in the United States, but with important Scots dialogue scenes, what had changed?

When Perry said what he said, there was a serious reaction. A number of people including writers, actors and critics argued that he was misunderstanding the position. His views were seen as actually culturally colonialist, not just anti-Scots, but anti-Scottish. Yet, I would argue now that, whatever his implicit or explicit political views about the place of Scots at the time he spoke, he did not misunderstand the creative linguistic situation then. In fact, I would argue he understood more than most and was reacting to what was there: a crisis existed in the direction of playwriting in Scots, whatever wishful thinking might wish to imagine. He saw that by 1968, the SCDA strand of Scots-language playwriting was largely sentimentalised beyond credibility, another strand seemed to many people historically regressive, and a third, the radical option, had been downtrodden. And, if that situation remained the way things were, there was surely no vibrant future for Scots on the stage. But it did not stay that way. If he was anything, Clive Perry was astute and, out of the reaction he got – and perhaps sought to cause – he found the idea of bringing in Bill Bryden, and meantime had begun to work with the likes of Stewart Conn. In 1971, Conn's *The Burning*, dealing in lively Scots dialogue with James VI and the witch trials of his time, is surely the first major play in the modern renaissance of plays written with substantial Scots dialogue. For, while, as I have said, it dealt with historical material, it often did so in a modern Scots and was focused on modern issues – no matter how filtered though a period perspective – of liberty, oppression and conscience. After that, came a considerable body of substantial work in a wide range of theatres including, at the Royal Lyceum, Bryden's own *Willie Rough* (1972), already mentioned, in whose cast was Glasgow Unity veteran Roddy McMillan, and McMillan's own *The Bevellers* (1973). Meantime, Hector MacMillan was writing plays for the radio and Stephen MacDonald at Dundee Rep presented plays likes his *The Rising* (1973), exploring the characters and events of the 1820 Radical Rising, and *The Royal Visit* (1974), quizzically presenting Walter Scott's instigation of and planning for George IV's 1822 visit to Scotland. It would be tedious to go on to list all the many modern plays worked in varieties of modern Scots since those. But that is the point. Alexander Reid had called it correctly: just as Unity had used 'the speech, 'redeemed for literary purposes of Argyle Street, Glasgow, or the Kirkgate, Leith', so did Conn and Bryden and McMillan and all the others that followed. This might mean – and often did – that the varieties used were not respectably approaching any standard or matching any style sheet – were not 'redeemed for literary purposes', but were, in that old categorisation, 'bad' rather than 'good' Scots. But they came from the creative listening and observation of the ways the Scots language was used by people. Now we see not only original drama in Scots; we have seen Liz Lochhead, Hector Macmillan, Edwin Morgan, Bill Findlay and Martin Bowman translating major plays, whether Greek tragedy, the classics of Molière, Rostand's *Cyrano de Bergerac* or the contemporary plays of Michel Tremblay, into a vibrant colloquial and demotic Scots. It is no coincidence that this effervescent and diverse approach to, and celebration of, Scots language accompanied the cultural and political developments that seem to have led inexorably through the process of mutual interaction of theatre, culture and political community from the launch of the current Scottish theatrical renaissance in the late 1960s to devolution and the independence referendum of 2014. However one reads the outcome of that vote, it is clear that the political culture of Scotland is now radically changed from what it was fifty years ago, in common with its theatrical landscape. Liberty of thought and linguistic freedom parallel one other.

In crude terms, what Perry had been seeing when he was interviewed in 1968 was that either drama in Scots was mired in a one-act form often with sentimental themes or locked into historical and nostalgic themes. Further, the companies for which such drama was written were themselves, often, despite the work of Corrie and the Unity playwrights, embedded in a particular view of 'Scotland' that was evading the realities of modern urban life. As Bill Findlay has put it in a passage quoted earlier,

> despite their 'national' aspirations, held with sincerity and integrity, the companies tended to have a limited sense of 'national' when it came to work in a Scots idiom, in that the playwrights avert their

gaze from the contemporary industrial and urban reality of Scotland, and therefore from the associated linguistic reality, too.[27]

Reid's vision, when he wrote, seemed hopelessly ambitious, but in the 1970s Perry's provocation and the production policies he then took forward, alongside those of Stephen MacDonald at Dundee from 1973 to 1976 and then, after Perry, from 1976 to 1979 at the Lyceum, have fulfilled that vision. Gregory Burke's *Black Watch* again and again tours the world; David Greig's and David Harrower's plays are translated into more and more languages in a way unthinkable in 1958. The medium of Scots on stage has again become an essential element in allowing writers to address what it is to be a modern Scot. It is not, of course, essential that writers exclusively use Scots – Greig and Harrower do sparingly – but Scots is a crucial part of a battery of linguistic resources available to the modern Scottish playwright. In the process of this coming about, the history of the staging of Ena Lamont Stewart's *Men Should Weep* marks significantly changing attitudes. This play, part of a tradition of drama implicitly dismissed by Perry in 1968, was revived, directed by the then Director of Glasgow Citizens', Giles Havergal, by 7:84 (Scotland) Theatre Company as part of its 1982 *Clydebuilt* season. This season revived popular drama from earlier in the century and also included *In Time o Strife*, *Gold in His Boots*, and Ewan MacColl's *Johnny Noble* (1954). *Men Should Weep* finally was recognised as a major twentieth-century classic when it was performed by the London National Theatre in 2010 and in the next year, in a separate production, by the National Theatre of Scotland.

This process has helped free up other linguistic and cultural vistas. Michelle Macleod and Moray Watson have written eloquently on the vitality of Gaelic-language drama in the 1960s and 1970s in their chapter in the *Edinburgh History of Scottish Literature* (2007).[28] Despite the failure to survive of the companies Fir Chlis (1978–81) and Tosg (1996–2006), attempts at Gaelic-language drama have been energetic and often in the form of soaps, like *Machair* (STV, 1992–98), have made a longer-term impression. Now, any vision of 'Scottish nationhood' expressed on the Scottish stage has achieved such a range of diversity and multiplicity of identities, not to mention languages and idiolects, that it is no longer possible to argue for any single vision of 'Scotland'. That has certainly freed the tongue in the sense both of language and of an organ of speech for Scottish playwriting. Twentieth-century Scots-language theatrical developments, after the early struggling of Wareing and Moffat before the First World War and in the 1920s of the Scottish National Players and Corrie's radical reaction to them, were reinforced by the work of Glasgow Unity, not to mention new writing presented by the Glasgow Citizens' and the Edinburgh Gateway Theatre Company. Since the 1970s, a diversification of topics, themes and language choice, whether English, Scots or Gaelic, has meant that Scottish theatre has embodied and led in the determination and celebration of the perception that there is no single Scottish 'identity'. Rather there is recognition of many identities which make up Scottish culture, or 'nationhood' – gender-based, sexual, regional, social – and linguistic. There is a real sense in which the twentieth century saw a new freedom for the Scots language on stage.

Notes

1. This chapter draws substantially, with significant additional material, on aspects of chapter 6, 'Twentieth-century drama, innovation and the Scots leid' in Ian Brown, *Scottish Theatre: Diversity, Language, Continuity* (Amsterdam: Rodopi, 2013), particularly pp. 134–63.
2. David Hutchison, '1900 to 1950', in *A History of Scottish Theatre* ed. by Bill Findlay (Edinburgh: Polygon, 1998), p. 208.
3. Pamphlet filed under 'Miscellaneous Items' in the Graham Moffat Collection, Mitchell Library, Glasgow, SR 225.
4. 'Press Opinions on Mr. Graham Moffat's Scottish Comedietta, "Till the Bells Ring"'. Filed under 'Miscellaneous Items' in the Graham Moffat Collection, Mitchell Library, Glasgow, SR 225.
5. Hutchison, '1900 to 1950', p. 212.
6. query.nytimes.com/mem/archive-free/pdf?res=FA0A1EF63A5517738DDDA80994 D8415B818DF1D3, [accessed 5 October 2012].
7. Graham Moffat, *Join me in remembering the life and reminiscences of the author of 'Bunty pulls the strings'* (Camps Bay: Winifred L. Moffat, 1955), pp. 25–26.
8. Ibid., p. 26.
9. Graham Moffat, *Bunty pulls the string and other plays* (London: Samuel French, 1934).
10. Ian Brown, 'Scots language in Theory and Practice in Graham Moffat's Playwriting', *Scottish Language* 33 (2014), pp. 65–81
11. David Hutchison, *The Modern Scottish Theatre* (Glasgow: Molendinar, 1977), p. 71.
12. John Brandane, *The Glen is Mine and The Lifting* (London: Constable, 1925), p. 202.
13. Ibid., p. 216.

14 Ibid., p. 217.
15 Bill Findlay, 'Modern Scots Drama and Language Planning: A Context and Caution', in *Towards our Goals in Broadcasting, the Press, the Performing Arts and the Economy*, ed. by John M. Kirk and Dónaill P. Ó Baoill (Belfast: Cló Ollscoil na Banríona, 2003), pp. 166–67.
16 Alasdair Cameron, 'Theatre in Scotland: 1214 to the Present', in Paul H. Scott (ed.), *Scotland: a concise cultural history* (Edinburgh: Mainstream Publishing, 1993), p. 152.
17 Hutchison, '1900 to 1950', pp. 227–28.
18 Ibid., pp. 246.
19 See for example, Ian Brown, '"Our multiform, our infinite Scotland": Scottish Literature as "Scottish", "English" and "World" Literature' (Glasgow: ASLS, 2012), esp. pp. 4–5, and 'Literary pilgrimage as cultural imperialism and "Scott-land"', in Ian Brown, ed., *Literary Tourism, The Trossachs and Walter Scott* (Glasgow: Scottish Literature International, 2012), esp. pp. 3–4.
20 For more information on this process, see Hutchison, *The Modern Scottish Theatre*, pp. 29–31.
21 Hutchison, *The Modern Scottish Theatre*, p. 36.
22 Craig and Stevenson, Ibid., p. x.
23 Katja Lenz, 'Modern Scottish Drama: Snakes in Iceland – Drama in Scotland?', *Zeitschrift für Anglistik und Amerikanistik*, XLIV, 4 (1996), p. 309.
24 Murray Pittock, 'Scottish Nationality in the Age of Fletcher', in *The Saltoun Papers: Reflections on Andrew Fletcher*, ed. by Paul Henderson Scott (Edinburgh: Saltire Society, 2003), p. 187.
25 Alexander Reid, 'Foreword', *Two Scots Plays* (London: Collins, 1958), pp. xii–xiii.
26 Quoted in Bill Findlay, ed., *Scots Plays of the Seventies* (Dalkeith: Scottish Cultural Press, 2003), p. xvi.
27 Bill Findlay, 'Modern Scots Drama and Language Planning', pp. 166–67.
28 Michelle Macleod and Moray Watson 'In the Shadow of the Bard: The Gaelic Short Story, Novel and Drama since the early Twentieth Century', in *The Edinburgh History of Scottish Literature*, ed. by Ian Brown (Edinburgh: Edinburgh University Press, 2007) vol. 3, pp. 273–82 (280–82).

6. The nature of aesthetics in the works of Mary Brunton, Hugh MacDiarmid and Alasdair Gray

ANDREW MONNICKENDAM

In the introduction to Hugh MacDiarmid's *Aesthetics in Scotland* (1984), Alan Bold comments that it is, for its author, 'an unusually contemplative piece'.[1] Contemplative it might be, but it is openly polemical in nature and extensive in scope, prone to sweeping generalisations about Scotland and its culture. Three points require a brief explanation. First, Bold dates the essay as written in 1950. Second, instead of an extended disquisition, the essay is best approached formally as if it were an early nineteenth-century review of a novel: a series of longish quotations joined at certain points by a series of brief interjections which therefore help to create a set of ideas. Third, the aesthetics in the title have less to do with literature and more to do with the visual arts.

Among his contemplations, two basic ones can be underlined. First, his point of departure is that '[f]ar too many Scots are still utterly insensitive to the arts – a higher proportion, I think, than can be found in any other Western European country'.[2] This deep-rooted anti-aestheticism is, in this instance, a result of the education system, as 'most teachers are not expected to have any standards of appreciation or knowledge beyond those of the general public'.[3] In contrast, he has positive things to say about the radio and its potential to spread the gospel of literature. This line of inquiry then entangles itself in a series of stereotypical arguments based on ethnicity. He positions in one corner – what for him epitomises Scottish neuroticism – the figure of John Ruskin, and in the other, the Celtic mind: 'the Gaelic people were gay and fantastic'.[4] Their position as lying outside the European mainstream is confirmed by their distance from the Bible. An additional problem for Scotland has been that the Enlightenment philosophers – he specifically mentions Adam Ferguson and Hugh Blair – 'knew and cared little or nothing about the arts'[5] due to their addiction to the 'emotive language of the Bible'.[6] This controversial hypothesis remains a very potent explanation for better comprehension of another phenomenon, namely the Kailyard, particularly in such stories as James Barrie's 'A Literary Club' (part of *Auld Licht Idylls* (1888)), where learning morphs into sentiment and then into national virtues.

That said, the major contemplation, one made several times in this short piece, is rather different, namely that

> [t]o blame all this on Calvinism in Scotland is stupid. It not only ignores the facts which are admirably set out in Dr Mary Ramsay's *Calvin And Art*. It ignores also the fact that it is quite unjust to attribute to Calvinism a crude Philistinism which was, in fact, bred by the Industrial Revolution and aggravated by the loss of our own national roots.[7]

As we shall see, both writers share a series of common concerns. Ramsay begins her account by proposing that the twinning of Scottish Calvinism and Philistinism is the consequence of a misunderstanding of the nature of Calvinism in Scotland and an over-emphasis on 'the influence of theology on art'.[8] Calvin believed in art which was 'protestant, realistic, moral',[9] and his attacks on art are, more often than not, attacks on 'certain practises of the church of Rome'.[10] The word 'certain' deserves underlining. The end result of St Gregory's adage, that images are the books of the illiterate, has been to keep people illiterate, or, if that is too strong wording, to justify criticism of certain practices of the Church of Rome. She adds that for Calvin 'one kind of "image" alone can be rightfully found in Christian temples, the sacred symbols of the Christian mysteries'.[11] For Ramsay, Calvin was not a suppressor of art, but he believed art should follow the above-mentioned directives.

Ramsay's argument is based on geography and religion, though which weighs more heavily is in the end not very clear. Both the opening and closing of the study contain assertions that echo MacDiarmid's on nationhood. Ramsay states that 'a Scottish art that is really national and not merely sporadic, individual, eccentric, must wait for the restoration of the Scottish nation',[12] and, as a conclusion, 'our art history seems to resolve itself into the story of individual artists or at best small groups [...]. The splendid "Modern Athens" period only serves to emphasise this. Burns and Scott to reach their true greatness had to be nourished by roots that spread back many hundred years'.[13] MacDiarmid might not have held Burns and Scott in such high standing, but the two fundamental assertions that their greatness stems from their national roots and that the Union only permits individuals and groups, thus pre-empting the formation of national artistic movements, would surely have met with his approval. After all, Ramsay's ideas themselves reiterate the arguments that led to the setting-up of the Abbey Theatre in Dublin.

To return to MacDiarmid, in an argument that harks back to the role of popular culture – the culture industry – in the writings of Walter Benjamin, and Adorno and Horkheimer, he suggests that things have not improved. The rise of modernism, with the corresponding challenge to the common reader or viewer's perception of aesthetics, has simply aggravated the situation, hence the level of the previously mentioned 'general public' is very low indeed; Philistinism, presumably, is far more extensive than ever before in Scotland. As a poet so deeply enmeshed in modernism, its aesthetics perhaps explain his own extremism as convincingly as those based on essentially national parameters. After all, Cleanth Brooks, T. S. Eliot, F. R. Leavis *et alia* would presumably have no problem in accepting the Caledonian antisyzygy as a template for poetry, as long as the geographical restrictions were removed, for linguistic collisions are essential to their understanding of good art. Perhaps the metaphysical conceit and the antisyzygy are more closely related than we have been led to believe.

However 'stupid' it might be to link Calvinism irredeemably to anti-aestheticism and consequently to an overt of latent suspicion of art in general or modernism in particular, this link is, we are all well aware, a strong one. To take an everyday example, let us imagine that one of the ignorant race of teachers took their class for a day-trip to St Andrews. In order to better prepare the outing, the website 'Undiscovered Scotland' is consulted:

> The wind of change wrought by the Reformation brought about the end of the cathedral. On 11 June 1559 John Knox preached a sermon

in St Andrews parish church that so aroused the congregation they immediately went to the cathedral and destroyed the splendid fittings and furnishings associated by the reformers with 'popery' [...]. The end followed quickly. The Church of St Mary on the Rock was probably completely destroyed shortly after it was first attacked. The cathedral and its friary effectively ceased to function on 14 June 1559 when further attacks took place, and within a week all the friars has been 'violently expelled' from St Andrews.[14]

Accordingly, the Reformation is instigated by intolerance, fiery rhetoric and destruction, which in turn suggests that the Reformation basically comprises these three qualities; there is nothing else to compensate for a status close to terrorism. Such an account certainly falls within the catchment area that MacDiarmid has identified: although it is stupid to blame everything on Calvin, it is a widespread habit.

MacDiarmid's contemporary, Fionn MacColla (Thomas MacDonald), who might have been instrumental in the former's idealist views of the glories of Gaeldom, must be, using the logic of *Aesthetics in Scotland*, someone who – at this juncture – verges on the 'stupid', as figure 1 shows.

MacColla's diagram provides a vivid picture of his personal view of the Protestant bunker. We just need a little imagination to capture the harmful influence of pervasive individualism by turning the page upside down: with a little prompting, it will help us recall that every herring must hang by its own tail, if we are to believe the Reverend Mr Struthers in George Douglas Brown's *The House with the Green Shutters*.[15] The potency of this image lies not simply in the importance of silver darlings to Scottish life and its economy, as illustrated in and by Neil Gunn's eponymous epic novel, nor simply to the implications of smoke and hell, but to the perverse abuse of fish, that embracing symbol of Christianity. It is almost as if Calvinism, from this view, is not only uncharitable – one should presumably question the good Samaritan's motives and behaviour – but suspiciously un-Christian. After all, every vestige of community is removed in the image of the gutted fish. MacColla himself had no doubts whatsoever on this subject, and adorns the cover of his polemical essay, *At the Sign of the Clenched First* (1967),

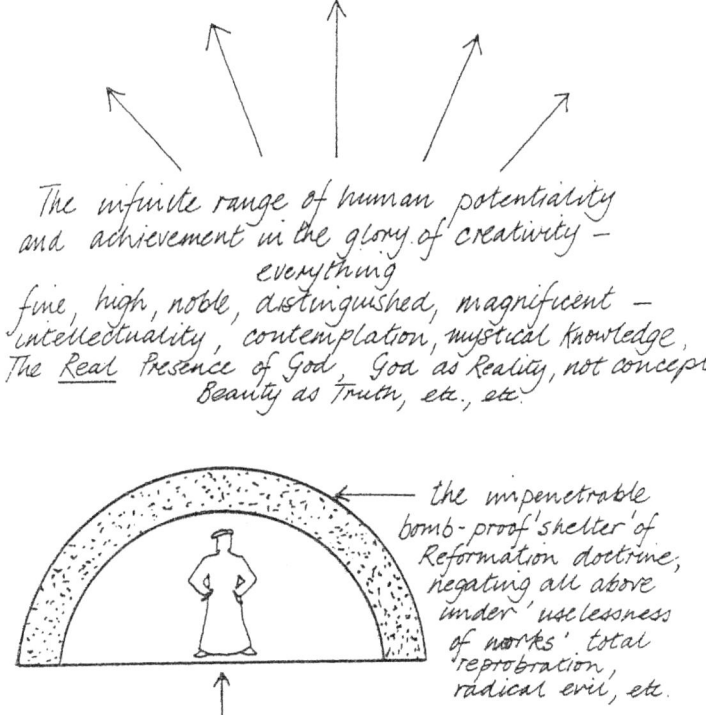

Fig. 1: from *Too Long in this Condition* by Fionn MacColla (Thurso: Caithness Books, 1975), p. 102. Reproduced by permission.

with the four objects of his almost illimitable ire: John Knox, Adolf Hitler, Henry VIII and Lenin.

One of the oddities in the MacDiarmid formulation is the ambivalent role of fiction in the arts. In this essay he shares the thinly disguised suspicion of the contemporary novel in English that so marks Virginia Woolf's critique: it is vastly inferior to its Russian cousin. If the Ian Watt hypothesis of the rise of the novel is valid, however leaky or imperfect it may be, then MacColla's drawings replicate Robinson Crusoe's self-glorification that he rules a kingdom: he is an island to himself, and therefore anyone else has to be, both physically and metaphorically, the other, and subsequently subservient. Nathaniel Hawthorne's gloomy figures in the custom house provide the preface to the obvious transatlantic extension of Crusoe-like ideology, namely, that the other to be most feared is woman, hence the logic of the *Scarlet Letter* (1850): woman is simultaneously the alpha and the omega of creation.

Consequently, after these broad theoretical points, we come to the enigma which I can describe and analyse but cannot solve. Hawthorne's gloomy Puritans would presumably have agreed with much that Alexander Brunton, the minister, wrote about his wife, the novelist Mary Brunton, in the memoir published alongside her incomplete but remarkable fragment *Emmeline* in 1819. As I have argued elsewhere,[16] at certain junctures the memoir attempts to construct a pious literary person at complete odds with the moral contradictions of her posthumous *Emmeline*, which evokes empathy with its eponymous heroine, who has walked out of her first marriage, abandoned her little children for love: in other words, it educes sympathy for someone who has broken all the rules of Christian conduct.

What does the memoir do to poor Mary? The basic stratagem is to foreground the compiler – the husband – at the expense of the wife, the biographer at the expense of his subject. A contemporary review went so far as to ask rhetorically 'if it is surpassed by any biographical writing in the language',[17] basically because it placed Mary so prominently in the picture. This innocent-looking comment, journalistic hyperbole, reverses roles and priorities because it is primarily if not exclusively due to the author's skill that Mary Brunton becomes a literary subject. Thus Alexander's role is never neutral. In fact he is given considerable credit not only for the memoir but for his wife's talent and success. A particularly pertinent example is provided by the description of their primetime together: '[a]fter her marriage, Mrs Brunton's whole leisure was devoted to the improvement of her mind;

in which her husband had a much larger share than he himself can properly record.'[18] We are told that she was particularly interested in languages and in the writers of the Scottish Enlightenment, which is possibly a gloss on Alexander Brunton's own comment that 'in the evening, I was in the habit of reading aloud to her, books chiefly of criticism and Belles Lettres'.[19] It is certainly true that her literary career was partly the result of this education; she did not turn to writing to some years after their marriage, or, in other words, to some years after this instruction had begun. The suggestion is an obvious one: he cultivated her taste.

The memoir records one dramatic failure: he could not teach her maths. Alexander Brunton is not very explicit about this,[20] and we are told that that academic fiasco is an anomaly.[21] Yet who is to blame, the student or the teacher? Nothing is stated explicitly, but it has to be pointed out that the husband gives us a brief inventory of her favourite reading matter, just a collection of pious texts. If the memoir is excellent, if the husband tried to educate her properly but could not teach her maths, it is inevitable that one arrives at the conclusion that a clear gender and genre bias is at work. Brunton could not teach her maths, as a female mind is not capable of acquiring such knowledge. Mary Brunton was certainly an admirable novelist, but, the memoir implies, fiction must be ranked way below Belles Lettres, religious tracts or maths. The academic pecking order would explain why Alexander Brunton only mentions religious reading while describing the virtues of a lady novelist. At the very least, fiction assumes the cloak of the genre which cannot be named.

To accuse Alexander Brunton of parochialism is simple enough, but while he tries to confine his wife to the home, a place she truly loved, her life reached out well beyond the confines of the Edinburgh Tron, first and most obviously, in the creation of her fictional worlds whose geography stretches over the border and across the Atlantic. As I have argued elsewhere, her Scotland is hallmarked by its spirituality; her patriotism is religious patriotism.[22] Second, the memoir contains records of her journeys to England, which combine both positive and displeasing comparisons with her homeland. Third, she delves into those other arts, the ignorance of which MacDiarmid felt to be a defining factor of Scotland's aesthetic poverty.

Alexander Brunton's list of his wife's favourite reading included John Newton's *Messiah* (1786), which has the lengthy subtitle *fifty expository discourses on the series of scriptural passages, which form the subject of the celebrated oratorio of Handel*. Consequently, on a visit to London they attend a performance of the *Messiah*. An anonymous acquaintance

> called to take us to an oratorio at Covent-Garden. As we are *nobody*, he advised us to go to the pit, that we might have some chance of seeing and hearing. We were no sooner placed, than the adjoining seats were occupied by some very drunk sailors, and their own true loves, whose expressions of affection made it necessary to change our quarters. The music was far superior to any thing I had heard before. But in such a place, and in such a company, the praise of God seemed almost blasphemy.[23]

It is quite noticeable that, covertly here and unequivocally in other parts of the memoir, Mary Brunton compounds her husband's erasure of her identity with a marked degree of self-deprecation, itself part of a prolonged exercise in insisting that a novelist who is somebody is actually nobody, evidenced here by the insistence that her group were '*nobody*'; this is one of many similar symptoms. The final sentence is thought-provoking, as it is not easy to identify why 'the praise of God seemed almost blasphemy' here. The drunken sailors and the prostitutes contribute to a certain extent, but there is also a suggestion that the music is so beautiful that the listener's attention to artistic perfection comes about at the expense of true spirituality. Handel also had, we should remember, a keen interest in the profane, the classics, as well as the sacred. Covent Garden was notorious for prostitution, so perhaps, we could argue that the true venue for Handel should be elsewhere, somewhere suitable for full appreciation of music 'far superior to any thing I had heard before'.

If her appreciation of Baroque music catches us unawares, we are completely unprepared for her love of Baroque art, exemplified in the following passage describing the Elizabethan pile, Burghley. Brunton states that:

> Cecil had as good a taste in houses as his mistress had in prime ministers. Admirable pictures! – A Magdalene, by Carlo Marrati; Domenichino's mistress, by himself – loveliness personified! Above all, the Salvator Mundi! […] But the magical expression of the countenance! The inimitable execution of every part! Such benevolence – such sensibility – so divine – so touching – cannot be conceived without the soul of Carlo Dolce! How blest must the creatures have been whose fancy was peopled with such images![24]

The enthusiasm shown her in the anaphoric sentence continues onto the next page. More follows. In her visit to Magdalene College, she again expresses her admiration for Carlo Dolce, as well as for Guido Reni's *Venus attired by the Graces*. The three artists she admires, Guido Reni (1575–1642), Carlo Dolci (1616–1686) and Carlo Maratta (1625–1713) cover the length and breadth of the Baroque period. Particularly significant is her description of Mary Magdalene's 'loveliness personified' and the coupling of art and religion in describing the 'the soul of Carlo Dolce'. The Reni picture, alternatively referred to as *The Toilet of Venus*, is basically a celebration of female nudity; it was sufficiently well known for engravings to be made. This unbounded admiration requires a rethinking of our basic assumptions about one particular woman novelist but also profoundly questions our assumptions about the appreciation and knowledge of the arts. In this instance, it refutes MacDiarmid's thesis, as laid out in *Aesthetics in Scotland*.

One could argue that this is just one incident, but that hardly takes us anywhere, for it is not simply the case that she spontaneously admires these paintings but that she also is knowledgeable, or, to abuse the MacDiarmid epithet, she represents a location where extremes meet. The Baroque, as a period, surely is at the farthest possible point from the three Calvinist requisites, as defined by Ramsay: protestant, realistic and moral. Nothing is more explosive and sensuous than its depiction of the female body, as in Reni, for example. If admiring the Virgin Mary is bad enough, what about Mary Magdalene! Madame Bovary (senior) thought it an offensive name for her future granddaughter, so she was named Berthe. Likewise, Brunton's final statement, 'How blest must the creatures have been whose fancy was peopled with such images', emphasises a semi-divine role for the artist; it is a phrase that could come from the pen of Samuel Taylor Coleridge or Percy Shelley for example, and, to cap it all, she ends with that most unholy component of paganism: images. The argument that, as in the case of Handel's *Messiah*, art is at the service of faith, surely is unconvincing in the extreme, as she has deliberately opted for both St Gregory and the visually erotic. What can be deduced from her remarks is that she is aware of a difference between reception or appreciation, on the one hand, and creation, on the other, as evident in that final sentence. The two concepts would normally coincide, but this is not an imperative. For example, Great Britain and the United States have plenty of foodies, to judge from the well-stocked section of cookbooks in mainstream bookstores, but that doesn't transmute into having a solid reputation for gastronomy. Outside the scope of this paper lies the gender question: she talks of Venus rather than Adonis, and Mary rather than Jesus or the apostles.

Sebastian Mitchell (2013) in an incisive account – of James Thomson, Tobias Smollett, Allan Ramsay, David Hume, James MacPherson, James Boswell, Walter Scott and William Turner – has not only linked the visual and the literary in the Romantic Century but has also tried to illustrate something which the Ramsay/MacDiarmid line of argument implies is impossible. In reading the close of Thomson's *The Castle of Indolence* (1748), Mitchell reiterates his central thesis that the poem underscores its author's economic integrationism,[25] in other words, a belief in work and prosperity that are accomplished only by the Union in contrast to, obviously, indolence. The poem upholds 'standard Whig virtues – endeavour, art, freedom of expression, commerce',[26] of which the inclusion of art is of particular relevance to our argument. Thomson, as a follower of Edmund Spenser and, more particularly of John Milton, is hence able 'to answer that fundamental question of why prelapsarian life included gardening: that the significant aspect of art in this view is not so much the work itself, but the labour of its creation'.[27] This, surely partly explains Brunton's response to the Baroque. Of course, her enthusiasm for the most effusive was no doubt designed to cause a few heads to shake, if her diary was ever intended for the public view, but that in no way detracts from the fact that the artists in question are blessed, but blessed to create when creation encompasses 'labour'. In retrospect, Brunton's love of both the creative and the divine spirit places her side by side with Coleridge, also expansive in his metaphors of creation and likewise deeply religious, often exasperated by the inability to complete or to create at all. This unlikely marriage of interests is what neither MacDiarmid nor Ramsay (to a lesser extent) can envisage.

It would be an exaggeration to suggest that Mitchell has discovered a magic formula, but undoubtedly he has gone a long way towards enabling us to focus on the problem and its inlaid polemics. Still, he is aware that this is a research question rather than an answer:

> It may be that the fundamental poetical tension of the Bower of Bliss between energetic protestant asceticism and seductive aestheticism is never fully resolved, either in this canto or in *The Faerie Queene* as a whole.[28]

That the riddle Brunton represents occurs similarly in Elizabethan protestant poetry illustrates, in the simplest of ways, how crucial the aesthetic problem was before, during and after the Reformation. It is easy to jump to the conclusion that subsequently there could be no history of the rise of art in Scotland equivalent to Ian Watt's account of the novel, hypothesising that art has suffered the same supposed fate as drama at the hands of the killjoys; I am claiming that that is not tenable at all. The comparison to Holland always springs to mind, and has been explored in great detail by Simon Schama in *The Embarrassment of Riches: An Interpretation of Dutch Culture in the Golden Age* (1987). Scott drew attention to the links between the novel and Flemish painting in his seminal review of *Emma* (1816), a subject developed at greater length by Mario Praz in *The Hero in Eclipse in Victorian Fiction* (1956). Notwithstanding, Mitchell proposes that there was a distinctive Scottish school at this time, defined in his epithet, 'empirical portraiture',[29] or what we could define as common sense painting. To close this section, he also stresses the highly visual nature of the afterlives of Ossian, that is to say tartanry springs from a literary source.

Such paradoxes, or what seem to be paradoxes, can be found in the work of modern or contemporary artists. For example, Henri Matisse paints an exotic, colourful, idealised fleshy world populated by odalisques, but he considered his masterpiece to be the Chapelle du Rosaire. Francis Poulenc alternated between the personality of the monk and the bad boy (*le voyou*), but this, added to his professed homosexuality, did not prevent him from writing possibly the most important Western religious music of the twentieth century, including the opera *Dialogues des Carmélites*. But if these examples seem to be too distant in tradition and location to be useful, *Lanark* provides a suitable rejoinder, when Duncan Thaw paints Cowlairs Parish Church, in real life, Greenhead Church, Glasgow. Like St Mary on the Rock, it was knocked down, on this occasion 'to make way for a new road'.[30]

The episode is described in detail in chapters 27 to 29. Alasdair Gray's biographer, Rodge Glass, comments that '[t]hough some of the facts are exaggerated, there is much in the way Thaw describes his working process that exists in Alasdair's own'.[31] The most striking of these is his dedication to the task at hand. In a 2007 interview, Gray explains, 'I always preferred to sleep on the premises – at Greenhead Church, I was quite comfy. I slept in the foetal position, and had a foot-warmer curling around me'.[32] 'The foetal position' is a noticeably Gray-like touch. In *Lanark*, following Glass's idea of life-plus-exaggeration, we find Thaw stating that Cowlairs is where he lives.[33] Brunton's insistence on the blessed mind of the creator and Mitchell's underscoring of the importance of the labour of creation are reflected in the closing dialogue of chapter 28, when the minister says

> 'It's beautiful, Duncan, but you could be an eternity on it. An eternity.'
>
> 'And if they say the events on the horizon distract from the big simple foreground shapes, tell them I'd begun to notice that, but this was my first mural, I'd seen nobody else paint one, and I'd to teach myself as I went along. Tell them I couldn't afford assistants.'
>
> The minister hesitated, then said firmly, 'Finish the mural when you like, Duncan. Pay no attention to them. Work on it as you like.'[34]

What makes this passage worthy of attention is not simply the tolerance that allows the minister to trust the atheist – or arguably pantheist – artist to depict the creation, but that they also discuss how God should be present yet somehow almost invisible.³⁵ In a similar fashion, 'them', though it initially refers to the parishioners, in fact turns out to be journalists and reporters. Their recording of his labours continually undermines his self-confidence and creativity, leading to the moment of crisis and breakdown that concludes book two. Thus it is easy to surmise that Gray's continuous habit of writing witty, misleading blurbs on his fiction has its roots in what Glass informs us was to be, hopefully, despite the many ups and downs, the execution of Gray's first masterpiece. What contributes most to the argument here is, again, the conflation of the creative and the religious. That paradigm of romanticism, the unfinished work, is here a mural, but it encompasses both that model and Mitchell's hypothesis. The beauty of the mural, of which images certainly exist, lies not simply in aesthetics but primarily in labour, after all the minister's command is 'Work on it'. What we witness is not just a process leading to maturity, as suggested by the foetal position, that is, the first creative step in a *Bildungs-* or *Künstlerroman*, but the creative process itself becomes the object of beauty. However, the abrupt close of book two that swiftly follows in chapter 30 turns development into trauma. The viewpoints of Brunton, the blessed mind, and Mitchell, labour, are radically different, yet both emphasise the process rather than focus exclusively on the artwork, the finished product.

The question who or what Alasdair Gray is might seem initially nonsensical. Ron Butlin eloquently states that

> *Lanark* made things possible. When we came across Marquez we thought, my God, the novel is not dead – a whole world opened up. That was localised with *Lanark*, a *Scottish* writer could do it. Alasdair was this living presence, from the older generation- there were ten fifteen years between us – someone just on the cusp of being our generation *had done it. Succeeded*.³⁶

In his estimation, Gray has succeeded in being both a local and universal writer, bridging that gap between national and international that Scottish Renaissance writers such as Gunn or MacDiarmid strove to contend was possible, but perhaps did not manage to achieve. Again, in the same way as the aforementioned writers are located in modernism, Gray leans on the artistic vanguard of his time, magic realism. It might be worth pointing out that if all three writers – MacDiarmid, Gunn and Gray – are successful in attaining an important artistic goal, this is overwhelmingly achieved, save for the early poetry of MacDiarmid, in a highly idiosyncratic English prose. An analysis of its constituent parts would undoubtedly provide a stimulating topic for a future chapter.

However interesting this debate might be, it is based on a supposition that Gray is a novelist and short-story writer. Is that the case? Initially, this would seem to be a ludicrous question: it is true that he studied art, but basically, as Butlin states, his major contribution to the arts has been, as Scotland's major contemporary prose writer, to inspire fellow writers to create on the epistemological basis that their national roots should not confine their artistic ambition to that small space. To use an apt Foucauldian phrase, Gray is a founder of discursivity. Yet, there is one book that is similar to the mural and to *Lanark* in both its ambition and the difficulty in its realisation, a.k.a. labour: the lengthy *The Book of Prefaces* (2002). It firmly defends literature in a way that is usually associated with Matthew Arnold:

> I consider this anthology a memorial to the kind of education British governments now think useless, especially for British working class children. But it has been my education, so I am bound to believe it one of the best in the world.[37]

It is debatable whether the final sentence contains a note of irony, but I would doubt that, as the enterprise is a labour of love that incorporates a highly canonical collection of prefaces or similar introductory material from Caedmon to Wilfred Owen. It is a book that depends heavily on graphic design: on the typeface, on colours, on the arrangement of drawings and prose. It contains a host of portraits of literary figures and his contemporaries. In short, the creative textual input is restricted to textual commentary à la Calvin, the selection of texts, the introduction and postscript, whereas the visual creative input is its reason for being.

A consideration of the status of Gray as primarily a visual or prose artist enables this chapter to reach a satisfactory conclusion. Glass, for example, on the final page of the biography, which, following typical Gray conventions, is not really the final page, pinpoints the issue by stating that he has been called alternatively 'Clydeside Michelangelo [...] Clydeside Dickens',[38] the painter of murals, the novelist of poverty; Dickens, needless to say, was a writer who depended greatly on the use of illustrations. In terms of form, not far away lies one of Gray's most widely appraised novels, *Poor Things* (1992). Again, it is heavily illustrated, citing as a precedent Henry Gray's *Anatomy* (1908 [1858]). The illustrations of bones, teeth and skulls are depictions of a physical reality that highlight the separation between reality and the page. At the same time, the major body of the text is preceded by an introduction, illustrations, and an allegedly handwritten exhortation to burn the manuscript. These devices sit well within the metafictional parameters that were so much part of the playful postmodernism active at the time of the novel's publication.

It would be highly unsatisfactory to stop at this point: everything boils down to the fact that Gray is a thoroughbred postmodernist. However valid a strategy that might be, it confines itself to the fiction of one author, leaving Brunton, Ramsay and MacDiarmid out of the picture altogether. The conclusion of this chapter tries to identify the common thread that binds an otherwise unlikely group of individuals, mostly. It is undeniable that Gray's fictional techniques have an identifiable pedigree in postmodern aesthetics, hence Butlin's point of departure is Gabriel García Márquez, who not only is the principal practitioner of magical realism, but who, like Gray in *Lanark*, also turns his fictional location, Macondo, into a universal theatre without sacrificing firm political opinions to textual *jouissance*: self-referentiality goes so far, but no farther. Nonetheless, this does not seem to me to be the only or the most convincing explanation of Gray's narrative strategies. The concept of embeddedness implies different levels of texture, like Russian dolls they fit neatly within each other, which provides one explanation of postmodern narrative which may very well apply to Gray. But if we change perspective, to the lineal form of the novel, it is clear that rather than form one neat structure, the constant deferral of the text creates a sense of distance between cover and content, author and text. It is precisely here, if we accept the analogy, that atheist Gray shares common ground with Presbyterian Brunton: both use different strategies to distance themselves from their fiction. Brunton's manifest but formulaic disdain of fiction leads her to believe the known female novelist is little better than a clown, suggesting that 'by a lady' enables women to remain hidden from the public eye, in her view, a very good thing too! Yet, I would argue, what both share, in evidently different ways, is a marked distrust of the imagination as a tool for fiction. Although that might ring true, or just about plausible for, say, *Poor Things*, does it have any validity for Gray's greatest work *Lanark*? That open question hinges on how we comprehend the relationship between the openly imaginative sections of the book and more realistic ones. If we believe that Gray desires their separation, then my argument is refuted, however I would propose that the overall purpose is to join them together, to use the imaginary world to illuminate the poverty of austerity Glasgow, hence the entry into the other world is through the ground: the world of science fiction is brought down to earth, or more truly, buried underneath it.

The frontispiece of *A History Maker* (1995) informs that 'Alasdair Gray is a stout, elderly, married Glaswegian who lives by painting and writing things'.[39] The fact that Gray is both visual and verbal artist – in that order – is significant precisely because this wariness of the imagination is limited to prose. The Greenhead Church mural reveals a completely different aesthetic mindset. Here, Gray is willing to sidestep his atheism and take on the ultimate challenge for a painter: to follow in the footsteps of a mighty predecessor and aspire to become the Clydeside Michelangelo. However wrong-footed his plan is in the novel or in his own life, in no way does it prevent him from taking on the role of St Gregory, going so far as to paint the divine presence itself. It is precisely this differing taxonomy that brings the aesthetics of Brunton, MacDiarmid (who showed impatience with the novel), Ramsay and Gray together. Their distrust of the imagination is apparent in their stance on fiction, but disappears almost completely when they turn to painting, leaving far behind Calvin's three precepts and the subject matter of Dutch painting of the Golden Age. What is left hanging in the air is whether their aesthetics can incorporate the novel as a work of art. From completely irreconcilable ideological standpoints, MacDiarmid and Brunton express doubts, whilst Gray's fiction formally incorporates distancing mechanisms. Ian Watt would surely have understood this enigma, as would one of the figures on the back cover of *The Book of Prefaces*, John Knox. All are wary of the emotive language of the novel.

Notes
1 Hugh MacDiarmid, *Aesthetics in Scotland*, ed. & intro. by Alan Bold (Edinburgh: Mainstream Publishing, 1984), p. 7.
2 MacDiarmid, p. 27.
3 Ibid., p. 30.
4 Ibid., p. 36.
5 Ibid., p. 42.
6 Ibid., p. 43.
7 Ibid., p. 27.
8 M. P. Ramsay, *Calvin and Art Considered in Relation to Scotland* (Edinburgh & London: Moray Press, 1938), p. 9.
9 Ramsay, p. 13.
10 Ibid., p. 12.
11 Ibid., p. 20.
12 Ibid., p. 11.
13 Ibid., p. 91.
14 www.undiscoveredscotland.co.uk/standrews/cathedral/index.html (Accessed 28 February 2104).
15 '"[…] at the Day of Judgment every herring must hang by his own tail!" Self-dependence was never more luridly expressed.' George Douglas Brown, *The House with the Green Shutters*. Intro. J. T. Low. (Edinburgh: Holmes McDougall, 1974), p. 32.
16 Andrew Monnickendam, *The Novels of Walter Scott and his Literary Relations Mary Brunton, Susan Ferrier and Christian Johnstone* (Basingstoke: Palgrave Macmillan, 2012), pp. 25–33.
17 Review of '*Emmeline and Other Pieces*'. *The Edinburgh Monthly Review* (7.2 (1819), p. 73.
18 Mary Brunton, *Emmeline: with Some Other Pieces* (Edinburgh: Archibald Constable, 1819), p. ix.
19 Brunton, p. ix.
20 Ibid., p. x.
21 Ibid., p. 76.
22 Monnickendam, p. 43.
23 Brunton, pp. 106–07.
24 Ibid., pp. 105–06.
25 Sebastian Mitchell, *Visions of Britain, 1730–1830 Anglo-Scottish Writing and Representation* (Basingstoke: Palgrave Macmillan, 2013), p. 15.

26 Mitchell, p. 42
27 Ibid., p. 42.
28 Ibid., p. 44.
29 Ibid., p. 104.
30 Rodge Glass, *Alasdair Gray. A Secretary's Biography* (London: Bloomsbury, 2009), p. 99.
31 Glass, p. 69.
32 Ibid., p. 84.
33 Alasdair Gray, *Lanark: A Life in Four Books* (London: Paladin, 1987), p. 333.
34 Gray, p. 334.
35 Ibid., p. 334.
36 Quoted in Glass, p. 167.
37 Alasdair Gray, *The Book of Prefaces* (London and New York: Bloomsbury, 2002), p. 631.
38 Glass, p. 313.
39 Alasdair Gray, *A History Maker* (London: Penguin Books, 1995), no pp.

II: INDIVIDUAL WRITERS AND FREEDOM

7. Scotland and the literary call to freedom in Mary Brunton's fiction[1]

MARÍA JESÚS LORENZO MODIA

Mary Brunton (1778–1818) was born in the Orkneys, spent most of her life in Scotland, died in the city of Edinburgh, and published novels in which her country was a key issue. She has perhaps not been as overlooked as Mary McKerrow, her most recent biographer, suggests:[2] all her works have been in print during the late twentieth century,[3] and a new edition of her first novel was published as recently as 2014. Her literary production consists of three core novels: *Self-Control* (1811),[4] *Discipline* (1815),[5] and *Emmeline* (1818),[6] a posthumous, unfinished text published by her husband as a tribute to her life, which was truncated following the birth of a stillborn son.

Brunton's place in the history of literature needs to be recognised, in that she occupies a prominent position in the formation and development of the so-called female novel. The degree of her literary success was also noteworthy, with her first novel going through three editions in the year of its publication; the book also commanded a high price, selling for twenty-one shillings, compared to fifteen for Jane Austen's *Sense and Sensibility*.[7] However, a further aspect of her work which requires consideration is Brunton's role in the creation of a Scottish literary canon and the story of the nation, one which makes sense of Scotland's relationship to England and thus to Great Britain (Ferris). In order to explore this issue, and how it was presented by an early nineteenth-century Scottish female writer, the theoretical framework to be used will be that of post-colonialism, drawing particularly on the work of Edward Said (1991),[8] Homi Bhabha (1994),[9] and Patrick Parrinder (2006),[10] as well as elements of gender studies, as in the work of Janet Todd (1989)[11] and Elaine Showalter (1984),[12] among others. As for the relationship between a writer and the nation to which he/she claims to be ascribed, the issues proposed by Parrinder in *Nation and Novel* are those of descent, nationality, domicile (p. 3), but also those of language and 'filiation,' or 'affiliation' according to Edward Said (pp. 19–20). In terms of the situation of Scotland in this period, the above factors should be complemented with the concept of 'cultural nation,' as opposed to that of 'nation state,' discussed by Friedrich Meinecke in 1908,[13] and re-elaborated by Kristan Kumar in *The Making of the English National Identity* (2003).[14] Brunton's contribution to the creation of the female Highland novel has already been studied by Sarah W. R. Smith, who considers her to be a writer inspired by Calvinism, one who contributed to the development of the role of women as active social agents pursuing economic independence as a social tool, for the benefit of both themselves and their families.[15] Brunton has been seen as a novelist who, in contrast to Walter Scott, pays due attention to women, whose works 'hold considerable political, social, and economic power, often by proxy for male leaders; she believably shows how the patriarchal and hierarchic society changes under post-Rebellion stresses',[16] and whose Highlanders are not only rural characters but leaders who are familiar both with the atmosphere of the capital of Scotland and that of the London metropolis, or even abroad.[17]

In contributing to the creation of the Scottish female novel genre, and to the national tale, as Andrew Monnickendam put it in *The Novels of Sir Walter Scott and his Literary Relations*,[18] Brunton was accompanied by other novelists and essay writers, these including Elizabeth Hamilton (1758–1816), who shared with her a moderate, progressive interest in transforming national domestic agendas, particularly poverty and educational reform,[19] and was followed by others, such as Jane Porter (1776–1850), Christian Isobel Johnstone (1781–1857), and Susan Ferrier (1782–1854), all of them labelled 'The Other Great Unknowns' by Carol Anderson and Aileen M. Riddell.[20] Brunton was moderately well received by her fellow writers and contemporary critics, in particular in post-Enlightenment Edinburgh, which was a centre of intellectual activity. One indication of her literary relations is the dedication of *Self-Control* to the London based Scottish writer Joanna Baillie (1762–1851), who later paid tribute to Brunton's memory with the following obituary:

No more shall bed-rid pauper watch
The gentle rising of the latch
And as she enters shift his place,
To hear her voice and see her face.
The helpless vagrant, oft relieved,
From her hath his last dole received.
The circle, social and enlightened,
Whose evening hours her converse brightened,
Have seen her quit the friendly door,
Whose threshold she shall cross no more.
And he, by holy ties endear'd,
Whose life her love so sweetly cheer'd,
Of her cold clay, the mind's voice cell,
Hath ta'en a speechless last farewell.
Yea, those who never saw her face,
Now did on blue horizon trace
One mountain of her native land,
Nor turn that leaf with eager hand,
On which appears the unfinish'd page,
Of her whose works did oft engage
Untired attention, interest deep,
While searching, healthful thoughts would creep
To the heart's core, like balmy air,
To leave a kindly feeling there,—
And gaze, till stain of fallen tears,
Upon the snowy blank appears,
Now all who did her friendship claim,
With alter'd voice pronounce her name,
And quickly turn, with wistful ear,
Her praise from stranger's lips to hear,
And hoard as saintly relics gain'd
Aught that to her hath e'er pertain'd.[21]

In the dedication of *Self-Control* 'To Miss Joanna Baillie', Brunton aligns her moral views on the passions and self-control, as depicted in her first novel, with those of Baillie in her *Plays on Passions* (1798–1812), and, using the conventional 'humilitas' rhetorical device, makes an apology of fiction as being useful for readers, and particularly for young ladies:

> Nor is a work of fiction necessarily unprofitable to the readers. When the vitiated appetite refuses its proper food, the alternative may be administered in a sweetmeat. It may be imprudent to confess the presence of the medicine, lest the sickly palate, thus warned, turn from it in loathing. But I rely in this instance on the philosopher, who avers that 'young ladies never read prefaces'; and I am not without hope, that with you, and with all who form exceptions to this rule, the avowal of a useful purpose may be an inducement to tolerate what otherwise might be thought unworthy of regard.[22]

Mary Brunton plays a liminal role both as a woman and as a Scottish novelist, writing from the margins of a male literary system centred largely in the London metropolis, and places herself in that third space known as hybridity, as a paradigm of colonial anxiety expressed by means of the discourse of mimicry 'constructed around an ambivalence',[23] evidently expressed indirectly by Brunton. Many of Jane Austen's fictional texts, as well as Anne Brontë's *The Tenant of Wildfell Hall* (1848), follow the pattern drawn by Brunton in the use of the 'forked tongue' which reflects, from a female perspective, the difficulties of the entrance of ladies into the world.[24] Such literary relationships may be easily tested when comparing the respective novels. However, Austen also wrote letters in which she expressed her discreet admiration for Brunton (Letter 91, 11–12 Oct 1813)[25] and how, being a contemporary of Brunton, she tried in her own work to develop the plots and situations found in the novels by this Caledonian writer.[26] In fact, the author of *Emma* went so far as to say she had avoided Brunton's books, fearing that she might discover in them the development of topics that she herself had in mind; indeed, she mentions one such novel by name in a letter written the same year as this novel was published:

> We have tried to get *Self-contoul* [sic], but in vain. – I should like to know what her Estimate is but am always half afraid of finding a clever novel too clever – & of finding my own story & my own people all forestalled. (Letter 72, 30 April 1811)[27]

Besides the possible influence of Brunton's work in the construction of the English novel, her texts are also permeated with another key issue, the concept of Scotland as a nation, although the political *status quo* of the country is not overtly discussed.[28] Her heroes and heroines in *Self-Control* are depicted as positive characters, and are considered Scots in every respect, including the way their nationality is described. Thus, the protagonist Laura Montreville is defined as 'entirely a Scotch woman' (p. 142) who sighs 'for a Scotch Strephon' (p. 232), that is, for a native shepherd lover, echoing the image from Greek pastoral that had already been used in Sir Philip Sydney's *Arcadia* (1504) and in Song 174 by Robert Burns, 'Ye gods, was Strephon's picture blest' (1787–1803). Laura's maternal family sticks to their Scottish roots, and consider education an issue related to the nation, this to be passed from generation to generation, as can be seen in the first page of the novel, where the topic is dealt with in relation to Laura's father: '[…] to the national opinions of a Scottish mother, he was indebted for an education, of which the liberality suited better with his birth than with his fortunes' (p. 1). On the contrary, bad or reprehensible characters in the novel are seen to disregard everything Scottish, which can lead to a compounding of this negativity. For instance, Laura's strict moral behaviour is despised by her cruel aunt on account of the Scottish, Presbyterian morals which underlie it, these described by her aunt as 'Scotch *gaucheries*,' thus dismissing Laura's Scots origin and religious persuasion as both awkward and rustic (p. 341).

Mary Brunton's novels are set in Scotland, and both the territory and the people are considered 'her all'. *Discipline* – published in 1814, the same year as Walter Scott's *Waverley* – includes Highland scenes, and refers to both the anti-slavery movement and the issue of poverty, and deals with how these questions were approached by society and religion. In *Self-Control* the country even causes the heroine to weep, in a rather sentimental way, when she 'first beheld romantic Edinburgh. "Is it not glorious!" She cried, tears of wonder and delight glittering in her eyes' (p. 45). In this novel Brunton uses binary oppositions presenting Scotland as genuine and morally positive, and everything related to colonial power as derogatory and externally imposed for Scots. Hence, London, as a far-away metropolis, is represented as a place where any problem may arise, and where the heroine's family is dispossessed of both fortune and honour. Moreover, the unknown dominating territories, that is, England, have a perverse, magnetic power for members of the household, since London is the emblem of a tempting and fascinating land, one which 'smiled rich and inviting from afar' (p. 48). The novelist is at pains to make a clear distinction between the different countries belonging to the United Kingdom and the asymmetries following the 1707 Act of Union, thus reflecting a common idea for many British citizens that the term England should be distinguished from that of Britain, even in the Regency period. Whenever characters are away from Scotland, they are always sighing for the Highlands, and consider that place not only their home (p. 106) but also a sanctuary to return to (p. 388), expressed in terms of a haven where everything has a positive connotation: 'she permitted De Courcy to follow her at the end of that time to Scotland. A few weeks they were to spend in wandering through the romantic scenes of her native land [...]' (p. 403). As Anderson and Riddell suggest, 'happiness and moral worth are associated with Scotland, specifically the Highlands [...] anticipating the work of Susan Ferrier'.[29]

Many eighteenth-century novels depict the entrance of a hero and/or a heroine into the world. Most of their plots present a female protagonist with no academic education, and whose virtue is in peril, that is, a young lady who over the course of the novel is pursued by a suitor, in a concerted attempt to seduce her and thus to destroy her innocence. Success on the part of the suitor, of course, would tarnish the heroine's reputation, dispossessing her of any claim to a normal, moral life. And so it is in *Self-Control*, where those women who are interested in cultural progress are discouraged from doing so by libertines, for whom the idea of promoting a woman's intellectual abilities is of little interest:

> She was convinced that 'of all studies that of mathematics must be the most delightful. She imagined it might not be quite impracticable

even for a lady, supposing she were so fortunate as to meet with a friend who could assist her.' De Courcy, laughing, offered his services, not, it must be owned, with an idea that they would be accepted. (p. 255)

Laura, the heroine of *Self-Control*, is passionately infatuated with the seducer, even physically so, yet surprisingly enough, after their first meeting she realises his dubious morals, and rejects him consistently, despite her inner feelings. In this clear sexual attraction for her potential partner, the protagonist follows the path trodden by Eliza Haywood in *Love in Excess* (1719–20), in which the heroine is sexually attracted to an aristocratic libertine, and in fact is eventually punished for it, having been unable to resist her passion. Mary Brunton, for her part, presents female sexuality in a fraught Scottish context, and channels it, by means of a proper marriage and the celebration of domesticity, back to her beloved Edinburgh; this after having controlled a mad passion and having escaped from the experience of a kidnapping abroad. At stake here are not only her honour and morals, but also her national identity. Although the rake – Colonel Hargrave – is of Scottish origin, he is the kind of villain who despises his own country, showing signs of self-hate and a lack of respect for the land and its inhabitants, as can be seen in the following example:

> […] thither he retired accordingly, not without some national misgivings of mind on the subject of Scottish nastiness and its consequences. His apartment, however, though small, was decent, his bed was clean, his sleep refreshing, and his dreams pleasant; nor was it till a late hour the following morning, that he rose to the homely comfort, and clumsy abundance of a Highland breakfast. (p. 39)

While at some points in the novel the use of a regional variety of the language is seen as affording characters an emotional link to their heartfelt identity, this is not the case with Colonel Hargrave, who despises it:

> […] he was answered, 'Wow, Sir, him an' Miss Laura's awa' at six o'clock this morning.' 'Away,' repeated the Colonel, – 'Where are they

gone?' 'To London, Sir; and I'm sure a lanely time we'll hae till they come hame again.' 'What stay do they intend making?' 'Hech, Sir, I dare say that's what they dinna ken themsels.' 'What is their address?' inquired the Colonel. 'What's your will, Sir:' 'Where are they to be found?' 'Am'n I tellan you they're in London, Sir, I'm sure ye ken whar that is?' 'But how are you to send them letters?' 'Wow! They never got mony letters but frae England; and now 'at they are in London, ye ken the folk may gie them into their ain hand.' 'But suppose you should have occasion to write to them yourself?' said Hargrave, whose small stock of patience wore fast to a close. 'Hech, Sir, sorrow a scrape I can write. They learn a' thae newfangled things now, but, trouth, i' my young days, we were na' sae upsettan.' Hargrave was in no humour to canvas the merits of the different modes of education; and, muttering an ejaculation, in which the word *devil* was distinctively audible, he turned away. (pp. 39–40)

It is also interesting to note that the racial or ethnic features of Scots, such as their red hair, and the consideration of these as positive, are also highlighted by the heroine's friends:

'Did you ever see anything so lovely as Miss Montreville?' said Sophia Bolingbroke to the young lady who sat next her. 'I never can think anybody pretty who has red hair,' was the reply. 'If her hair be red,' returned Sophia, 'it is the most pardonable red hair in the world, for it is more nearly black […]' (p. 317)

Other traditions, such as wearing kilts, are also mentioned ironically when Laura's father, an Englishman living in Scotland, is asked if he had been forced to wear one, to which he answered with a positive opinion of Scots: 'they never interfered with my dress' (p. 107).

Finally, the main exaltation of Caledonia appears in the heroine's words on first sight of the coast during her voyage back to the Clyde from Canada:

> In a clear, frosty morning towards the end of September, she heard once more the cry of the land! – now music to her ear. Now with a beating breast she ran to gaze upon a ridge of mountains indenting the disc of the rising sun; but the tears of rapture dimmed her eyes, when every voice at once shouted, 'Scotland!' (p. 428)

Notwithstanding this conception of her country as home, she is capable of irony regarding her countrymen:

> In general, nothing is more ridiculous than a Highlander's description of his maladies. It is such a mixture of shrewdness, confidence, and total ignorance; it is so absurdly minute, and yet so loaded with apologies to the delicacy of the listener, that I have many a time been obliged to laugh, at the expense of being thought a monster of insensibility.[30]

Thus Scotland, together with the different perceptions of its national identity, is a key topic in Mary Brunton's narrative, particularly in *Self-Control*. Additionally, the issue of national identity, embodied by the heroine, is intertwined with that of the plight of women. Hence we see her suffer the effects of double standards in two ways, discriminated against both as a Scot and as a poor woman.[31]

In *Self-Control*, then, the heroine suffers from both psychological and physical persecution and abuse, to the extent that she is confined, kidnapped, and taken to America so that the rake can possess her (p. 172). The influence of Samuel Richardson's novels on Mary Brunton seems evident here, and indeed she mentions them in *Self-Control* (pp. 135–36). However, this latter novel presents a heroine who is far more credible to its own contemporary female readership than those of Richardson would have been, immolated as they usually were in their virtue. In *Self-Control*, by contrast, pervasive sexual harassment is rejected by the protagonist through religious but also moral rectitude: her love for her potential seducer is passionate, and even physical, yet she is able to reject the union on account of the extreme moral turpitude with which he initiates the relationship. Unable to confess the sexual harassment suffered at home, which borders on paedophilia, the female protagonist has to confront not only the seducer and his accomplices but also her own father, who considers the rake to be a true friend and urges her to accept the marriage proposal made by this supposedly reformed libertine. But the innovative element here is that the effects of male chauvinism are clearly identified as the cause of the heroine's malady and self-denial. As we know, women's illnesses have been explored extensively in the field of gender studies and criticism, especially given the domestic confinement and reduced perspective on life in which women often found themselves. For example, in *The Female Malady: Women, Madness and English Culture 1830–1980*,[32] Elaine Showalter showed misogyny to be among the principal causes of women's insanity. In this regard, Captain Montreville, the heroine's father *Self-Control*, seems to understand this, verbalising it thus: 'The world's opinion affixes just disgrace to the vices in your sex, which in ours it views with more indulgent eyes' (p. 176). Unlike earlier heroines, Laura is an active woman, capable of coming back to life after drowning in a river when escaping her persecutor, and even recovering from mental illness caused by the same man. She represents the personal and social insecurity of women at the time, specifically those who are not in possession of a personal fortune yet who society does not allow to earn their own living. However, once the problem is identified, she defies her own destiny in every respect. She not only rejects an unacceptable marriage proposal, but also attempts to become a professional artist in an attempt to attain both public recognition and economic independence. Hence, the heroine is finally able to overcome constant assault, becomes mistress of her own life, marries a true lover, and lives contentedly in Scotland, a haven for her permanent happiness.

This novel may represent the reversal of the male literary tradition, in the sense that the heroine subverts an unappealing future, one which is depicted in other novels of the period. In such texts the protagonist either rejects her seducer and dies – physically or metaphorically – or accepts a reformed rake, complying with normal patriarchal power relations, and accepting that males can find social acceptance, even if there are sexual sins in their past, whereas such acceptance is not available for women. Ironically enough, the libertine in *Self-Control* is within the Scottish literary tradition, in that he is a fan of Tobias Smollett's picaresque novel *Peregrine Pickle*, 'which he devoured with great eagerness' (p. 41). In Smollett's novel, the egotistical dandy has a dissipated life, but in the end the female protagonist accepts his repentance of past sins, and marries him devotedly. On the contrary, through Laura's attitude, Mary Brunton seems to reject this traditional plot as misogynistic, given the moral standard it conveys, and makes her heroine fight for a different solution to the plight of women. The life of the protagonist proves that women need not, indeed must not, accept suitors who are known for their base actions towards women, thus denying libertines the kind of respectable existence which is, effectively, a reward for their dark and sinful past.

Mary Brunton's narratives show how the issue of gender and the nation are inextricably interwoven, with Scotland serving as a positive background, an emblem of shelter for a character in distress who yearns to return to her homeland. Moreover, her Scottish moral education and religious background might be considered an essential factor in her permanent fight for freedom in life, both regarding her economic independence, and in the choice of a partner who respects not only her but also her country. Fiction of this type, then, presents a somewhat conservative ideology, stressing morals, duty and religion, but on closer analysis can be seen as transcending the limits of most Evangelical novels, revealing a subversive agenda in terms of both gender and nation, showing that self-control is used as a means of verbalising change and as a strategy of dutiful disobedience to old patriarchal roles.

Notes

1. This research falls within the MINECO projects FFI-2012–35872, FEM2015–66937-P and FFI2015–71025-REDT. This support is hereby gratefully acknowledged.
2. Mary McKerrow, *Mary Brunton: The Forgotten Scottish Novelist* (Orkney: The Orcadian, 2001), p. 1.
3. Anthony A. Mandal, *Jane Austen and the Popular Novel: The Determined Author* (Basingstoke and New York: Palgrave Macmillan, 2007).
4. Mary Brunton, *Self-Control*, Intro. Sarah Maitland (London: Pandora, 1986).

5   Mary Brunton, *Discipline*, Intro. Fay Weldon (London: Pandora, 1986).
6   Mary Brunton, *Emmeline* (London: Routledge, 1992).
7   Antony Mandal, 'Introduction', in Mary Brunton, *Self-Control* (London: Pickering and Chatto & Chawton House Library) pp. xiii–xliii, (p. xxv).
8   Edward W. Said, *The World, The Text, The Critic* (Cambridge, MA: Harvard University Press, 1983).
9   Homi K. Bhabha, 'Of Mimicry and Man: The Ambivalence of Colonial Discourse', in *The Location of Culture* (London and New York: Routledge, 1994) pp. 85–92.
10 Patrick Parrinder, *Nation and the Novel: The English Novel from its Origins to the Present Day* (Oxford: Oxford University Press, 2006).
11 Janet Todd, *The Sign of Angelica: Women, Writing and Fiction, 1660–1800* (London: Virago, 1989).
12 Elaine Showalter, *A Literature of their Own: British Women Novelists from Brontë to Lessing* (London: Virago, 1984).
13 Friedrich Meinecke, *Cosmopolitanism and the Nation State* (Princeton, New Jersey: Princeton University Press, 1970).
14 Krishan Kumar, *The Making of the English National Identity*, 2nd edn. (Cambridge: Cambridge University Press, repr. 2005).
15 Sarah W. R. Smith, 'Men, Women, and Money: The Case of Mary Brunton', in *Fetter'd or Free? British Women Novelists, 1670–1815*, ed. by Mary Anne Schofield and Cecilia Macheski (Athens: Ohio University Press, 1986) pp. 40–57, (p. 48).
16 Smith, p. 54.
17 Ibid.
18 Andrew Monnickendam, *The Novels of Sir Walter Scott and his Literary Relations: Mary Brunton, Susan Ferrier and Christian Johnstone* (Basingstoke: Palgrave Macmillan, 2013), p. 1.
19 Susan B. Egenolf, *The Art of Political Fiction in Hamilton, Edgeworth, and Owenson* (Farnham: Ashgate, 2009), pp. 13–16.
20 Carol Anderson, and Aileen M. Riddell, 'The Other Great Unknowns: Women Fiction Writers of the Early Nineteenth Century', in *A History of Scottish Women's Writing*, ed. by Douglas Gifford and Dorothy Macmillan (Edinburgh: Edinburgh University Press, 1977), pp. 179–95, (p. 179).
21 Joanna Baillie, 'Mary Brunton's Obituary' In Bryce, Rev. Alexander, *Biographical Dictionary of Eminent Scotsmen* (Glasgow, Edinburgh and London: Blackie and Son, 1855) vol. 1, pp. 390–92, (p. 392).
22 Brunton, *Self-Control*, p. vi.
23 Bhabha, p. 86.
24 Ibid, p. 85.
25 Robert William Chapman, ed., *Jane Austen's Letters* (Oxford: Clarendon, 1932), p. 344.
26 Ellen Moers, *Literary Women: The Great Writers* (New York: Anchor Books, Doubleday, 1977), p. 77; Dale Spender, *Mothers of the Novel. 100 Good Women Writers before Jane Austen* (London: Pandora, 1986), p. 149.
27 Chapman, p. 320.
28 Margaret H. Bruce, 'Mary Brunton (1778–1818): An Assessment', *Journal of Women's Studies in Literature*, 1 (1979), pp. 1–15 (p. 14).

29 Anderson and. Riddell, 'The Other Great Unknowns', p. 187.
30 Alexander Brunton, *Memoir*, in *Emmeline with Some Other Pieces, By Mary Brunton* (Edinburgh: Archibald Constable, 1819) p. lxiii.
31 Sharon Alker, 'The Business of Romance: Mary Brunton and the Virtue of Commerce', *European Romantic Review*, 13.2 (June 2002), pp. 199–205 (p. 202).
32 Elaine Showalter, *The Female Malady: Women, Madness and English Culture 1830–1980* (London: Penguin, 1987).

8. Rivers, freedom and constraint in some of Stevenson's autobiographical writing

LESLEY GRAHAM

This chapter examines the various ways in which Robert Louis Stevenson, in a selection of essays from the 1880s, expresses the idea of freedom and its contrary through the image of rivers and their flow. The freedoms in question are multiple – the freedom to move forward professionally, to travel unfettered, to explore the world. The constraints are just as varied – the feeling of being hemmed in geographically; of being locked into the logic of family heredity; of being condemned to long periods of convalescence and subject to the constraints of family life. Resentment about this lack of freedom is keenly expressed, for example, in the essays written during the time that he spent convalescing in Davos in the Swiss Alps; a period of enforced isolation, hemmed in on all sides by high mountains, surrounded by snow and condemned to follow the valetudinarian lifestyle. It seems that the essay form offered Stevenson a freedom of content and style that allowed him to explore the tensions between the extremes of freedom and dependence and this, very often, through images of flux, of flowing rivers, held in on both sides by river-banks but constantly moving forwards, bringing with them the traces of the places and times through which they have passed; of the tyranny of inheritance cascading down generations.

When Stevenson set out to write an essay about his ideal house, his first requisite was that there should be water nearby. 'The house must be within hail of either a little river or the sea', he writes. His preference is specifically for a modest watercourse because 'a lively burn gives us, in the space of a few yards, a greater variety of promontory and islet, of cascade, shallow goil, and boiling pool, with answerable changes both of song and colour, than a navigable stream in many hundred miles.'[1] As we shall see, this flow of liveliness and of variety is deployed by Stevenson in several essays where he uses the river as an organising and pacing device especially in the opening paragraphs: his fluctuating flow of ideas and words mimicking the river's irregular course but occasionally drifting into calmer pools of reflection – an opening that reflects the irregular and unpredictable flow of ideas in the essay itself.

This is the case in two essays that recall Stevenson's Edinburgh childhood. These pieces illustrate both the importance of rivers in general for Stevenson and the influence that they had on his imagination, in particular the extent to which he identified his Edinburgh childhood with the Water of Leith, the title of one of the essays. 'It is not possible to exaggerate the hold that is taken on the mind of men by a familiar river,'[2] he writes. The river in question is a modest waterway but an interesting one, running down from the Pentland Hills through a varied urban and rural landscape: 'Such as it was, […] it was the river whose streams made glad my childhood and for that reason ever memorable to me.' It 'skirted the outposts, vacant lots, and half-rural slums of a great city, and at last, running between the repose of a graveyard and the clatter of engine factory, lapsed, between dark gates and groves of masts and a long alley of weedy piers, into an islanded salt estuary' (45). The Water of Leith is thus entrusted with Stevenson's sense of his childhood identity and with the memory of the variety and industry of his native city: they are braided rivers.

The Water of Leith is also celebrated in the essay 'The Manse: A Fragment'. In the opening paragraph, Stevenson approaches Colinton Manse, the home of his maternal grandfather, by way of the river, describing the exact time and spot from which he dreams of the old manse.

> I have named, among many rivers that make music in my memory, that dirty Water of Leith. Often and often I desire to look upon it again; and the choice of a point of view is easy to me. It should be at a certain water-door, embowered in shrubbery. The river is there dammed back for the service of the flour-mill just below, so that it lies deep and darkling, and the sand slopes into brown obscurity with a glint of gold; and it has but newly been recruited by the borrowings of the snuff-mill just above, and these, tumbling merrily in, shake the pool to its black heart, fill it with drowsy eddies, and

set the curded froth of many other mills solemnly steering to and fro upon the surface.³

As the passage develops there is an overwhelming sense that the old Water of Leith, the site of Stevenson's happy childhood has been irretrievably polluted; a sense that the river is a locus of change, degradation and loss.

> Or so it was when I was young; for change, and the masons, and the pruning-knife, have been busy; and if I could hope to repeat a cherished experience, it must be on many and impossible conditions. I must choose, as well as the point of view, a certain moment in my growth, so that the scale may be exaggerated, and the trees on the steep opposite side may seem to climb to heaven, and the sand by the water-door, where I am standing, seem as low as Styx. And I must choose the season also, so that the valley may be brimmed like a cup with sunshine and the songs of birds; – and the year of grace, so that when I turn to leave the riverside I may find the old manse and its inhabitants unchanged. (155–56)

Although the permanency of the existence of the riverscape might suggest otherwise, Stevenson knows that however much he would like to view the scene again from a child's physical perspective with towering trees and low water, a return to the cherished place is no more possible than a return to his boyhood.

Just as the Water of Leith flows through the opening paragraphs of the eponymous essay fragment and 'The Manse', establishing their course, drawing the reader in to the current of the essay as the sentences gather mass and momentum, so the remembered river branches out inter-textually into letters, poems and no doubt other genres too. He expresses a similar desire to return to Swanston in a letter to his nurse Alison Cunningham written at almost exactly the same time as he was writing those essays: 'I would like fine to go up the burnside a bit, and sit by the pool and be young again – or no, be what I am still, only there instead of here, for just a little' (16 April 1887).⁴ A similar sentiment acknowledging the impossibility of the enterprise is expressed in 'To Minnie,' a poem in *A Child's Garden of Verses*, written for his now grown-up girl cousin:

> The river, on from mill to mill,
> Flows past our childhood's garden still;
> But ah! we children never more
> Shall watch it from the water-door![5]

Stevenson means this in a Heraclitian sense. Fresh waters now flow in the Water of Leith and he shows a keen awareness that absolutely everything changes, nothing remains still and one can never step twice into the same stream. As Denis Denisoff observes, 'This active, transhistorical self-engagement constructs the narrator as both child and adult simultaneously. [...] To try and unravel the temporal conflations is to fight the spirit of the piece.'[6] What Denisoff calls the 'temporal conflation' of the piece is made possible by the permanence of the river as a feature of the landscape but also by its slipperiness – it is here and it is elsewhere at the same time, it flowed through this place in the past just as it does now and will continue to do in the future.

Rivers continued to irrigate Stevenson's sense of place and self throughout his young adulthood as attested by the subject matter of his first published book *An Inland Voyage* which recounts his adventures paddling along the waterways of northern France delighting in the forward impulsion through tranquil scenery. He poses in the persona of an experienced man of the world, recruiting the river of life topos as he recounts shouting out to some young women by the river who had blown kisses and asked him and his companion Walter Simpson to come back. 'Come back? There is no coming back, young ladies, on the impetuous stream of life' he retorts.[7] The faux-experienced Stevenson also strikes a pose when he rather startlingly declares that 'After a good woman, and a good book, and tobacco, there is nothing so agreeable on earth as a river' (146–47). Again, something less sunny and straightforward lurks below the surface of this perfect vehicle for the insouciance of young adulthood and when after heavy rain, Stevenson's canoe capsizes, he finds himself dragged under discovering that the river can take away freedom just as easily as it gives it: 'You can never know, till you try it, what a dead pull a river makes against a man' (112–13). The narrative takes on a serious tone, as in the words of Oliver Buckton 'the journey down the river becomes a metaphor for the vagaries of life and the deferral of death.'[8] The traveller Stevenson depicts the river-journey as a futile struggle against death until the very shape of his canoe becomes a *memento mori* as people call out to him that it is like a coffin (122) and he warns the reader that:

> [...] we must all set our pocket-watches by the clock of fate. There is a headlong, forthright tide, that bears away man with his fancies like a straw, and runs fast in time and space. It is full of curves like this, your winding river of the *Oise*; and lingers and returns in pleasant pastorals; and yet, rightly thought upon, never returns at all. For though it should revisit the same acre of meadow in the same hour, it will have made an ample sweep between-whiles; many little streams will have fallen in; many exhalations risen towards the sun; and even although it were the same acre, it will no more be the same river of *Oise*. And thus, O graces of *Origny*, although the wandering fortune of my life should carry me back again to where you await death's whistle by the river, that will not be the old I who walks the street; and those wives and mothers, say, will those be you? (145–46)

The same image – that of life as a turbulent river – is used in the essay 'Crabbed Age and Youth' when Stevenson writes: 'we may compare the headlong course of our years to a swift torrent in which a man is carried away; now he is dashed against a boulder, now he grapples for a moment to a trailing spray; at the end, he is hurled out and overwhelmed in a dark and bottomless ocean.'[9]

During Stevenson's next journey in France – the one that provided the subject matter of *Travels with a Donkey in the Cévennes* – rivers and streams are associated with no such impending watery graves, but rather with variety in the landscape and the promise of possible relief from the weariness of walking. As he follows the Tarn to Pont de Montvert he admires its crystal clear hues and at every pool longs to bathe his 'naked body in the mountain air and water'.[10] The river bathing is a semi-pagan act of worship. Physical contact with the river water is then a thrilling way of paying homage to nature and to the landscape he is moving through: a way of circumventing the thorny question of religion that was so much on his mind during this long walk through Camisard Country. The joyful celebration of bathing continues in 'Fontainebleau'[11] an essay recalling the time Stevenson spent in the artists' colonies in and around the Forest of Fontainebleau, choosing to live in Gretz because unlike many of the other artists' colonies it actually had a 'bright river' running through it. 'It is vastly different to awake in Gretz, to go down the green inn-garden, to find the river streaming through the bridge, and to see the dawn begin across the poplared level' (134), a river ready to receive the author's body in the sultry noon.

These laughing rivers, trotting rivers, cool embracing rivers in France all reflect uncomplicated freedom of movement, freedom from the shackles of everyday life and the insouciance is later called upon in his textualised memories of the period. But as the writer grew older the very concept of freedom became more complicated for the mature adult that Stevenson now was. He had left his bohemian days in Fontainebleau behind, for the time being at least, and surrounded himself with a wife and ready-made family in need of financial support. He was also fettered by the climatic requirements of his own health problems, and increasingly those of his wife. It was clear that a healthy, stable, adult life came at a price, as he was to write in the essay 'Gentlemen' in 1888:

> Freedom we now know for a thing incompatible with corporate life and a blessing probably peculiar to the solitary robber; we know besides that every advance in richness of existence, whether moral or material, is paid for by a loss of liberty; that liberty is man's coin in which he pays his way; that luxury and knowledge and virtue, and love and the family affections, are all so many fresh fetters on the naked and solitary freeman.[12]

The experience of this new lack of freedom is acutely expressed in a series of five somewhat discontented essays written during a sojourn in Davos in Switzerland and published in the *Pall Mall Gazette*. Stevenson had come to Davos for the invigorating mountain air but immediately felt hemmed in and imprisoned in this mountain sanatorium, bored by the sameness of so much white landscape. This sentiment is reflected in his resentment of the joyless river which runs through the valley but is never named. In the first of the five essays, 'Health and Mountains', Stevenson briefly delineates the main features of a mountain sanatorium surrounded by walls of mountains; hotels and black pinewoods contrasting with the white curd of snow that covers the mountains, the whole scene populated with invalids going about their health-seeking activities:

> A certain furious river runs curving down the valley; its pace never varies, it has not a pool for as far as you can follow it; and its unchanging, senseless hurry is strangely tedious to witness. It is a river that a man could grow to hate. Day after day breaks with the rarest gold upon the mountain spires, and creeps, growing and glowing, down into the valley. From end to end the snow reverberates the sunshine; from end to end the air tingles with the light, clear and dry like crystal. Only along the course of the river, but high above it, there hangs far into the noon, one waving scarf of vapour. It were hard to fancy a more engaging feature in a landscape; perhaps it is harder to believe that delicate, long-lasting phantom of the atmosphere, a creature of the incontinent stream whose course it follows.[13]

This is a far cry from the qualified release expressed in the more famous 'Ordered South',[14] the first of Stevenson's essays to explore the experience of seeking a healthier climate abroad. The Mediterranean somehow heightened the exotic nature of the release from family tension which, to some extent at least, compensated for the humiliation of being incapacitated. In 'Davos in Winter', the river is unsatisfactory because it is neither an interesting, varied, meandering river nor the sea. It offers no promising vista with an unseen shore only the unbending logic of its monotonous course; a constant reminder of a present locked into the logic of the ill person's ritual occupations. Not even in the neighbouring valleys is there any escape:

> [...] as the hour proceeds, [...] you will find yourself upon the farther side in yet another Alpine valley, snow white and coal black, with such another long-drawn congeries of hamlets and such another senseless watercourse bickering along the foot. You have had your moment; but you have not changed the scene. The mountains are about you like a trap; you cannot foot it up a hillside and behold the sea as a great plain, but live in holes and corners, and can change only one for another.[15]

The 'senseless river' provides him with no inspiration. It has no name that means anything to him, unlike the association-laden rivers of his youth, the names of which all tumble out in a joyful gazetteer-like list in one of the opening paragraphs of 'Pastoral' (1887).

> How often and willingly do I not look again in fancy on Tummel, or Manor, or the talking Airdle, or Dee swirling in its Lynn; on the bright burn of Kinnaird, or the golden burn that pours and sulks in the den behind Kingussie! I think shame to leave out one of these enchantresses, but the list would grow too long if I remembered all; only I may not forget Allan Water, nor birch-wetting Rogie, nor yet Almond; nor, for all its pollutions, that Water of Leith of the many and well-named mills – Bell's Mills, and Canon Mills, and Silver Mills; nor Redford Burn of pleasant memories; nor yet, for all its smallness, that nameless trickle that springs in the green bosom of Allermuir, and is fed from Halkerside with a perennial teacupful, and threads the moss under the Shearer's Knowe, and makes one pool there, overhung by a rock, where I loved to sit and make bad verses, and is then kidnapped in its infancy by subterranean pipes for the service of the sea-beholding city in the plain. From many points in the moss you may see at one glance its whole course and that of all its tributaries; [...][16]

A good river (or even better, a litany of good rivers) provides him with enough flow to carry his essay along through landscapes and ideas as in 'The Water of Leith' or in 'Forest Notes'. It ensures continuity and coherence but also variety. It also provides him with an image for the thing that flows perhaps most easily in his life: words. He relishes the flow of words in conversation and in text, regularly comparing their movement to that of a river. An old lady in Gondet, whose acquaintance he made during the trip to the Cévennes made a particular impression on him due to her 'unwearying flow of oaths and obscenities, endless like a river'.[17] The more gentlemanly talk of the Savile Club in London – where Stevenson himself was an admired conversationalist – is submitted to the same metaphor in the two-part essay 'Talk and Talkers', a celebration of Stevenson's friends and their talking styles: 'The genuine artist follows the stream of conversation as an angler follows the windings of a brook, not dallying where he fails to "kill"'.[18] Not only words but consciousness also can flow, not like a stream of consciousness but more like a mind that has freed itself of imperious physical needs and desires. As the essay 'Lay Morals' suggests, if a man learns to love a woman he overcomes 'betrayals and regrets; for the man now lives as a whole; his consciousness now moves on uninterrupted like a river; through all the extremes and ups and downs of passion, he remains approvingly conscious of himself'.[19] Clearly for Stevenson a liberated mind flows: it is an internalised river.

And the language of the essay flows river-like too within the structural banks imposed by the genre. Ann Colley writes 'the sentences not only move in delicate gradations and pause in pools of meaning but also progress through brusque juxtapositions, irregularities, or even through outlandish use of words [...] his sentences break their continuity for a moment by submerging themselves in reviving figures of speech or by dipping into images that invigorate meaning'.[20]

In the dedication to *Catriona*, Stevenson addresses his friend Charles Baxter and recalls the Edinburgh of their shared boyhood memories expressing the hope that there exists in Edinburgh 'some seed of the elect; some long-legged, hot-headed youth must repeat to-day our dreams and wanderings of so many years ago; he will relish the pleasure, which should have been ours, to follow among named streets and numbered houses the country walks of David Balfour'.[21] This notion of passing the baton on down the stream to future generations is also expressed in the poem 'Where Go the Boats?' from the collection *A Child's Garden of Verses* in which the child wonders what will happen to the boats he launches.

> Away down the river,
> A hundred miles or more,
> Other little children
> Shall bring my boats ashore. (32)

Stevenson releases his thoughts in his work and sends them out into the world to be picked up by others, future readers and here a connection seems to be established between Stevenson's professional life as a writer and his childhood: literature as play by the riverside.[22]

Stevenson was obviously keenly aware of personal and professional posterity – the downstream – but he was just as preoccupied with upstream identities, and in the continuation of the dedication to *Catriona*, composed in Samoa in 1892, he includes an explicit reference to the metaphor of the river and its upper reaches:

> I have come so far; and the sights and thoughts of my youth pursue me; and I see like a vision the youth of my father, and of his father, and the whole stream of lives flowing down there far in the north, with the sound of laughter and tears, to cast me out in the end, as by a sudden freshet, on these ultimate islands. And I admire and bow my head before the romance of destiny. (vi)

This is a familiar trope in Stevenson's essays: the establishment of a chain of inheritance —a river – linking past, present and future generations through their familiarity with a given place. We find it notably in 'College Memories', in 'Fontainebleau: Village Communities of Painters' and in 'The Manse'.

After the opening paragraph structured around an evocation of the Water of Leith quoted earlier, 'The Manse' moves on to a consideration of the concepts and confusions of heredity. In the words of Colley, 'The water's motions, to and fro upon the surface, help him find his way back to memories of his grandfather, as well as to the revered crannies of his own childhood. Stevenson's recollections of his grandfather flow in and out of the river's interrupted streams' (211). The author wonders whether the things he thought he learned to love through experiences at the manse are not rather the result of the influence of his ancestors' professions or perhaps some atavistic hangover from his grandfather's childhood experiences. Might his grandfather's experiences be nothing more, in fact, than memories that he has forgotten? The sense of strangeness is heightened with the contemplation of the fact that the mini-Stevenson being carried around Edinburgh in the body of his Balfour ancestor must have been meeting other potential mini-Stevensons embodied in other ancestors so that one quarter of the future Stevenson was meeting the other future quarters. Stevenson's ancestors go about their business with never a thought for the possibility of the embedded existence of their future descendants. The evocation of a flowing river in the essay was a preparation for this rumination on the question of heredity with characteristic traits pouring down the generations.

Alongside the obvious nostalgia for youth expressed in the dedication to *Catriona* we also perceive how restricting the weight of heredity might have been for Stevenson had he stayed in Edinburgh as the last in a long line of weel-kent faces in the streets of the city and a dead-end in a long line of river experts. For let us not forget that the river and the management of its course fell within the area of expertise of the Stevenson family of engineers: always ready, as Stevenson states in *Records of a Family of Engineers*, to take on the problem of training and guiding a river in its course (83). So that while a river was certainly a pleasant sight for the young Stevenson, he was always aware of how much more it represented for his father:

> To my father it was a chequer-board of lively forces, which he traced from pool to shallow with minute appreciation and enduring interest. [...] Thus he pored over the engineer's voluminous handy-book of nature; thus must, too, have pored my grandfather and uncles.[23]

Release from the weight of his lineage, that 'whole stream of lives flowing down there far in the north' had only come for Stevenson through being cast out by that freshet into a life of exile.

Stevenson approached his own profession in much the same way as his engineering forebears had gone about potamology, understanding and decoding literature as they had rivers and then applying that knowledge to his own creative work. The text of his essays in particular were mapped and engineered after long observation and training just as Stevenson's father and grandfather had mapped and engineered rivers.

The image of the river is a good representation too of the freedom that the essay form provided for Stevenson. Montaigne invented the word 'essay' to designate a new type of literature that allowed him to go with the strange flow of his contemplations. This strangeness, central to the essay as practised by Montaigne, implies, in the words of Kenneth White, 'leaving the harbour of a fixed identity in order to plunge into the floating life, following the transformations of the self and the meanderings of thought'.[24] The essay flows forward like a river, but stops in pools from time to time to accommodate longer reflections ; it is free too to deviate from the path initially suggested, to branch out then come back and join the main waterway. Ideas are floated and come together, forming a system rather than a merely linear progression. The essay, as practised by Stevenson, is a space for flux and freedom – freedom to float, to meander, to shift, to be unsettling, to draw the reader under, to be haphazard, to be creative, and in the end to open out into possible seas of reflection, the aim of the essay having been not to reach a cut-and-dry conclusion, an ultimate truth, but to provoke free-flowing thought.

Notes

1   R. L. Stevenson, 'The Ideal House', in *The Works of R. L. Stevenson*, vol. 28 (London: Chatto & Windus, 1898), p. 42.
2   R. L. Stevenson, 'Water of Leith', in *Stevenson's Scotland*, ed. by T. Hubbard and D. Glen (Edinburgh: Mercat Press, 2003), p. 45.
3   R. L. Stevenson, 'The Manse', in *The Works of R. L. Stevenson*, vol. 1 (London: Chatto & Windus, 1894), p. 155.
4   B. A. Booth, and E. Mehew (eds), *The Letters of Robert Louis Stevenson: Vol. 5* (New Haven: Yale University Press, 1995), p. 393.

5 R. L. Stevenson, *A Child's Garden of Verses* (London: Penguin Books, 1952), p. 116.
6 D. Denisoff, 'Pleasurable subjectivities and temporal conflation in Stevenson's aesthetics', *Journal of Stevenson Studies*, 4 (2007), pp. 227–46, (p. 238).
7 R. L. Stevenson, *An Inland Voyage* (London: C. Kegan Paul & Co, 1878), p. 145.
8 O. S. Buckton, 'Reanimating Stevenson's Corpus', *Nineteenth-Century Literature*, 55, 1 (Jun., 2000), pp. 22–58, (p. 45).
9 R. L. Stevenson, 'Crabbed Age and Youth', in *Virginibus Puerisque and other Papers* (London: C. Kegan Paul & Co, 1881), p. 97.
10 R. L. Stevenson, *Travels With a Donkey in the Cévennes* (London, Chatto & Windus, 1916), p. 115.
11 R. L. Stevenson, 'Fontainebleau: Villages Communities of Painters', in *Across The Plains* (London: Chatto & Windus, 1892). First published in two parts in the *Magazine of Art* 7, May 1884.
12 R. L. Stevenson, 'Gentlemen', in *Scribner's Magazine* III, (January–June 1888), pp. 635–40 (p. 635).
13 R. L. Stevenson, 'Health and Mountains', in *Essays of Travel* (London: Chatto & Windus, 1905), pp. 214–15.
14 R. L. Stevenson, 'Ordered South', in *Virginibus Puerisque and other Papers* (London: C. Kegan Paul & Co, 1881), pp. 137–64.
15 R. L. Stevenson, 'Davos in Winter', in *Essays of Travel* (London: Chatto & Windus, 1905), pp. 210–11.
16 R. L. Stevenson, 'Pastoral', in *The Works of R. L. Stevenson*, vol. 1 (London: Chatto & Windus, 1894), p. 145.
17 R. L. Stevenson, 'A Mountain Town in France', in *The Works of R. L. Stevenson*, vol. 21 (London: Chatto & Windus, 1896), p. 226.
18 R. L. Stevenson, 'Talk and Talkers, 1', in *The Works of R. L. Stevenson*, vol. 1 (London: Chatto & Windus, 1894), p. 181.
19 R. L. Stevenson, 'Lay Morals', in *The Works of R. L. Stevenson*, vol. 21 (London: Chatto & Windus, 1896), p. 346.
20 A. C. Colley, *Victorians in the Mountains: Sinking the Sublime* (Farnham: Ashgate, 2010), p. 210.
21 R. L. Stevenson, *Catriona* (London: Cassell, 1893), p. v.
22 We might be reminded here also of Joseph Conrad and the desire he expressed to return to his early years: 'when I launched my first paper boats in the days of my literary childhood.' (Preface to *The Shorter Tales of Joseph Conrad* quoted by Nathalie Jaëck, 'Conrad's and Stevenson's Logbooks and 'Paperboats': Attempts in Textual Wreckage', in *Stevenson and Conrad: Writers of Land and Sea*, ed. by Linda Dryden (Texas: Texas Tech University Press, 2009), pp. 39–51.
23 R. L. Stevenson, *Records of a Family of Engineers* (London: Chatto & Windus, 1912), p. 85.
24 K. White, *The Wanderer and his Charts: Exploring the Fields of Vagrant Thought and Vagabond Beauty. Essays on Cultural Renewal* (Edinburgh: Polygon, 2004), p. 58.

9. Freedom and subservience in Lewis Grassic Gibbon's *Sunset Song*

PHILIPPE LAPLACE

> O thou who lived for Freedom when the Night
> Had hardly yet begun: when little light
> Blinded the eyes of men and dawntime seemed
> So fair and faint – a foolish dream half-dreamed!
> (Gibbon 2001: 185)

Sunset Song, the first novel of the trilogy *A Scots Quair*, has enjoyed a wide readership and general esteem in Scotland and throughout the world, in spite of its linguistic difficulties and its abrasive social and political standpoints. Voted 'the best Scottish book of all time' in 2005 in a survey backed by BBC Scotland, it is undoubtedly *the* novel (along with *Cloud Howe* and *Grey Granite*, the subsequent two novels of the trilogy) which gave the thirty-two-year-old Anarcho-Marxist James Leslie Mitchell – Lewis Grassic Gibbon's real name – his nearly iconic status in the Scottish Literary Renaissance. The so-called English novels written by Mitchell are not as well-known – *Spartacus* where the desire for freedom is of course at the heart of the novel and maybe *Stained Radiance* are the exceptions – whereas he has remained famous and celebrated for the work he produced as Lewis Grassic Gibbon – namely a collection of essays with Hugh MacDiarmid, some short stories and *A Scots Quair* which he set in his home region, the Mearns in Kincardineshire.

The novelist famously wrote shortly before his death: 'I hate capitalism; all my books are explicit or implicit propaganda.'[1] The first two volumes of *A Scots Quair* reflect Gibbon's main concerns about society and the burden imposed by capitalist values upon farmers and farming communities before turning his attention towards workers in the final volume. This chapter considers how the theme of freedom, and its necessary component, subservience, can be studied in the first novel of the trilogy. We will consider what freedom meant from a personal and artistic point of view before studying Gibbon's characters and their confrontation with freedom and subservience through Gramsci's notion of contradictory consciousness: we will also consider how Gibbon cleverly handled the demotic and turned it into a compelling narratological device in order to articulate his characters' ideological dispositions. We will finally see how Gibbon expressed the basic dichotomy freedom/subservience through the image of the Land. This will give us the necessary paradigm in order to understand how successfully his ideology is developed in *Sunset Song*.

Personal and narrative freedom for Grassic Gibbon

The first element one should note is that *Sunset Song* meant narrative distance and freedom for James Leslie Mitchell. Using a pseudonym made up of his mother's maiden name and an adaptation of her first name – Lilias Grassic Gibbon – gave him the possibility to separate this new fictional work from the previous English novels he had so far published. He could write a novel about Scotland and more particularly about his homeland, the Mearns, and leave little doubts as to his origin and identity. The genuine Scottish voice he adopted also gave him the opportunity of 'crying out louder'. This new local and authentic voice allowed him to be heard not only as a genuine Scottish novelist in *Sunset Song* and in the short stories he thereafter wrote, but also in the essays he published with MacDiarmid where he bitterly attacks the Scottish Nationalists, challenges the artistic conceptions of his fellow Scottish writers of the Literary Renaissance and denounces the dismal conditions experienced by the working-class in Glasgow.[2] The English Mitchell and the Scottish Gibbon went on to publish the incredible number of nine books in the following two years until the highly prolific author's untimely death at the age of thirty-four shortly after the publication of *Grey Granite*.

Not only did *Sunset Song* mean personal distance and freedom for Mitchell under his Scottish persona, but the novel also had more comprehensive and literary side effects by allowing him to clearly mark a break with popular Scottish writing: it meant artistic freedom and a clear split from traditional narrative voices and discourse in Scotland at the end of the nineteenth and at the beginning of the twentieth centuries. The Kailyard had in a way imprisoned Scotland into a very particular and restrictive representation. Mitchell uses traditional Kailyard motifs in *Sunset Song* but only to distort them to suit his own narratological agenda and to proclaim the release from a restrictive standard. The protagonist is a female and the death of her mother and brothers is not turned into the emotional or pathetic scenes the reader could have expected, but they mark the end of an era for the young girl: she is then flung into the world of adults, full of dangers and devoid of the innocence and naiveté she has so far tried to enjoy:

> It was not mother only that died with the twins, something died in your heart and went down with her to lie in Kinraddie kirkyard – the child in your heart died then, the bairn that believed the hills were made for its play, every road set fair with its warning posts, hands ready to snatch you back from the brink of danger when the play grew over-rough. That died, and the Chris of the books and the dreams died with it, or you folded them up in their paper of tissue and laid them away by the dark, quiet corpse that was your childhood. (63–64)[3]

Neither is the protagonist's family as genteel as it would have been expected in a standard Kailyard novel: Chris's mother committed filicide, then suicide, in order to avoid a sixth pregnancy. Life in the village is beset with malice and gossip which Gibbon refers to with a word from the Doric dialect spoken in the Mearns *claik*, as if to stress the very local distinctiveness of a universal mode of communication and distortion. *Sunset Song* is therefore to be considered as a sarcastic reaction to a traditional literary feature that had constricted literary expression for so long in Scotland.

Chris Guthrie is the highly endearing protagonist of the trilogy and we follow her life, from adolescence to womanhood, in search of emancipation, freedom and fulfillment, these three words underlying her personal objectives. She is keen, as a young woman, to gain her own autonomy far from the spiritual and moral coercion exerted by religion and by the villagers' traditional values. But her freedom is also attained on a more personal and intimate level. *Sunset Song* could indeed be read as a *Bildungsroman*, a *Bildungsroman* being, according to a definition (Buckley 1974: viii): 'the novel of youth, the novel of education, of apprenticeship, of adolescence, of initiation, even the life-novel'. However, the main protagonist's gender does not correspond to the traditional features of a genre whose plots, themes and motifs are usually male-centred through education and self-achievement. Catherine Carswell had in Scotland already used the thematic features of the *Bildungsroman* for a female character in her 1920 novel set in Glasgow, *Open the Door!* However *Sunset Song* has the particularity of being written from a male point of view, albeit very sympathetic to the plight of women, and is also set in a rural community where cultural and educational opportunities are highly restricted.

Chris, from a very first age, is torn between her love for the land and her community and her desire to study to become a schoolteacher. The English Chris and the Scottish Chris, as she says, toy with her feelings and her emotions. She realises the vacuity of her life in the Kinraddie community: '[...] suddenly Chris hated the lot, the English Chris came back in her skin a minute, she saw them the yokels and clowns everlasting, dull-brained and crude' (85). However, contrary to what would have been expected in any *Bildungsroman* – even in a female *Bildungsroman* – she decides not to pursue her education after her father's death. Despite her resentful feelings for the dullness and the passivity of her fellow-villagers, she feels irresistibly drawn to the land and it is that land that will provide her with the education and understanding of life she seeks, and not the books she would have read at college.

> Sea and sky and the folk who wrote and fought and were learnéd, teaching and saying and praying, they lasted but as a breath, a mist of fog in the hills, but the land was forever, it moved and changed below you, but was forever, you were close to it and it to you, not at a bleak remove it held you and hurted you. And she had thought to leave it all! (119)

The Scottish Chris got the better of her. Gibbon therefore used the motifs of two major literary genres in his novel, the typically Scottish Kailyard and the traditional *Bildungsroman*, but only to diverge from what would have been the expected conclusions in both cases. His novel is distinctly different from previous fictional accounts of life in a village which could, from the outside, resemble any of those described in a traditional nineteenth-century Scottish novel. Gibbon therefore asserts his individuality and his refusal to belong to any well-trodden literary current.

There are numerous ways in which Chris Guthrie is entrapped in the small Kinraddie community, but her body is her first prison. Women, at the beginning of the twentieth century – especially in a rural Presbyterian environment – did not enjoy equal treatment with men and were often confined to demeaning tasks: 'If only she'd been born a boy she'd never had such hatings vexing her, she'd have ploughed up parks and seen to their draining, lived and lived, gone up the hills a shepherd and never had to scunner herself with the making of beds or the scouring of pots.' She however concludes: 'But neither would she ever have had Ewan hold her as last night he had' (41). As many critics noticed, Chris witnesses her physical evolution from adolescence to womanhood by staring at her naked reflection in a full-length mirror. These unavoidable changes reflect a physical emancipation she cannot express easily and which her father regards as shameful from a public point of view. On the other hand, John Guthrie clearly expresses his incestuous desire for his daughter, using religion as the excuse which would give him permission to sexually abuse his daughter. John Guthrie is a man Gibbon is keen to present as a rebel in front of social hierarchy, somebody hating the ruling class. He is however prisoner of a dogmatic system of thinking which has corrupted his idiolect – he often quotes from the Bible and sings hymns – and which has perverted his nature. Religion has still a strong grip and influence on people in spite of their social inclinations.

> But a worse thing came as that slow September dragged to its end, a thing she would never tell a soul, festering away in a closet of her mind the memory lay, it would die sometime, everything died, love

and hate; fainter and fainter it had grown this year till but half she believed it a fancy, those evening fancies when father lay with the red in his face and his eyes on her, whispering and whispering at her, the harvest in his blood, whispering her to come to him, they'd done it in the Old Testament times, whispering *You're my flesh and blood, I can do with you what I will, come to me, Chris, do you hear?* (108)

The very word freedom or the adjective free do not appear very often in the novel: only one time for 'freedom' in *Sunset Song* and three times altogether in *A Scots Quair*. However Chris uses it in two occasions after what one could see as the tragic events in her life: namely the death of her father and her husband's departure for the war. Both men have imprisoned Chris into what could appear as restricted stereotypical roles and their leaving is undoubtedly perceived as a welcome liberation and release for Chris: 'But Chris walked *free* and uncaring, soon as the burial was over she'd be *free* as never in her life she'd been, she lifted her face to the blow of the wet September wind and the world that was *free* to her' (114, my italics). Language and Gibbon's écriture are also keys to the understanding of the novel and to the social and political message it conveys.

Ideological discourses

a) Vološinov's analysis of ideological discourse

Gibbon's use of italics for dialogue, a point which the *TLS* reviewer held against the author,[4] means that the narrative flows unhampered by any of the standard punctuation marks for dialogue. The reader moves spontaneously from the narrator's point of view to the characters'. This is, for example, a passage in which Gibbon's genuine concern for Scots is made obvious through Long Rob's statement:

> But Rob was just saying what a shame it was that folk should be shamed nowadays to speak Scotch – or they called it Scots if they did, the split-tongued sourocks! [...] And Rob said *You can tell me, man, what's the English for sotter, or greip, or smore, or pleiter, gloaming*

> or glunching or well-kenspeckled? And if you said gloaming was sunset you'd fair be a liar; and you're hardly that, Mr Gordon.
> But Gordon was real decent and reasonable, *You can't help it, Rob. If folk are to get on in the world nowadays, away from the ploughshafts and out of the pleiter, they must use the English, orra though it be.* And Chae cried out that was right enough, and God! Who could you blame? And a fair bit breeze got up about it all, every soul in the parlour seemed speaking at once; [...] (156)

Gibbon reveals his characters' ideological bias through their dialogue and thoughts and through the voice of the community, not through the heterodiegetic narrator's interventions. Ideology is inextricably linked to language and to the characters' rhetoric in *The Scots Quair*. Gibbon's narrative technique may be likened to what the Marxist philosopher of language Valentin Vološinov concluded about language and its ideological construction and functions.

Vološinov – a member of the so-called Bakhtin circle – developed his linguistic theories in two books first published in 1927 and 1929. Language, according to the Russian formalist, should be studied in a global social context, and not as single utterances. The first characteristic of language is that it is ideological and that it cannot be defined or analysed otherwise. It is certainly not, as Saussure had previously declared, part of a more complicated sign-system involving the accidental combination of a *signified* and a *signifier* whose relation to the sign was therefore purely arbitrary.[5] Diachronicity was also a necessary tool to achieve a good understanding of the ideological make-up of words. Words reflect the speaker's social standpoint which will be opposed to, confirmed or challenged by other ideological markers and positions in any discussion.

An example, related to sacred vocabulary, is provided early in *Sunset Song* by Chris's brother, Will. Having heard the word 'Jehovah' used so cogently by the Minister in church, Will decides to call his new horse by that name. John Guthrie, having heard Will utter the word, strikes him and then snaps at him: 'And mind, my mannie, if I ever hear you again take your Maker's name in vain, if I ever hear you use that word again, I'll libb you.

Mind that. I'll libb you like a lamb'. (30) The word is nonetheless also used out of context by Chris's mum a week later while taunting John Guthrie's concern about calling a doctor, the subtext being Guthrie's thoughts about birth control: '*Don't worry about that. No doubt your friend Jehovah will see to it all.* Father seemed to freeze up, then, his face grew black, he said never a word, and Chris had wondered at that, [...]' (29).

The person listening processes the message according to his or her ideological system of thought before replying, still according to his or her ideological system of thought. John Guthrie's idiolect is based on the Bible and his speech, whether he tells his wife that he does not agree with any form of birth control, strikes his son for having pronounced a sacred word or begs his daughter for incestuous relationships, reflects his commitment – or his submissiveness – to the Presbyterian dogma. Guthrie's language is not a structure of thought that can be considered analytically outside his social background and Kinraddie – as most rural communities at the time – is clearly imbued with religious language and imagery. As Vološinov expresses it,

> Language reflects, not subjective, psychological vacillations, but stable social interrelationships among speakers. Various linguistic forms of these interrelationships, and various modifications of these forms, prevail in different languages at different periods of time within different social groups and under the effect of different contextual aims. What this attests to is the relative strength or weakness of those tendencies in the social interorientation of a community of speakers, of which the given linguistic forms themselves are stabilized and age-old crystallizations.[6]

Chris Guthrie herself cannot get rid of this religious language and often uses mystical and allegorical vocabulary to describe the Standing Stones above Kinraddie and the land where she seeks comfort.

Another major feature introduced by Gibbon in *Sunset Song* is his use of dialect and how he weaves the voice of the community into a chorus to the main events. The frequent use of the pronoun *You* by Chris or by the folk voice also creates a closeness between characters and readers and can be taken as a generic use or a self-referent use according to the context. The community, often referred to as 'the body' in *Sunset Song*, is given a voice through a shapeless and nameless comment punctuating the villagers' life. Vološinov also studied the third person narrative voice mainly in German and French literatures, but the general conclusions he reaches may also be used for Gibbon. He saw it as an authorial device in order to introduce reflections and attitudes which would have been impossible to convey by other means of discourse.[7] Gibbon of course used this device all through the novel as a negative comment, the reflection and gossip and envy – the *cleik* – of the community. This is the community's interior monologue, instable and unreliable as the narrator tells us:

> About what happened after that some told one thing and some another and some told both together. […] you couldn't believe every lie you heard. […] Most of the story till then was maybe but guessing, ill-natured guessing at that, but the porter at the Bridge of Dunn, a good twenty miles south of Fordoun, swore to the rest. (83)

The voice of the community adopts paradoxical viewpoints depending on the situation and the current social reaction expected from them. It is certainly not reliable because of its hyperbolic nature and its tendency to transform the information to suit the preconception of the audience. The minister and his drunken or sexual antics, for instance, cause great mirth in the village, but nearly everybody attends the Sunday service and steadfastly follows the minister's instructions, whatever they may be. The minister's passionate calls for joining the War, his anti-German rhetoric and his casting out of Long Rob as a pro-German pacifist certainly influence the Kinraddie community's behaviour. Gibbon wants to show that the Church of Scotland, the Kirk, has taken a firm grip on the Scottish rural communities. Its hegemony is total, influencing the way people speak and what people do and think. The only solution to release them from this ideological domination is cultural and comprehensive: individual reactions are bound to come to nothing. The Kirk, as an institution, needs to be denounced for the dogmatic veil it imposes on society. As a novelist and as a propagandist, Gibbon clearly saw that this was one of his missions and that he, as a novelist, had to contribute to the denunciation of the cultural and intellectual hegemony the Kirk had exercised for so long in Scotland. People, even though aware of some of the ministers' malpractice were too apprehensive to clash openly with the institution. It remained an innocent subject of general amusement but not of serious critical analysis.

b) Gramsci's 'Contradictory Consciousness'

This paradoxical attitude can be linked to what the Italian Marxist critic and activist Antonio Gramsci called 'contradictory consciousness' when he studied the ideologies of the working-class in Italy. Even if Gramsci mostly disregarded farming communities, as he insisted that they did not have a clear conception of the class system, his visions are nonetheless relevant to Kinraddie which Gibbon saw as the forerunner of *Grey Granite*'s working-class society. As the narrator tells us, Kinraddie's traditional farm-workers are the last of an old order which will all have disappeared by the end of the First World War, replaced by a new breed of manual workers. The farm-workers, as part of a fundamentally peasant economy, therefore, belong to a class system soon defunct because of the arrival of new machines and new values.

Gramsci observed that on the one hand the working-class consideration and language were aimed at class struggle and revolt: they were conscious of their fate and alienation and of the need to change society and the social apparatus. But on the other hand there was a blind respect and agreement with rules and values that were part of inherited traditions, or which had been decreed by the omnipotent ruling-class and which people did not dare question, even they clearly went against their own living and working conditions.[8] Both contradictory sentiments – this rebellious spirit and the acceptance of their domination – coexisted and had to be taken into account when considering the consciousness, views and discourse of working-class people.

As we have seen before, religion can clearly be part of this 'contradictory consciousness'. On the one hand ministers are mocked for their indecent behaviour while on the other hand, what they represent and their ideological stance are uncritically accepted by most of the community.

The traditional farming life of the community – in a way a traditional Kailyard feature – is shattered with the arrival of an international event which sends the whole community into chaos: the First World War. Ewan Tavendale, despite his position as a farmer which could exempt him from military service, decides to enlist in 1916. Grassic Gibbon's harsh condemnation of the army is somehow surprising given that he had spent ten years serving in the British army, even if he was careful to note that he did it only in order to earn some money and to get the financial stability he needed.[9] Anyway, just as his knowledge of farming toil cannot be doubted, the descriptions of the army also bear an authentic stamp.

The army has clearly transformed Ewan Tavendale: from the kind, even sweet, man who married Chris Guthrie, he has become, once he returns from the town barracks, a coarse drunkard who has no qualms about sexually abusing his wife, telling her about his sexual prowess with prostitutes and screaming at their child. This image is far from any First World War hero imagery.

The only characters who, in Gramsci's words would not have this contradictory consciousness and would not be torn between respect for the authority and social class, are Long Rob of the Mill and, to a certain extent, Chae Strachan. From the start Long Rob clearly opposes the Kirk, which he never attends, and Gibbon is keen to define him by his intellectual readings and his philosophical positions. Long Rob is, according to Gramsci's definitions, an 'organic intellectual', that is to say, even if his education and profession have no connection with the intellectual sphere, he is deeply committed to the evolution of society:[10] his aspirations are related to social class and to the improvement of the conditions of living for Kinraddie's farm-workers. Chae Strachan is a more ambivalent character who, in spite of his Marxist political leanings and his clear advocacy of class struggle, does not manage to keep away from the Kirk or from the ruling class's authority. Chae's 'excitement' (186, 191) about the War leads him to enlist amongst the first. Long Rob resists far longer and it is only when his anti-war position is untenable in the community that he finally resigns himself to enlisting. Gibbon's conclusion seems pretty bleak: it is impossible, in a rural community like Kinraddie, to oppose the cultural hegemony of church and state. Evolution – or Revolution – will come from the outside.

c) *Freedom and subservience: the Land as a* pharmakon

The land – so central a theme in the novel – is seen as a comfort and a blessing for Chris – this is where she finds relief and happiness and her personal motto all through the trilogy concerns the everlasting presence of the land, a true beacon which has survived and endured through all personal, human and social upheaval and will for ever remain. But the land, or more precisely toiling the land, that is to say farming, is also seen as a tormentor, and this ambivalent image is common to many of the *Sunset Song* characters who revel in the land but who are also enslaved by farming activities. Chris discovers this after her father's death when she has to do all the physical tasks he used to do. Her only solution is to hire somebody to relieve her of the physically exhausting farmwork.

I would suggest that the land, in *Sunset Song*, has assumed the role of a *Pharmakon*. The *Pharmakon* is, according to Plato's *Phaedrus*, a substance – what we would now call a drug – which can save and kill: small doses will cure people whereas an overdose will kill or harm somebody. It is of course to be taken metaphorically as two-dimensional or as a binary opposition. There is no such thing as a legal or illegal substance in *Sunset Song*, but the Land, present in all discourse and in the narrative fabric of the novel, can be likened to a *Pharmakon*.

> So hurt and dazed, she turned to the land, close to it and the smell of it, kind and kind it was, it didn't rise up and torment your heart, you could keep at peace with the land if you gave it your heart and hands, tended it and slaved for it, it was wild and a tyrant, but it was not cruel. (230)

It epitomises this dichotomy between freedom and subservience which the characters of *Sunset Song* illustrate through their actions and their conceptions about the land. Jacques Derrida constructed a close-reading of Plato's *Pharmakon* by highlighting this dichotomy; he analysed the ambivalent features of this metaphorical substance by drawing a parallel between spoken and written discourses; this is, after all, the basic subject of Plato's *Phaedrus*. Plato wants to highlight the specificity and the significance of the spoken language, what Derrida calls the Logos – which stands for speech, logic, reason[11] – and its superiority over written language. In *Sunset Song*, spoken language also takes a significant part of the narrative structure due to Gibbon's idiosyncratic linguistic approach.

> À peine plus loin, Socrate compare à une drogue (*pharmakon*) les textes écrits que Phèdre a apportés avec lui. Ce *pharmakon*, cette 'médecine', ce philtre, à la fois remède et poison, s'introduit déjà dans le corps du discours avec toute son ambivalence. Ce charme, cette vertu de fascination, cette puissance d'envoûtement peuvent être – tour à tour ou simultanément – bénéfiques et maléfiques. Le *pharmakon* serait une *substance*, avec tout ce que ce mot pourra connoter, en fait de matière aux vertus occultes, de profondeur cryptée refusant son ambivalence à l'analyse [...]. (Derrida 2004: 264)[12]

> (Only a little further on, Socrates compares the written texts Phaedrus has brought along to a drug (*pharmakon*). This *pharmakon*, this 'medicine', this philtre, which acts as both remedy and poison, already introduces itself into the body of the discourse with all its ambivalence. This charm, this spellbinding virtue, this power of fascination, can be – alternately or simultaneously – beneficent or maleficent. The *pharmakon* would be a *substance*, with all that that word can connote in terms of matter with occult virtues, cryptic depths refusing to submit their ambivalence to analysis [...].)[13]

The land – considered in its physical, metaphysical and metaphorical senses – is a source of pleasure and pain for Chris. This is first of all where she finds relief and joy; Gibbon is careful to turn her visits to the Standing Stones which overlook Kinraddie into a pilgrimage and a mystical experience for her. But the land is also the very source of her hardship. This is the land the English Chris wants to leave, with its coarse creatures and language. This is a land of hardship and toil where Chris has to fight to overcome people's prejudice. This is also the land whose wind, smell and memory come to haunt Ewan Tavendale while fighting in France and which drive him to desert and lead him to the firing squad.

Conclusion

Gibbon's conclusions are grim: as the newly appointed minister Robert Colquohoun declares that the old farming world is dead (1999: 256), replaced by another world comprising proceeds and profit. Religion has been phased out but subservience to other masters has already started. And this is what Gibbon, as a 'revolutionary writer' (2001: 738), is keen to point out. Indeed, the First World War has not been a tragedy for all the inhabitants of Kinraddie: some have clearly made money and intend to carry on. Subservience, albeit to a new form of servility – monetary obsession – seems to have gained the upper hand in the 'tormented place' (1) that is Kinraddie; this will be the subject explored by Gibbon in the last two novels of his trilogy. The Land, this *pharmakon* which held the Kinraddie community together and between which the Kinraddie folk had to try to find their own way, has become the latest victim of the new spirit blown by the profiteers. Not only did the old Scots way of working farms die, but the ideologists who embodied expectancy for society are also dead: Chae and Long Rob have finally succumbed to social pressure and social coercion and were killed in the trenches. Only Chris is left, widowed but free: free to abandon her life on the farm and free to love, even if she resigns herself to marrying once again, so conforming to one of society's standard patriarchal rules.

Notes
1. James Leslie Mitchell, *The Left Review*, 1.5 (February 1935), p. 180.
2. Lewis Grassic Gibbon, *Smeddum: A Lewis Grassic Gibbon Anthology*. Edited and Introduced by Valentina Bold (Edinburgh: Canongate, 2001), pp. 1–169.
3. Quotations are taken from Lewis Grassic Gibbon, *Sunset Song*, ed. with an intro. by Tom Crawford (Edinburgh: Canongate, 1999).
4. *The Times Literary Supplement* 1601, October 6, 1932, p. 713.
5. Valentin Nikolaevic Vološinov, *Marxism and the Philosophy of Language*. Translated by Ladislav Matejka and I. R. Titunik (New York and London: Seminar Press, 1973), pp. 59–63.

6   Vološinov, p. 118.
7   Vološinov, pp. 131–32.
8   Antonio Gramsci, *Selections from the Prison Notebooks*. Edited and translated by Quentin Hoare and Geoffrey Nowell Smith (London: Elecbook, 1999), p. 641.
9   Ian S. Munro, *Leslie Mitchell: Lewis Grassic Gibbon* (Edinburgh: Oliver & Boyd, 1966), pp. 32, 56.
10 Gramsci, pp. 142–47.
11 Barbara Johnson, 'Translator's Introduction', in Jacques Derrida, *Dissemination*. Translated, with an Introduction and Additional Notes by Barbara Johnson (London: The Athlone Press, 1981), p. ix.
12 Jacques Derrida, 'La pharmacie de Platon', in Platon, *Phèdre*. Traduction inédite, introduction et notes par Luc Bisson (Paris: Flammarion, 2004), p. 264.
13 Derrida, 'Plato's Pharmacy', trans. Johnson (London: The Athlone Press, 1981), p. 73.

10. Women and freedom in Muriel Spark's fiction

MARGARITA ESTÉVEZ-SAÁ

Dame Muriel Spark's oeuvre is, together with that of Doris Lessing and A. S. Byatt, among the greatest representations of women's salient contribution to literature in English in the twentieth century. Furthermore, her wide and prolific literary legacy can and should be considered as a privileged testimony of the vicissitudes of the last century and an acute reflection on the evolution of women's history during that period. The influence of her Scottish background and of the education received in her native Edinburgh, together with her frequent travels and stays in other European countries, add universal value to her views on art, women and identity issues, topics that she dealt with widely in her creative work.

Spark excelled in different genres and her literary output includes novels, short stories, critical works (on Mary Shelley, Emily Brontë, John Masefield, William Wordsworth, and Henry Newman), poetry and an autobiographical volume. Since my intention is to focus on women and freedom in relation to her Scottish origins, I have chosen to delve into the partial autobiography she wrote, *Curriculum Vitae. A Volume of Autobiography* (1992), as well as such representative novels as *The Prime of Miss Jean Brodie* (1961), *The Public Image* (1968), *Loitering with Intent* (1981), and *Symposium* (1990). Occasional references to other works will be made, but this selection broadly covers the most fruitful decades of her literary trajectory. Besides, all of these novels feature prominently reflections on women and on women's identity (some of these set within the spatial framework of Edinburgh) and, studied in chronological order, throw light on the changes in women's circumstances brought about by the advance of the century that Muriel Spark so carefully recorded.

In March 2003 I was honoured with an invitation by James Brooker, former professor at the University of the Algarve, to give a lecture on Muriel Spark's fiction and to interview the author on occasion of her participation in the *Second Workshop in Anglophone Culture: 'Identity'*, organised by the Departamento de Letras Clássicas e Modernas of the University of the Algarve in Portugal. Dame Muriel came accompanied by her faithful friend Penelope Jardine, whom I recall remaining in a discreet position without interfering with the work of the scholars, despite Spark's noticeable sight difficulties. The author was kind and grateful, and did not avoid any question, even the most difficult or controversial ones (such as those related to her religious conversion to Catholicism or the allegedly dubious purpose of her partial autobiography). Part of the interview was published in 2004 in the academic journal *Women's Studies*. In that interview Dame Muriel agreed with two general comments I made to her and that are of particular interest for the purposes of this chapter.

First, Spark acknowledged that her novels and short stories display a specific interest in female characters and prove her being more at ease when imagining and characterising female protagonists in her fiction: 'I think I write better about women than I do about men. I don't give men quite the individual identity. I've tried to treat men and I think, sometimes, succeeded, but I feel happier when I'm dealing with a woman or with women and I don't know why. Probably because I know what it feels like.'[1]

Her concern with the female condition led her to portray in her fiction women at different ages (young girls, adolescents, middle-aged women and, most interestingly, old women); belonging to different social classes; reflecting diverse economic circumstances, levels of education and marital status; and evincing varied political and religious affiliations. Taken as a whole, the literary legacy left by Muriel Spark offers a wide canvas on which the reader can see the possibilities enjoyed by women as well as the limits imposed on females throughout the twentieth century.

Secondly, when asked during the interview about the nationality she would choose for herself, she did not hesitate to assert that she would be Scottish if she could. This is particularly interesting in the case of a writer who has lived in South Africa, London, the United States and Italy, among other places.

Not surprisingly, Scotland and Edinburgh feature prominently in her fiction and in her autobiography. Thus, in *Curriculum Vitae* she recalls becoming aware, when she was very young, of being the daughter of a Scottish father and an English mother:

> 'The English' in the Edinburgh of my childhood were considered to be superficial and hypocritical. And over-dressed. My mother, who was English, used to come and fetch me from school. It was my daily dread that she should open her mouth and thus betray her suspect origins. 'Foreigners' were fairly tolerated but 'the English' were something quite different. [...]
>
> My father spoke with a strong Edinburgh accent, and although he was a Jew, having been born and educated in Edinburgh of Scottish–Jewish parents, he wore the same sort of clothes as the other fathers and spoke as they did, about the same things. So he was no problem.[2]

This double ascendancy is noticed at a linguistic level by a young Muriel when she mentions that 'At home, if I left the tap running in the bathroom, my mother would say, "Turn off the tap," but my father's command was, "Turn off the well."'[3] At that time adolescent Muriel Spark was undoubtedly more at ease with her Scottish ancestry.

Since the main interest of this chapter is women and freedom in Spark's work, I propose to pay particular attention to the influence of her Scottish upbringing in relation to these two issues. In her autobiography, and among the different allusions to the Edinburgh of her childhood years, the aspects that Spark emphasises again and again are the importance of education, the free and happy coexistence of people with different religions and the active participation of women in the vindication of their rights. She devotes several pages to praise the educational possibilities that her native Edinburgh offered to young people:

> From the sixteenth century to the nineteenth, the worthy and prosperous merchants and burghers of Edinburgh vied with each other to leave their fortunes for the founding of schools throughout the city. Education was held in awe, and the Scottish idea was

that nobody should be denied this privilege. The schools, only a few of them having undergone change in nature and in buildings, still exist.[4]

The enlightened atmosphere provided by these schools favored the education of girls with slender means such as Spark herself, who was able to attend James Gillespie's High School for Girls, and that offered her 'the most formative years of my life, and in many ways the most fortunate for a future writer'.[5] After those years, Spark attended Heriot-Watt College, an institution that offered her 'a more scientific atmosphere in general, and a more scientific approach to English, in contrast to the broad, humane, poetry-loving approach of Gillespie's'.[6] One of the indelible traces left by her education at Heriot-Watt College was the economical prose so characteristic of her work: 'The use of language in the daily life of commerce, of trade, banking, even politics, was plainly more genuinely based in proportion as it was less rhetorical'.[7]

To the importance of education should be added the freedom in religious choices that Spark also explicitly mentions:

> Many religious persuasions were represented among the pupils. There were Jewish girls in practically every class. I remember one Hindu Indian named Coti whom we made much of. There were lots of Catholics. Some girls were of mixed faiths – mother Protestant, father Jewish; Irish Catholic mother, Episcopalian father. It meant very little in practical terms to us.[8]

The young Spark also became aware of the efforts in favour of the vindication of women's rights. Among her family members, one who features prominently in the autobiography is her maternal grandmother Adelaide, whom she considered 'extremely witty'[9] and an 'outspoken champion for the rights of women',[10] who 'had marched with Mrs. Pankhurst, carrying an umbrella as they all did'[11] and who used to recall 'her meetings with the suffragettes and the memorable day in Watford when she marched up the High Street for the women's vote'.[12]

This enlightened and enlightening educational, religious and social atmosphere of her native Scotland was taken for granted by a young Muriel Spark who, nevertheless, realised after leaving the country that the freedom enjoyed in her native place was not shared in other countries:

> I'll tell you what I felt when I left Scotland to go abroad for the first time as a girl, when I was a young girl. I found that I didn't realize that men were supposed to be superior to women. In Scotland, the equality of the sexes was much more. It was almost a necessity in a mountainous country. I think that everyone's work was equally valid and valuable and maybe the protestant ethic was very much more for the equality of the sexes, I found. I wasn't aware of it at the time but when I went away from Scotland, I realized that there had been quite an advantage in having been born there. There was a freedom of expression open to women that wasn't available in other countries.[13]

This liberating atmosphere and the unrestrained nature of the education received certainly inform both the vital and the artistic experience of the Scottish author.

At a biographical level, it is undeniable that Spark led an unconventionally liberated life, travelling to Africa and touring through Europe and the States, abandoning a depressed husband, leaving her infant son to the care of her parents, and having occasional extramarital affairs. Even her conversion to Catholicism is tinged with her typical disentangled attitude. Her unorthodoxy is displayed in some of her peculiar habits such as attending mass after the sermon has taken place, or her ambiguous conception of truth: 'I don't know that I'm committed to absolute truth. I know that is a doctrinal fact but I wouldn't be too sure that advanced Catholic thought is not becoming more relative in its attitude to truth.'[14] In general terms, she has vindicated 'that more freedom should be given to the individual conscience [...] I think that the whole opening of religion is a much better thing'.[15]

Her opinions about nationalist attitudes are as difficult to catalogue as her religious stance. After defining herself as Scottish in every single interview

– 'I'm Scottish as far as I can claim to be anything'[16]– she has exposed her ambiguous attitude towards nationalist policies. Thus, on the one hand, she has declared that she does not like nationalism as a phenomenon since 'It shuts too many doors, far more doors than it ever opens […] there's no Nationalist foreign policy as far as I can see. I don't know what their economic policy is.'[17] On the other hand, she considered that 'devolution might work'[18] and that she thinks 'the Scots have a point in that they've been neglected by the English parliament, who really don't take Scottish affairs seriously enough.'[19] Consequently, she seems to opt for championing a sort of cultural nationalism that vindicates folklore and traditions and pays particular attention to linguistic issues as in her reference to liking the 'Scottish turns of phrase.'[20]

From an artistic point of view, Spark should be also considered a herald of freedom. Her literary output is certainly difficult to encapsulate under a predetermined label. If we take her novelistic production, for instance, she has surpassed notions and markers such as, among others, realist, metafictional, Catholic, postmodern, Gothic, or detective fiction. The author expressed her unease when considered, for instance, a Catholic writer, a Scottish author or even a feminist artist, always trying to evade the nets that have been employed to capture her inherently slippery nature and artistry. In fact, as is well known, she had alluded to exile as inherent to her condition as an artist:

> She belonged nowhere, was determined to belong nowhere and to no one. 'It was Edinburgh,' she wrote, 'that bred within me the condition of exiledom: and what have I being doing since then but moving from exile into exile?' This was not a lament. Exile for her, as for James Joyce, was the natural condition of the artist. 'It has ceased,' she wrote, 'to be a fate, it has become a calling.' Edinburgh was her Dublin, redolent of escaped impositions yet bred in the bone of her art. It was the locus of conflicting memories.[21]

To this vindication of exile we should add her undeniable cosmopolitanism both as a vital experience and as an artistic stance that was materialised in the various places she chose to live in and the diverse settings used in her novels and short stories (set in different European countries, in America and in Africa), as well as in the international and universal topics dealt with in her fiction (women's place in society, the relationship between truth and art, or the existence of good and evil, among many others).

Her self-imposed exile and cosmopolitan bias have led some critics to argue that 'Though claiming herself to be "Scottish by formation", efforts to identify Spark as a Scottish writer have proved difficult, and not only because of her distant relation to her birthplace.'[22] Notwithstanding, as the author herself had stated in relation to her national ascription, 'One wouldn't know if "Scottish" is applied to the writer or the writing,'[23] and in her case critics have gone as far as to interpret her conversion to Catholicism as a 'radical national act as well as a religious realignment – a return to a certain Scottish history,'[24] and they have not failed to comment on the pervasive influence of Spark's Scottish origins and of her native city in her art. Therefore, the 'stereotype of the cold dour Scottish metaphysical mind' has been related to her persona and to some of her protagonists,[25] the detectable indigenous tradition of supernatural ballads has been mentioned in relation to her fiction,[26] 'a Scottish preoccupation with the grotesque and surreal,'[27] as well as the echoes in her work of Scottish authors such as James Hogg and his *Memoirs and Confessions of a Justified Sinner*,[28] or the importance of the city and its mores in the characterisation of her protagonist Jean Brodie.[29] Even the orthographic excesses, and a playful concern with the borders of speech and type, that Michael Gardiner notices in *Robinson* and *The Comforters*, are related to 'a long-term anxiety for Scottish writers dealing with a state standard form.'[30]

Despite the indelible trace left by her Scottish origins in both her formation and her art, Spark stood at a distance with regard to her native place: her 'Edinburgh Villanelle' states 'Heart of Midlothian, never mine.'[31] The city became a suffocating place that, whenever visited, caused the artist great anxiety, mainly because of the pressure of family and friends. Something similar happened to her in London and she seemed to be more at ease in Italy where she was anonymous, as we learn from Stannard's biography.

Notwithstanding, Muriel Spark's vital and artistic stances seemed to be presided over by what she herself called 'the nevertheless principle,' that she described in her article 'Edinburgh-born', and that applies both to her origins and to her conception of the female condition, including her own self:

> All grades of society constructed sentences bridged by 'nevertheless.' It is my own instinct to associate the word, as the core of thought-pattern, with Edinburgh particularly. [...] I believe myself to be fairly indoctrinated by the habit of thought which calls for this word. In fact I approve of the ceremonious accumulation of weather forecasts and barometer-readings that pronounce for a fine day, before letting rip on the statement 'nevertheless, it's raining.' I find that much of my literary composition is based on the nevertheless idea. I act upon it. It was on the nevertheless principle that I turned Catholic.[32]

This 'nevertheless principle' she associates with her native place, describing her relationship with Scotland and Edinburgh, as well as her Catholic religious affiliation, applies also to her conception of women and her depiction of the female condition in her fiction. As we have already mentioned, women feature prominently in her novels, and her female protagonists are characterised as complex, ambiguous, multi-faceted human representatives. They are usually presented from an ironic and comic distance that makes the reader recognise, as well as sympathise with, their foibles. Theirs is a never-ending identity quest, one not exempt from risks.

She learned about the plight for women's rights in her native city, and by means of the figure of her grandmother, Adelaide, who had actively participated in the vindications for women's vote. Her autobiographic story 'The Gentile Jewesses', in which her maternal grandmother features prominently, describes the impact that this enlightened female figure had on a young Muriel Spark during the girl's visits to Watford, where Adelaide run a shop. Later on, it will be in Edinburgh where she would continue to learn about feminism and feminist principles:

> Edinburgh [...] It was a grand European city; nevertheless, it was provincial. It was her home, had given her a strong civic pride; [...] It had instilled in her a fundamental feminism and exactness of mind;

> nevertheless, she was not a 'political' feminist and was, first, last, and always, a poet.[33]

Her interest in women's issues led her to plan several book proposals related to the topic, such as one on 'the intellectual and social emancipation of women during the nineteenth century', a book on contemporary women's poetry or another on 'Women Novelists of the Nineteenth Century'.[34] These books were ultimately not written and it is in Spark's own fiction where the reader observes her deep concern with the condition of women in the twentieth century. Notwithstanding, as we shall see, following her Edinburgh 'nevertheless principle', her feminist bias was also controversial, due to Spark's deployment of what have been considered conventional manifestations of woman's femininity and also because of the highly ambivalent female characters she portrayed in her fiction.

Her representative canvas of female characters famously opened with the figure of Jean Brodie, the protagonist of her best-known novel, *The Prime of Miss Jean Brodie,* an educated spinster whose main aim in life is the formation of her pupils at the Marcia Blaine School for girls. Her experimental methods in the education of the young girls are not exempt from contradictions. Thus, her liberal conception of her professional activity – 'The word "education" comes from the root *e* from *ex*, out, and *duco*, I lead. It means a leading out. To me education is a leading out of what is already there in the pupil's soul. To Miss Mackay it is a putting in of something that is not there, and that is not what I call education, I call it intrusion, from the Latin root prefix *in* meaning in and the stem *trudo*, I thrust'[35] – contrasts with some more radical attitudes and commentaries: 'Give me a girl at an impressionable age, and she is mine for life.'[36] Brodie is a very complex and highly contradictory character who, despite her progressive methods, also features traditional and highly conservative attitudes that the reader detects. The novel includes a sound reflection on the possibilities and limits that 1930s Edinburgh offered these young women:

> It is not to be supposed that Miss Brodie was unique at this point of her prime. […] The progressive spinsters of Edinburgh did not teach

in schools, especially in schools of traditional character like Marcia Blaine's School for Girls. It was in this that Miss Brodie was, as the rest of the staff spinsterhood put it, a trifle out of place. But she was not out of place among her own kind, the vigorous daughters of dead or enfeebled merchants, of ministers of religion, University professors, doctors, [...] who had endowed these daughters with shrewd wits, high-coloured cheeks, constitutions like horses, logical educations, hearty spirits and private means.[37]

Miss Jean Brodie inaugurates a series of portraits of female characters who will combine, in a typical Sparkian fashion, positive features and negative traits; who will become responsible for their life choices as well as subjects of social mores and gender prejudices; and who will be, in any case, mysterious and ungraspable – 'We can never describe a person fully. Human beings are infinitely mysterious.'[38]

In *The Public Image,* Annabel Christopher is another example of a trapped female figure, torn between her public image as a successful actress and the private self she intends to keep as mother and wife. Her public image as a lady-tiger destroys her marriage and her husband who ends hating her and committing suicide. Annabel, who questions this public image that she nevertheless favours and promotes, decides finally to break free. Despite the enormity of her husband's enmity and treason, some readers might have difficulties in sympathising with an Annabel that has sacrificed her marriage in favour of her acting career. Nevertheless, it is certainly her choice, just as it is at the end of the novel to end her career and abandon her previous life: 'She had the baby on her lap. She said, "I want to be free like my baby." [...] In fact, she had felt, as she still felt, neither free nor unfree. She was not sure what those words meant. But she was entirely satisfied, now to be waiting with the baby at the airport for a plane to Greece';[39] 'Waiting for the order to board, she felt both free and unfree.'[40]

The doubts that Annabel displays in relation to the question of freedom are shared by the protagonist of *Loitering with Intent,* Fleur Talbot, a young woman whose motto in life is 'What a wonderful thing it was to be a woman and an artist in the twentieth century'.[41] Fleur wants to be a writer and is more than ready to abandon any personal attachment in favor of her profession: she says, for instance, that marriage would interfere with her artistic aspirations. Meanwhile she writes her first novel, and accepts work at a mysterious Autobiographical Association. The novel certainly plays with and subverts the dichotomy truth versus fiction, since Fleur's job at the Society consists mainly in making up the stories about its protagonists: 'You should easily be able to rectify any lack or lapse in form, syntax, style, characterization, invention, local colour, description, dialogue, construction and other trivialities.'[42] At the end of the novel the reader regards Fleur with suspicion. She is accused of libel and we are not sure whether she has been profiting from the Society and getting information and inspiration for her own novel *Warrender Chase*. Fleur remains a mysterious and inconsistent character who defies concepts such as truth and, in the end, we are left with the idea that the novel is playing with and questioning traditional dichotomies such as life versus fiction: 'The story of a life is a very informal party; there are no rules of precedence and hospitality, no invitations.'[43]

In *Symposium*, Muriel Spark focuses on the upper classes and renews her interest in Scottish folklore. Rich widows, professional women, and liberated female characters feature prominently in a novel that tells the lives of a series of characters attending a glamorous dinner party. A middle-aged rich widow and a mysterious young woman stand out among these upper-class protagonists. Hilda Damien has made a fortune by her own means and thanks to her entrepreneurial spirit. Her economic independence and lack of family or social attachments are to be put side by side with her desire to find a male partner and marry again at middle age: 'At fifty-three, unbeknown to her children, she wanted to get married again [...]. Hilda was not a feminist. She was above and beyond feminism. She had no need of a tame husband to help her with domestic chores, she had no domestic chores. She needed an equal, a mate.'[44] Hilda Damien is a good instance of how Sparkian female protagonists defy easy classification and certainly oppose any essentialist conception of women's identity.

Another example in *Symposium* is Margaret Murchie, Hilda's daughter-in-law, a sweet young bride from a traditional Scottish family. Margaret has been mysteriously involved in the murder of a childhood friend, of her grandmother and of a nun at a convent she was staying in, as well as related to the disappearance of a teacher. Once again the reader is left with doubts in relation to Margaret's condition as victim or culprit. Thus, we do not know if she has been directly or indirectly involved in the deaths or if it has been a mere coincidence that she has always been near those dying people. What is certain is that, at a given point in the novel, Margaret seems desperate and tired of being a passive witness of disaster and tragedy: 'I'm tired of being the passive carrier of disaster. I feel frustrated. I almost think it's time for me to take my life and destiny in my own hands, and actively make disasters come about. I would like to do something like that.'[45]

Elsewhere I have written about how many of Spark's protagonists tend to consciously and actively project a positive image of their own selves:[46] Brodie's prime, Annabel's lady-tiger public image, Fleur's self-projection as a twentieth-century woman artist, Margaret's mask of goodness and sweetness. It was my contention that more than mere 'delusions of grandeur' on the part of the protagonists this seems to be a recourse they have so as to assert their position and their value in a society that was intent on underrating them.

All Spark's female characters attempt to live freely and actively project selves and images that suit them. Similarly, all seem certainly frustrated in their attempts and subject to a sort of deterministic law that prevents them from absolute liberation. At the level of narrative the protagonists' aims and prospects as well as the images they positively project of themselves are constantly undermined and subverted by anticipatory passages that disclose their efforts' irony and sometimes futility. This dichotomy of freedom versus determinism detectable in Muriel Spark's works and the portrayal of her female protagonists has been acknowledged by the author herself in the following terms:

> I think that we ought to value our freedom because, in fact, we have very little. There is a limit, certainly, to our freedom. We have the law of gravity, just to start with. But we have other freedoms that we have to give up in order to live together. We can't just go around as some people think they can saying 'I'm free, I can do what I like.' We

can't do that. We have to sacrifice some of our free will to the good of the community. But I think we are born free within certain limits.[47]

The sociologist Anthony Elliott has reflected on the internal and external frames of reference that are involved in the creation of selves and in the process of identity formation. Elliott mentions that individuals try to interpret, fashion and forge their own selves but that they are inevitably limited by social practices, cultural conventions and even political relations in the staging of self-identity.[48] According to Elliott, 'neither internal nor external frames of reference should be privileged'.[49] I would argue that Muriel Spark has taken into account both these internal and external frames of reference when dealing with the issue of women and freedom both in the vital account she offered in *Curriculum Vitae* as well as in the portrayal of her protagonists. Her Scottish origins and the education received in her native Edinburgh left an indelible trace in her that is noticeable in her fiction. The city of David Hume instilled in her an enlightened mind that favoured notions such as education, tolerance, freedom, and a self-disciplined analytical attitude that led her continuously to assess and reassess nationality, religion, art, life and freedom. It is precisely this revisionary, 'nevertheless' stance which has prevented her from offering her readers a naïve view of women's liberation throughout the twentieth century, or from renouncing the portrayal and vindication of their progressive achievement of freedom.

Notes
1   James Brooker and Margarita Estévez Saá, 'Interview with Dame Muriel Spark', *Women's Studies* 33.8 (2004), 1035–46 (p. 1040).
2   Muriel Spark, *Curriculum Vitae. A Volume of Autobiography* (London: Penguin Books, 1992), pp.21–22.
3   Ibid., p. 22.
4   Ibid., p. 49.
5   Ibid., p. 50.
6   Ibid., p. 103.
7   Ibid., p. 103.
8   Ibid., p. 53.
9   Ibid., p. 91.
10 Ibid., p. 93.

11 Ibid., p. 28.
12 Ibid., p. 91.
13 Brooker and Estévez Saá, p.1039.
14 Robert Hosmer, 'An Interview with Dame Muriel Spark', *Salmagundi* 146–147 (2005), pp. 127–58 (p. 147).
15 Ibid., p. 132.
16 Martin McQuillan, '"The Same Informed Air": An Interview with Muriel Spark', in *Theorising Muriel Spark: Gender, Race, Deconstruction,* ed. by Martin McQuillan (New York: Palgrave MacMillan, 2002), pp. 210–29 (p. 226).
17 Ibid., p. 227.
18 Ibid., p. 227.
19 Ibid., p. 227.
20 Ibid., p. 227.
21 Martin Stannard, *Muriel Spark. The Biography* (London: Phoenix, 2010), p. 2.
22 Marilyn Reizbaum, 'The Stranger Spark', in *The Edinburgh Companion to Muriel Spark,* ed. by Michael Gardiner and Willy Maley (Edinburgh: Edinburgh University Press, 2010), pp. 40–51 (p. 45).
23 Quoted in Alan Bold, *Muriel Spark,* Contemporary Writers (London: Methuen, 1986), p. 26.
24 Reizbaum, pp. 45–46.
25 Gerard Carruthers, '"Fully to Savour Her Position": Muriel Spark and Scottish Identity', in *Muriel Spark: Twenty-First Century Interpretations,* ed. by David Herman (Baltimore: The Johns Hopkins University Press, 2010), pp. 21–38 (p. 33).
26 David Herman, 'Introduction', in *Muriel Spark,* ed. by David Herman, pp. 1–18 (p. 7).
27 Douglas Gifford, *et al.,* 'Scottish Fiction Since 1945: I. Continuity, Despair and Change', in *Scottish Literature: in English and Scots* (Edinburgh: Edinburgh University Press, 2002), pp. 834–98 (p. 861).
28 Carruthers, p. 29.
29 Philip E. Ray, 'Jean Brodie and Edinburgh: Personality and Place in Muriel Spark's *The Prime of Miss Jean Brodie', Studies in Scottish Literature* 13.1 (1978), pp. 23–31 (p. 24).
30 Michael Gardiner, 'Body and State in Spark's Early Fiction', in Gardiner and Maley, *Edinburgh Companion,* p. 35.
31 Muriel Spark, 'Edinburgh Villanelle', in *All the Poems: Collected Poems* (Manchester: Carcanet, 2004), p. 10.
32 Muriel Spark, 'Edinburgh-born', *New Statesman,* 10 August 1962, p. 180.
33 Stannard, p. 3.
34 Stannard, p. 118.
35 Muriel Spark, *The Prime of Miss Jean Brodie* (Harmondsworth: Penguin, 1961), p. 36.
36 Ibid., p. 9.
37 Ibid., p. 42.
38 Brooker and Estévez Saá, p. 1041.
39 Muriel Spark, *The Public Image* (Harmondsworth: Penguin, 1982), p. 123.
40 Ibid., p. 124.
41 Muriel Spark, *Loitering with Intent* (Harmondsworth: Penguin, 1995), p. 129.
42 Ibid., p. 18.
43 Ibid., p. 43.

44 Muriel Spark, *Symposium* (London: Virago, 2010), p. 35.
45 Ibid., p. 110.
46 This is a recurrent feature of Spark's female characters mentioned to the author in Brooker and Estévez-Saá, pp. 1035–1046 *passim*, and analysed at large in Margarita Estévez-Saá, 'Caracterización e identidad femenina en la obra de Muriel Spark', *Garoza* 7 (Septembee 2007), pp. 99–110.
47 Brooker and Estévez Saá, pp. 1043–44.
48 Anthony Elliott, *Concepts of the Self* (Cambridge: Polity Press, 2008), p. 10.
49 Ibid., p. 10.

11. Looking at America from Edinburgh Castle: postcolonial dislocations in Alice Munro's and Ann-Marie MacDonald's Scottish fictions

PILAR SOMACARRERA

Postcolonialism and the study of Scottish and Canadian literature

The vista referred to in the title of Alice Munro's short story collection *The View from Castle Rock* is not, as expected, that of the county of Fife, but that of America. This geographical incongruity which, according to Scott Hames, could be considered a drunken prank or a transatlantic fantasy,[1] is symptomatic of the postcolonial sense of geographical unease and mirroring which pervades Munro's stories about Scottish–Canadian connections. That Scotland and Canada are linked by their historical and literary connections is a given and has already been the subject of critical discussion.[2] However, less attention has been paid to their status as settler-invader nations who were complicit in the expansion of the British Empire, as John McGrath asserts in his political play *The Cheviot, the Stag and the Black, Black Oil*:

> STURDY HIGHLANDER *(out of character)*: But we came, more and more of us, from all over Europe, in the interests of a trade war between two lots of shareholders, and, in time, the Red Indians were reduced to the same state as our fathers after Culloden – defeated, hunted, treated like the scum of the earth, their culture polluted and torn out with slow deliberation and their land no longer their own.[3]

As Liam Connell points out, the idea that Scotland is a postcolonial nation has gained a certain popular currency in contemporary discussions, with commentary in major national newspapers describing Scotland as 'England's last colony' and the Scots as colonised people.[4] However, Connell also argues that the use of postcolonial theory in relation to Scottish literature forms a strategic effort to raise the profile of Scottish literary studies within the context of its institutional marginalisation as an area of study in British and North American Universities.[5] Michael Gardiner counters this argument by stating that these supposedly academically fashionable claims for postcoloniality can powerfully locate Scotland within a longer history of postcolonial subjectivity travelling through Caribbean and African anti-colonialism.[6]

Although Scottish literature and postcolonial literature are separate fields, they both have the critique of imperialist ideas present in British state culture as one of their main objectives. In this sense a postcolonial framework is useful to understanding Scottish literature, as Michael Gardiner and Graeme MacDonald demonstrate in *Scottish Literature and Postcolonial Literature*,[7] the first book-length study of Scottish literature using a post-devolutionary understanding of postcolonial studies. Another volume which places the field of postcolonial studies beyond its traditional core subject of Europe's former overseas colonies, and encompasses the study of margins, minorities and emerging nations within Europe itself is Silke Stroh's *Uneasy Subjects: Postcolonialism and Scottish Gaelic Poetry* (2011). Stroh focuses on the case of Scottish 'fringe postcolonialism'[8] and explores Scotland's political status as both an intra-British marginalised Other and an integral part of the British mainstream and Britain's sense of self,[9] a consequence of its complicity in the English/British imperialist project.

The debate about Canada's postcolonial status has been going on for approximately two decades. Donna Bennett's observes that English-Canada has played an oddly double role as a territory which is both subjected to an imperial power and also as agent of that power in the control it has exercised over populations (Quebecois and First Nations) within Canada's boundaries.[10] Another useful contribution to the debate is Laura Moss's edited volume *Is Canada Postcolonial? Unsettling Canadian Literature* where she argues that the position of Canada and Canadian culture had still not been fully addressed from a postcolonial point of view.[11] In fact, as Eva Darias-Beautell explains, until the 1980s Canadian literary criticism and university courses had been reluctant to acknowledge both their colonial past and their neo/postcolonial present.[12]

Consequently, and in the light of the similarities between Scotland and Canada as settler-invader nations,[13] a very productive field opens up in the comparative study of these literary traditions because, just as Scotland is, Canada is an Other, and an integral part with respect to the British Empire, and stands in a complex relation of dependence and subversion with respect to the culture inherited from the British Empire. This chapter explores the issues of place, language and history in the fictional works of two contemporary Canadian authors of Scottish descent. Scottish allusions in their texts, therefore, should be read as signs of Canada's postcolonial dependence with respect to other cultural traditions. The works chosen for study are Alice Munro's short-story collection *The View from Castle Rock* (2006) and Ann-Marie MacDonald's novel *Fall on Your Knees* (1996). Other texts by Munro and MacDonald will occasionally be referred to, as will some works of contemporary Scottish literature[14] which are thematically related and can also be read from a postcolonial point of view. As the winner of the 2013 Nobel Prize for Literature and the first Canadian to obtain such literary honour, Munro – an author of mixed Scottish, Irish and English origins – whose literary roots are Canadian but have an international dimension at the same time – epitomises the current canonical status of English-Canadian literature. Novelist, playwright and film-director Ann-Marie MacDonald (of Scottish-Lebanese descent), winner of the 1997 Commonwealth Writers Prize for her first novel *Fall on Your Knees*, is also an internationally renowned writer although she does not occupy the central position of Munro in the CanLit canon.

By contrast with earlier studies that have approached Scottish-Canadian writing only thematically,[15] this chapter's reading will be informed by the theoretical insights of postcolonial literary theory. Both *The View from Castle Rock* and *Fall on Your Knees* are made up of a compendium of memoir, history and autobiography. In her book *Lives of Mothers and Daughters*, Alice Munro's daughter Sheila explains that she has found herself unable to 'unravel the truth of my mother's fiction from the reality of what actually happened'.[16] As for *Fall on Your Knees*, in an interview with Eva Tinhayi,

MacDonald admits that the richness of her parents' heritage was really inspiring for her fiction.[17]

The two novels are concerned with issues commonly studied by postcolonial literary theory, such as history, place, language, diaspora and intertextuality. Both feature a family saga (the Pipers in *Fall on Your Knees* and the Laidlaws in *The View from Castle Rock*) and a genealogical tree reconstructed in a journey: Lily's fictional journey to New York to meet the remaining members of her family (Rose, her mother's partner, and her cousin Anthony) and Alice Munro's journey to the Ettrick Valley in Scotland, the place where her ancestors sprang from and left to emigrate to Southern Ontario, Canada. Both family trees are 'covered with the names of dead Scottish people'.[18] Presiding over the Piper saga in *Fall on Your Knees* is James Piper, a man of Scottish-Irish descent born in Inverness County, Cape Breton Island, Nova Scotia, whose ancestors had been expelled from Scotland during the Highland clearances. More explicitly autobiographical than *Fall on Your Knees*, the key elements of Munro's fictional memoir in *The View from Castle Rock* are drawn directly from family letters, official documents and the writings of her ancestor James Hogg. However, she remains rather elusive (or 'cagey,'[19] as Hames puts it) about the distinction between stories and truth:

> These are *stories*.
> You could say that such stories pay more attention to the truth of a life than fiction usually does. But not enough to swear on. And the part of this book that might be called family history has expanded into fiction, but always within the outlines of a true narrative.[20]

As I have explained elsewhere, *Fall on Your Knees* relies heavily on its Brontë intertexts while at the same time rewriting them.[21] Most conveniently for my comparative approach, an allusion to the Brontë sisters can be traced in 'No Advantages,' the first story of *The View from Castle Rock*: the narrator relates a description of a storm in the Ettrick Valley published by James Hogg in *Blackwood's Magazine* – known to be read by the Brontë sisters – with the first scene of Emily Brontë's *Wuthering Heights*.[22]

'Out of Place': Geographical Dislocations

Entering the Ettrick Church where his ancestor William Laidlaw is buried, the narrator of *The View from Castle Rock*, 'felt conspicuous, out of place' because 'Having been built in 1834, it did not compare, in historic appearance, or grim character, to the churches [she] had already seen in Scotland'.[23] She had probably arrived in Scotland with pre-conceived notions of the country as ancient territory of Gothic dimensions. The issue of recognition and misrecognition will be pivotal in my postcolonial discussion of place in Munro's and MacDonald's texts through the notion of place. In postcolonial studies, 'place,' does not simply mean 'landscape,' but a complex interaction between language, history and environment,[24] which became a concept of contention and struggle after the profound discursive interference of colonialism.[25] Andrew Teverson and Sara Upstone insist that the idea of place plays a significant role in how one defines one's own identity.[26] Similarly, the way in which that identity is defined by others, is continually foregrounded in postcolonial studies. The characters of Alice Munro's *The View from Castle Rock* and Ann-Marie MacDonald's *Fall on Your Knees* are torn between the 'Old country' and the 'New country', home and their country of adoption. The confusion of Scottish and North American locations alluded to in the title story of Munro's collection appears in 'No Advantages.' After listing the famous Scottish men who had been linked to the Ettrick Valley (Michael Scott – a philosopher from the Middle Ages – William Wallace and even Merlin from the Arthurian legend), the narrator expresses her disillusionment with a place she had often imagined: 'Neverthelesss the valley disappointed me the first time I saw it. Places are apt to do that when you've set them up in your imagination. The time of the year was very early spring, and the hills were brown, or a kind of lilac brown, reminding me of the hills around Calgary.'[27] The narrator's disappointment at the viewing of the Scottish ancestral landscape comes from a feeling of recognition which she did not expect to have, rather, than from the fact that she was 'underwhelmed by its banality'.[28] This expectation of recognition is what leads another ancestor of Munro's, Mary Laidlaw, to think that her North American destination will be 'some place inland, among the hills, some place like Ettrick'.[29]

Confusion of locations also features prominently of *Fall on Your Knees*. Mr and Mrs Mahmoud disembark at Cape Breton Island instead of in New York, where they expected to arrive, 'because of the lying mongrel of a sea captain who took their money and dumped them in this barren rock'.[30] The initial mistake committed at their relocation changes the lives of the Piper family to the extent that James will not rest until he is able to send his eldest daughter Kathleen to the 'blessed isle of Manhattan',[31] where she can escape the oppressive atmosphere of Cape Breton described as a 'God-forsaken island'[32] located in Nova Scotia. Once there, Kathleen feels that she will adapt to her new life in New York City and her education as an opera singer because '[it] is just another island'.[33] An imaginative connection is also established between the island of Barbados and that of Cape Breton when Teresa, the Mahmouds' maid, 'moved from a lush island to a stark one'.[34] The fuzzy distinction between places and the mapping of one location into another is a recurrent motif in these narratives by Scottish–Canadian women writers, which encompasses the uneasiness of diasporic and postcolonial subjects.

Another important motif related to place is that of naming. The issue of place names runs through the history of every colonised and postcolonial country, often involving the name of the country itself.[35] MacDonald's and Munro's novels and short stories are often concerned with names of places. In her second novel, *The Way the Crow Flies*, MacDonald traces the genealogy of place names in North America, starting with Canada itself which some say it is an Indian word meaning '"village of small huts" [and] Others say Portuguese fishermen named it Ca Nada: there, nothing'.[36] In settler colonies and postcolonies such as Australia, Canada and New Zealand place names such as Sidney, Victoria, London, Nova Scotia and Wellington indicate the concern to make the land familiar and to mark its ownership by the settlers.[37] James Piper was born in a town called Egypt, in Inverness County, a territory named after the capital of the Highlands. The names embody a paradox between East and West and Biblical allusion – James fled from Egypt, like the Jews to the Promised Land in the Biblical story. As Marta Dvorak and Coral Ann Howells observe, the names of the Old World places relocated in Canada induce a geographical dizziness, as we are confronted with the traces of a colonial settlement history.[38] Even the naming of the Canadian province 'Nova Scotia,' instead of simply 'New Scotland' evokes double imperial echoes of which James Laidlaw's children are unaware:

> Mary holds Young James up so that he may always remember this first sight of the continent that will forever be his home. She tells him the name of this land – Nova Scotia.
> 'It means New Scotland,' she says.
> Agnes hears her. 'Then why doesn't it say so?'
> Mary says, 'It's Latin, I think.'[39]

The presence of an imperial language (Latin) instead of English, Scots or Gaelic in a name like Nova Scotia given to a North American territory named after the original Scotland evokes the Romans' attempt to purge the native languages of the island they named Britannia.

In 'No Advantages', the narrator ponders the etymology of insignificant places, like Far-Hope, the farm where Munro's ancestors lived in the Ettrick Valley. The word 'hope' is one which most English speakers would associate with the meaning of 'expectation or something desired'.[40] 'Hope' is here a word from Scots or Northern English meaning small valley, especially one branching up from a main valley to higher ground.[41] The narrator of 'No Advantages' also explains its etymology: 'a Norse word [… which] means a bay, not a bay filled with water but with land, partly enclosed by the hills'.[42] Munro's ancestor, William Laidlaw, commonly known as Will O'Phaup, was named after a place because 'Phaup was simply the local version of Far-Hope, the name of the farm he took over at the head of Ettrick Valley'.[43] If through the names of places in postcolonial countries location becomes metonymic of those processes of travel, annexation and colonisation,[44] Will O'Phaup becomes a metonym for the landscape of the Ettrick Valley, as evinced by the fact that his first name (Will) became toponym in 'Will's Leap' to commemorate a certain spot in the Ettrick River where he had made a famous jump.[45]

Linguistic Dislocations

As the narrator of 'No Advantages' explains, the Ettrick Valley had always been a site for language contact: 'Norse, Anglo-Saxon and Gaelic words being all mixed up together in that part of the country [...] with some old Brythonic thrown in to indicate early Welsh presence'.[46] In her earlier stories about Scotland, published in her collection *Friend of My Youth*, a certain degree of quaintness is attached to the Scots language. In the title story, 'Friend of My Youth', Flora, the eldest of the Cameronian sisters with whom the protagonist-narrator boards, 'read stories in Scots dialect'.[47] In 'Hold me Fast, Don't Let Me Pass,' Hazel, who travels to Scotland to meet the woman her husband had had an affair with, is fascinated by Scots words although she has trouble recognising them in the locals' speech or even interpreting their tone:

> [Dudley] nodded to Hazel and to Antoinette: 'I'm off now, my lamb. Did he really say that—'lamb'? Whatever it was, it had the satirical inflection that an endearment would need between him and Antoinette. People did say 'lass' here. The driver on the bus from Edinburgh had said it to Hazel, that afternoon'.[48]

This anecdote is symptomatic of the way in which Canadians base their perceptions of Scotland in romanticised fantasies derived from what Magdalene Redekop calls the 'Scottish nostalgic grotesque as a tourist destination'.[49]

Upon his arrival in Canada, James Laidlaw is faced with the usual questions diasporic subjects ask themselves when they arrive in the 'New Country': 'How shall we sing the Lord's song in a strange land?'[50] He writes to his son Robert to explain his difficulties with the 'imperial' variety of English he has encountered in Canada which makes communication difficult: '[...] the people here speaks very good English there is many of our Scots words they cannot understand what we are saying and live far more independent than King George'.[51] The irony is that speaking the language of the Empire, 'English' with a capital letter,[52] allows them more 'independence' than using Scots which had for long been considered a variety of English or even just a dialect.[53]

In *Fall on Your Knees*, James's need to decide between communicating in the peripheral language of a dispossessed people (Gaelic, his mother's tongue) or in the language of the metropolis (English, his father's language): 'It used to make his father angry when James and his mother spoke Gaelic together, for his father spoke only English. Gaelic was James's mother tongue. English felt flat and harsh, like daylight after night-fishing, but his mother made sure he was proficient as a little prince, for they were part of the British Empire and he had his way to make.'[54] As Daniel Coleman observes, Piper's beliefs are based on the Scottish Presbyterian values of self-improvement through the English language which later become generalised onto English Canada as a whole.[55]

Although in contemporary Scotland Gaelic language and literature have a strong relationship with nationalism,[56] this principle does not apply to the way Gaelic is used in *Fall on Your Knees*. Gaelic is the *lingua franca* which the Mahmouds use for their trading activities with their neighbours, which pleasantly surprises James because 'Gaelic speakers were mostly out of the country'.[57] National sentiment is absent from in the way James Piper uses his mother tongue in MacDonald's novel. He uses Gaelic as a linguistic register for affectionate relations. He sings Gaelic songs to his wife during their honeymoon because 'he loved her more in his mother tongue'.[58] It was Gaelic he spoke to his daughter Kathleen when they went on walks but he sternly repressed it in her education, replacing it by English. Like Chris Guthrie's Janus-faced identity (the 'English Chris' and 'the other Chris – the Scottish one') in Lewis Grassic Gibbon's *Sunset Song*,[59] discussed in Philippe Laplace's chapter, James feels split up into two languages and identities, English and Gaelic. After repressing his first language for a long time, at the end of the novel James suffers a stroke and recovers Gaelic and the 'old-fashioned music'[60] he heard his mother play when he was a child. Significantly, he hears music and his mother speak to him in Gaelic while he is sleeping or just unconscious, an episode which, according to Gabriella Parro,[61] transforms him:

> He lies down, curled beneath the birch, and hears her voice, *Hello*. [...] and she speaks to him in Gaelic: '*Hello Seamus. Mo ghraidh. M'eudail*. His tears soothe his face, parched to kindling.

He speaks to her. He tells her he is sorry. He feels her hand, cool on the side of his face. He knows she is healing him, but he also realizes that with this she is preparing to send him away from her, 'No!' He feels she is condemning him back to a *hell* [my italics] he can't quite recall, 'No!' He opens his eyes.[62]

'Seamus' is 'James' in Gaelic; '*Mo ghraidh*' means 'my sweetheart' and '*M'eudail*' would be a similar term of endearment in Gaelic, a language which has numerous words meaning 'love'.[63] However, the dream-scene distils a disturbing ambiguity: the vision of the mother – being an embodiment of 'the abject' as understood by Julia Kristeva – is both blissful and disturbing at the same time.[64] I have italicised the word 'hell' in the earlier quotation because one of James's worst personal hells in *Fall on Your Knees* is his experience in First World War. He was forced to fight for the Cape Breton Highlanders 85th Overseas Battalion of the Canadian Expeditionary Force for which he is given 'a dress kilt of bright Macdonald tartan'[65] as part of his uniform as a soldier of a Highland regiment[66] in which 'eighty per cent of the unit spoke Gaelic'.[67] Perhaps the tartan design was the same as that in the tartan blanket his mother had woven and he took with him when he left Egypt.[68] James's mother represents the mother tongue but also the motherland, both loving and possessing the ability to condemn him by sending him to a pointless war.

Historical Dislocations

Postcolonial nations have felt the need to recover their lost or hidden histories, or to root theirs with that of their former metropolis, in order to find legitimation or to 'write back' to official versions. In the stories analysed in this essay, Munro and MacDonald challenge the idea of history implied in romance structure and opt for a more-open ended, almost improvisational approach.[69] *Fall on Your Knees* does not focus on the history of the British Empire, but on the personal stories of James Piper, his Scottish-Irish-Lebanese family, and those of the many immigrants who live in Cape Breton Island, who, in Katarzyna Rukszto's words, resist the normative racial, sexual, and gender categories of identification in favor of what she calls 'queer' identities.⁷⁰ *Fall on Your Knees* chronicles some of the most pressing social, political, economic, and racial issues faced by the Cape Breton community over the course of the twentieth century. James's life is interwoven with these events: he strikes; his three years in the trenches during the First World War; and his bootlegging activities during the 1920s and 1930s, a period of prohibition in Nova Scotia.

As for *The View from Castle Rock,* it perfectly illustrates the connections between the histories of Canada and Scotland as it traces the journey of James Laidlaw's family from the Ettrick Valley – that 'very small, dispersed and lonely place'⁷¹ – to 'America, which includes Canada'.⁷² The coincidence of Alice Munro being a distant relative of the Scottish author James Hogg contributes to building the transatlantic connection between the Scottish author and his distant Canadian relative. Hogg is in fact the source of some of the stories of Munro's ancestors, as she herself acknowledges in her Foreword to *The View from Castle Rock*: 'I was able to find their names in the local histories of Selkirk and Galashiels Public Libraries, and to find out what Hogg had to say about them in *Blackwood's Magazine*'.⁷³ As Alistair Moffat notes, *Blackwood's Magazine* (originally entitled *The Edinburgh Blackwood's Magazine*) was launched by William Blackwood in 1817 taking advantage of the general appetite for magazines, review articles and general columns.⁷⁴ It was one of the many magazines which started to be published as a result of Walter Scott's concern for the preservation of Scottishness. The 'Magazine' or 'Maga', as it was also known, had a wide readership across the British Empire, evidence of which is that it is the mentioned in *Fall on Your Knees* as read by the Piper sisters.⁷⁵

Alice Munro traces the history of her ancestors through three generations: the first is that of William Laidlaw / Will O'Phaup, the man who was named after his farm; the second, that of his daughter, Margaret Laidlaw Hogg and the third, that of James Hogg and James Laidlaw, son and nephew of the former, respectively. As an ancestor, William Laidlaw had the convenient quality of existing in the blurry limits between history and legend. As Munro points out, the story of Will, a shepherd from the Ettrick Valley who was also a very fast runner and beat a visiting English champion is a classic story of which she had heard numerous versions while growing up in

Huron County, Ontario.[76] In 'No Advantages,' the reader is introduced to James Hogg – Munro's 'trickster' ancestor[77] and James Laidlaw – Munro's great-great grandfather who left Scotland for North America when he was sixty. In addition to their first names, these character share their poverty (emphasised in the title of the story), eccentricity and penchant for writing. Munro skillfully presents the co-existence of the two Jameses (who become local historians) by having one comment about the other. Hogg considered his cousin an eccentric man for emigrating to America '– actually to Canada –'[78] as the narrator clarifies: '[…] for a number of years bygone he [James Laidlaw] talked and read about America, till he grew perfectly unhappy, and at last when approaching his sixtieth year actually set out to seek a temporary home and a grave in the new world'.[79] According to his cousin Laidlaw, 'Hogg spent most of his life conning lies', and Tibbie Shiel, the innkeeper, said he was a 'very sensible man, for a' the nonsense he wrat'.[80]

Another Scottish ancestor of Alice Munro's who further bonds the Canadian author with the history of Scotland and its writers is Margaret Laidlaw, Will O'Phaup's daughter and James Hogg's mother. Margaret Laidlaw provided Water Scott with some of the verses of *The Minstrelsy of the Scottish Border* (1802), even if 'there would be some trimming and embroidering of material in Hogg's part',[81] since it was Hogg himself who took Scott to see his mother. Munro's narrator retells the famous anecdote about Laidlaw's complaint to Scott, reproducing her words in Scots, that the verses 'were made for singin and no for prentin […]. And noo they'll never be sung mair.'[82] As simple as this anecdote about this uneducated countrywoman might appear, it epitomises the disappearance of oral history and literature and its substitution for what Penny Fielding calls 'a ballad literature made for a fashionable readership'[83] in Britain and its overseas colonies, including, of course, Canada.

Conclusion

The View from Castle Rock is dedicated to Douglas Gibson, Alice Munro's editor *'whose enthusiasm for this particular book has even sent him prowling through the graveyard of Ettrick Kirk, probably in the rain'* (ix).

This dedication seems to suggest that Alice Munro was prompted by Gibson to write a book about her Scottish ancestors following the habit of tracing the problem of Canadian identity 'elsewhere'[84] in other cultural traditions – in this case the Scottish one. The dedication of the book and its first story demonstrate that Gibson and Munro are accomplices in the strategy of attracting readers by using a literary-tour version of Scotland.[85] For this purpose Alice Munro relies on two traits of Scottish literature: first, nostalgia, what Redekop calls 'an inevitable part of the Scottish baggage', and, secondly, the pride Scots feel about historical figures, writers and philosophers like William Wallace, John Knox, Mary Queen of Scots, David Hume, James Hogg, Robert Burns and Walter Scott. These are mentioned in 'No Advantages', the essayistic story/prologue to *The View from Castle Rock*, where Munro, in a distinctive postcolonial manner, legitimises herself as a writer by highlighting her family connections with James Hogg. Similarly, Ann-Marie MacDonald uses the texts of Robert Louis Stevenson (especially *Treasure Island* and 'The Land of Nod') and *Jane Eyre* (a novel whose language and intertextual components are, to a great extent, influenced by Scottish culture) as the 'proto-texts'[86] which allow her to put forward her ideas about race, evolution and the subversion of Victorian images of women.

Postcolonial fictions root themselves in a strong sense of place. The idea of landscape is predicated upon a particular philosophic tradition in which the objective world is separated from the viewing subject.[87] Augustin Berque also uses the word 'landscape' with a restricted meaning. For Berque, a landscape is not an object *per se* but 'a médiance', that is, the outcome of a series of mediations between a perceiving subject, perceived surroundings and a fund of cultural, social and historical representations.[88] The way in which landscape is presented in these fictions, exemplified by the pun in the Norse word 'Hope' – meaning 'bay' and expectation – can be read through Berque's views about landscape.

Place and the past in these two Scottish-Canadian texts are pervaded by the uncanny. Joel Baetz has written about the presence of uncanny in *Fall on Your Knees*[89] and provides an example of a scene of the novel, in which James recognises the past (the repressed) as he suddenly sees a photograph of Kathleen on the piano and suddenly feels terrified as past and present converge: 'Now is the dim past. Then was the shining present'.[90] Similarly, reading the inscriptions at Ettrick cemetery, the narrator of 'No Advantages, 'was struck with a feeling familiar [...] to many people whose long history goes back to a country far away from the place where they grew up [...] Past and present lumped together here made a reality that was a commonplace and yet disturbing beyond anything I had imagined'.[91] The narrator – who at this point can be identified as a kind of alter ego of Alice Munro – attributes this feeling to her identity as 'a naïve North American'.[92] This and other recurrent allusions which emphasise the relationship, based on the rhetorical device of synecdoche, between America and Canada (Canada is just a part of America) foreground Canada's inferiority complex. In Munro's stories Canadians in Europe are often taken for Americans. The tension between Americanness and Canadianness and the image of Scottish people transplanted to America is dramatically inscribed in a passage from the story 'Illinois' in which the third generation of Laidlaws in Munro's collection (James Laidlaw's sons, William and Andrew) are the protagonists. William Laidlaw's wife and children have to emigrate to Upper Canada after his death from cholera, and Andrew, who has travelled to the United States to help them in their move, makes the following reflection about his brother Will: 'He had seen enough of the Yankee people by now to know what had tempted Will to live among them. The push and noise and rawness of them, the need to get on the jumpwagon. Though some were decent enough and some, and maybe some of the worst, were Scots, Will had something in him drawing to such a life' (*VCR*, 110).[93] The narrator sees in Scottish immigrants to Canada the rowdiness and interestedness of Americans.

The use of derogatory expressions to describe Cape Breton island ('God-forsaken island,' 'barren rock') and the constant opposition with Manhattan (New York City) which is presented as cosmopolitan and sophisticated emphasise Cape Breton's condition as a kind of colony within a country which is still not politically or culturally independent. In contrast with the prolific details of Munro's ancestors, the only allusion to the Highland Clearances, the dramatic episode in Scottish history which explains the diasporic process leading James's ancestors to emigrate to Scotland, appears in the following passage about Cape Breton, which describes it as 'The island familiar to famished Irish and gnarly-kneed Scots who had been replaced by sheep in their Old Country' (*FYK*, 87). The absence of a more precise reference to the Clearances leaves a gap which hinders the understanding of the novel for lay readers unfamiliar with Scottish history, and disturbingly speaks of MacDonald's lack of political commitment in relation to the land of her paternal ancestors.

Languages different from English spoken in Scotland (Scots, Gaelic) whose present status as literary language is no longer questioned are not attributed the status of literary or national languages, but rather, they are considered registers for affection or nostalgic quaintness in the narratives here analysed. In *Fall on Your Knees* the only literary language which James acknowledges is English. In his household, R. L. Stevenson is deprived of his Scottish identity as he is read as another writer in the English language. James Piper is another example of what Alistair MacLeod, another Canadian writer of Scottish ancestry, has called 'Highland Darwinism', the process by which Scottish characters 'become' more English by going into and mastering the English world.[94] Although Munro avoids the use of printed dialect in her works in order to avoid slipping into the quaintness of the oral realm, the few Scots words or allusions to the Scots language have that inevitable effect of quaintness which Canadians identify with speakers of Scots. Given that pre-colonial culture is usually oral, the suppression of oral traditions and its replacement by written accounts of history is part of the colonial processes undergone by subjected nations, which often continue in subsequent postcolonial stages. Walter Scott, James Hogg – and Alice Munro after them – create a fantasy of orality in their works. But true orality, as Margaret Laidlaw famously pointed out to Scott, was lost with the written version of the ballads which became a marketing product of English and North American readers.

In the light of the aforementioned arguments, I have to conclude that Alice Munro and Ann-Marie MacDonald, despite their canonical status in the CanLit system, should be considered as postcolonial authors in what one may regard as their Scottish fictions, *The View from Castle Rock* and *Fall on Your Knees*, because of the ways in which they rely on narratives that are highly dependent on Scottish cultural traditions which are eventually anglicised. Although one of the main traditions evoked in English-Canada is the Scottish one, this tradition is treated superficially and dependent on a higher and more accomplished one, which is the British. As Hames rightly points out, currently discredited forms of national imagining, like the romantic vision of the Borders, pan-Gaelic blood bonds or balladic enchantment, are resurrected in Canadian fictions which project anxieties internal to the national literary self-image of Canada onto a static Scotland.[95] The Canadian canon thus reduces itself to 'a canonic anxiety',[96] which props itself up thanks to allusions to Scotland and its culture and literary traditions.

This chapter began with some comments on the relevance of postcolonialism for both Canadian and Scottish literature. In the aftermath of the 2014 referendum about Scottish independence, a discussion of whether Scottish culture can be considered postcolonial or studied under the framework of postcolonial theory becomes more relevant than ever. Likewise, Canada, a nation which only recently freed itself from symbolic political links with Great Britain, but which, under the previous conservative government, had revived its connections with the British monarchy, must inevitably acknowledge its postcolonial condition if it intends to enfranchise itself psychologically and culturally.

Notes

1. Scott Hames, 'Diasporic Narcisism. De-sublimating Scotland in Alice Munro and Alistair MacLeod', *Anglistik: International Journal of English Studies*, 23.2 (September 2012), pp. 73–82.
2. See Elizabeth Waterston, *Rapt in Plaid. Canadian Literature and the Scottish Tradition* (Toronto: Toronto University Press, 2001).
3. John McGrath, *The Cheviot, the Stag and the Black, Black Oil* (London: Methuen Drama, 1974), p. 29.
4. Liam Connell, 'Modes of Marginality: Scottish Literature and the Uses of Postcolonial Theory', *Comparative Studies of South Asia, Africa and the Middle East*, XXIII, 1 (2003), pp. 4–17 (p. 5).
5. Connell, p. 3.
6. Michael Gardiner, 'Democracy and Scottish Postcoloniality', *Scotlands*, 3, 2 (1996), pp. 24–41 (p. 25).
7. Michael Gardiner, Graeme MacDonald and Niall O'Gallagher, *Scottish Literature and Postcolonial Literature: Comparative Texts and Critical Perspectives* (Edinburgh: Edinburgh University Press, 2011).

8   Silke Stroh,, *Uneasy Subjects. Postcolonialism and Scottish Gaelic Poetry* (Amsterdam: Rodopi, 2011). p. 11.
9   Ibid., p. 12.
10 Donna Bennet, 'English-Canada's Postcolonial Complexities', in *Unhomely States. Theorizing English-Canadian Postcolonialism*, ed. by Cynthia Sugars (Ontario: Broadview Press, 2004), pp. 107–36 (p. 116).
11 Laura Moss, 'Is Canada Postcolonial? Introducing the Question', in *Is Canada Postcolonial: Unsettling Canadian Literature*, ed. by Laura Moss (Waterloo: Wilfrid Laurier University Press, 2003), pp. 1–23 (p. 2).
12 Eva Darias-Beautell, 'Home Truths. Teaching Canadian Literature in Spanish Universities', in *Made in Canada, Read in Spain. Essays on the Translation and Circulation of English-Canadian Literature*, ed. by Pilar Somacarrera (London: Versita, 2013), pp. 164–78 (p. 177).
13 Waterston lists some of these similarities: 'two northern nations, ironic and sentimental, each quietly resentful of the stronger, more affluent neighbour lying south of the national border' (p. 8).
14 This essay would not have been possible without the background on contemporary Scottish literature and Scottish criticism I obtained in in the Scottish Literature module of the 'Text and Context' course organised by the Scottish Universities International Summer School at the University of Edinburgh and its subsequent week of research, for which I was awarded a Saltire Scholarship in 2013. My thanks go to the SUISS committee and team, as well as to all the lecturers and tutors.
15 See Waterston and Hames.
16 Quoted in Karl Miller, 'The Passion of Alice Laidlaw', *Changing English*, 14 (April 2007), pp. 17–22 (p. 17)
17 Eva Tihanyi, 'Jane Eyre in a Cape Breton Attic: Eva Tihanyi speaks with Ann-Marie MacDonald', *Books in Canada*, 25, 8 (1996), pp. 21–22 (p. 21).
18 Ann-Marie MacDonald, *Fall on Your Knees* (London: Vintage, 1996), p. 199.
19 Hames, p. 73.
20 Alice Munro, *The View from Castle Rock* (Toronto: Penguin Canada, 2006), p. xiv.
21 Pilar Somacarrera, 'A Madwoman in a Cape Breton Attic: Jane Eyre in Ann-Marie MacDonald's *Fall on Your Knees*', *Journal of Commonwealth Literature*, 39,1 (2004), pp. 55–75.
22 Munro, *The View from Castle Rock*, p. 24.
23 Ibid., p. 6
24 Bill Ashcroft, Gareth Griffiths and Helen Tiffin, *The Post-Colonial Studies Reader* (New York Routledge, 2006), p. 345.
25 Bill Ashcroft, Gareth Griffiths and Helen Tiffin, *Post-Colonial Studies: The Key Concepts* (Routledge: New York, 2007), p. 161.
26 Andrew Teverson and Sara Upstone, *Postcolonial Spaces. The Politics of Place in Contemporary Culture* (London: Palgrave, 2011), p. 3.
27 Munro, *The View from Castle Rock*, p. 5.
28 Hames, p. 75.
29 Munro, *The View from Castle Rock*, p. 38.
30 MacDonald, *Fall on your Knees*, p. 38. It is worth pointing out here that MacDonald never considers New York as a postcolonial location in her fiction. In *The Way the Crow*

Flies, the narrator states that 'New York was named after York in England, but no one ever thinks of York, England, when they think of New York' (13).
31 Ibid., p. 339.
32 Ibid., p. 19.
33 Ibid., p. 456.
34 Ibid., p. 118.
35 C. L. Innes, *The Cambridge Introduction to Postcolonial Literatures in English* (Cambridge: Cambridge University Press, 2007), p. 72.
36 Ann-Marie MacDonald, *For Whom the Crow Flies* (New York: Harper Collins, 2003), p. 13.
37 Innes, p. 72.
38 Marta Dvorak and Coral Ann Howells, 'The Literature of Atlantic Canada,' *Canadian Literature*, 186 (Summer 2006), pp. 6–13 (p. 8).
39 Munro, *The View from Castle Rock*, p. 56.
40 A semantic connection seems to emerge between the name of the farm, 'Far-Hope' and the title of the first story in *The View from Castle Rock*, 'No Advantages.' Munro found the phrase in the Statistical Account of Scotland (1799) which described the Ettrick Valley 'as having *no advantages*' (*The View from Castle Rock*, p. xiii).
41 *Shorter Oxford English Dictionary on CD-ROM*. Version 3.0. (Oxford: Oxford University Press, 2007).
42 Munro, *The View from Castle Rock*, p. 4.
43 Ibid., p 7.
44 Ashcroft et al., *The Post-Colonial Studies Reader*, p. 165.
45 Munro, *The View from Castle Rock*, p. 10.
46 Ibid., p. 45.
47 Alice Munro, *Friend of my Youth* (Toronto: Penguin Canada, 1990), p. 13.
48 Ibid., p. 83.
49 Magdalene Redekop. 'Alice Munro and the Scottish Nostalgic Grotesque', in *Essays on Canadian Writing*, 66 (Winter 1998), 1–15 (p. 15).
50 Munro, *The View from Castle Rock*, p. 82.
51 Ibid., p. 82.
52 Ashcroft et al., *The Post-Colonial Studies Reader*, p. 8.
53 Ronald Carter and John McRae, *The Routledge History of Literature in English*, Britain and Ireland. (London: Routledge, 1997), pp. 532–33.
54 MacDonald, *Fall on Your Knees*, p. 7.
55 Daniel Coleman, *White Civility. The Literary Project of English Canada* (Toronto: University of Toronto Press, 2006), p. 123.
56 Ismail S. Talib, *The Languages of Postcolonial Literatures* (Routledge: London, 2003), p. 42.
57 MacDonald, *Fall on Your Knees*, p. 274.
58 Ibid., p.15.
59 Lewis Grassic Gibbon, A Scots Quair. (1932,1933, 1934) (Edinburgh: Polygon, 2006), p. 41.
60 MacDonald, *Fall on Your Knees*, p. 418.
61 Gabriella Parro, '"Who is your Father, Dear?" Haunted Bloodlines and Miscegenation in Ann-Marie MacDonald's *Fall on Your Knees*', *Canadian Review of American Studies*, 35, 2 (2005), pp. 177–193 (p. 191).

62 MacDonald, *Fall on Your Knees*, p. 219.
63 I am grateful to Ian MacDonald, a Gaelic speaker from the Isle of Skye now living in Glasgow, for the English translations of the Gaelic words in MacDonald's text.
64 Julia Kristeva, *Powers of Horror. An Essay on Abjection* (New York: Columbia University Press, 1982), p. 60.
65 MacDonald, *Fall on Your Knees*, p. 84.
66 The fact that the Germans called the Highland Regiments '"*Die Damen von Hölle*" – the ladies from Hell.' (Ibid., p. 85) foregrounds the idea that of the hardships suffered by Scottish soldiers who were fearful aggressors and helpless victims at the same time.
67 Ibid., p. 83.
68 Ibid., p. 8.
69 Magdalene Redekop, *Mothers and Other Clowns. The Stories of Alice Munro* (New York: Routledge, 1992), p. 177.
70 Katarzyna Rukszto, 'Out of Bounds: Perverse Longings, Transgressive Desire and the Limits of Multiculturalism: A Reading of *Fall on Your Knees*', *International Journal of Canadian Studies*, 21 (Spring 2000), 17–34 (pp. 21, 25).
71 Miller, p. 20.
72 Munro, *The View from Castle Rock*, p. 25.
73 Ibid., p. xiii.
74 Alistair Moffat, *The Borders. A History of the Borders from the Earliest Times* (Edinburgh: Birlinn, 2007), p. 438.
75 MacDonald, *Fall on Your Knees*, p. 111.
76 Munro, *The View from Castle Rock*, p. 9,
77 Redekop, 'Alice Munro and the Scottish Grotesque', p. 7.
78 Munro, *The View from Castle Rock*, p. 20.
79 Ibid., p. 19.
80 Ibid., p. 19.
81 Ibid., p. 21.
82 Ibid., p. 22.
83 Penny Fielding, *Writing and Orality: Nationality, Culture, and Nineteenth-Century Scottish Fiction* (Oxford: Clarendon, 1996), p. 14.
84 Hames, p. 73.
85 I felt prompted to tour the Scottish Borders and the Ettrick Valley myself after reading Munro's collection. I was able to go on this tour in the summer of 2013.
86 Atef Layouene, 'Canadian Gothic and the Work of Ghosting in Ann-Marie MacDonald's *Fall on Your Knees*', in *Unsettled Remains: Canadian Literature and the Postcolonial Gothic*, ed. by Cynthia Sugars and Gerry Turcotte (Waterloo: Wilfrid Laurier University Press, 2009), pp. 125–54 (p. 129).
87 Ashcroft et al., *The Post-Colonial Studies Reader*, p. 344.
88 Augustin Berque, *Les Raisons du paysage de la Chine antique aux environments de synthèse* (Paris: Hazan, 1995), p. 50.
89 Joel Baetz, 'Tales from the Canadian Crypt: Canadian Ghosts, the Cultural Uncanny, and the Necessity of Haunting in Ann-Marie MacDonald's *Fall on Your Knees*', *Studies in Canadian Literature*, 39, 2 (2004), journals.hil.unb.ca/index.php/scl/article/view/12749/13695 [accessed October 15, 2014].
90 MacDonald, *Fall on Your Knees*, p. 260.

91 Munro, *The View from Castle Rock*, p. 7.
92 Ibid., p. 7.
93 Ibid., p 110
94 Alistair MacLeod, 'The Writings of Hugh MacLennan', *Brick*, 44 (Summer 1992), pp. 72–77 (p. 74).
95 Hames, p. 82.
96 Dermot McCarthy, 'Early Canadian Literary Histories in Canadian Canons', in *Canadian Canons: Essays in Literary Value*, ed. by Robert. Lecker (Toronto: University of Toronto Press, 1991), pp. 40–55 (p. 45).

12. Scottish and Galician background in Pearse Hutchinson's poetry: freedom, identity and literary landscapes

JOSÉ-MIGUEL ALONSO-GIRÁLDEZ

'The only word a poet must never commit is the word must.'[1]

This chapter pays tribute to the memory of the outstanding poet Pearse Hutchinson, born in Glasgow in 1927, who died in Dublin on 14 January 2012, aged eighty-four. A Scottish writer, though deeply linked to Irish culture, Hutchinson is a key figure in twentieth-century European literature, especially with regards to so-called peripheral literature and languages. The *Herald* obituary (19 January 2012) sets out his background:

> [Hutchinson] was born into an Irish republican family in central Glasgow. His 'deeply loving but strong-minded and puritanical' mother was from Cowcaddens but his father, a printer whose own father had left Dublin to find work in Scotland, was a Sinn Féin treasurer in Glasgow. He was interned in the Frongoch internment camp in north Wales as an Irish Republican prisoner between 1919–1921. [...] The family moved to Dublin when Hutchinson was five. [...] Due to his family's experience in the 1930s, Hutchinson had an 'ambivalent approach to elements in Scotland' but never towards the Scots or Scotland. He was an early visitor in the Scottish/Irish cultural exchanges that started in 1971, appearing with Crichton Smith in 1973. His last appearance was in 1992 with Crichton Smith and the Welsh poet Menna Elfyn in St Cecilia's Hall, Edinburgh, organised by the then fledgling Scottish Poetry Library for the Edinburgh International Festival.[2]

Indeed, Hutchinson's long life was entirely devoted to preserving cultural exchange, to understanding others and, above all, to understanding them in their own languages.

During his life, Hutchinson defended and promoted national identities, particularly those which derived from minority cultures, always emphasising the importance of local or native language, a vehicle which in his view was absolutely necessary in order to establish cultural links and even political relations. He was a champion of freedom in all the places he lived. His life was marked by friendship, solidarity and generosity. Here, we will deal with these real and metaphorical landscapes (territories of the mind) in which his literary production was deeply involved, beside, obviously, his Irish background. There are many aspects of his strong relationship with Catalonia and Galicia that have not yet been completely revealed. He spent several years in touch with both Galician and Catalonian writers and intellectuals, but also met other people living in both places, who helped him, as he regularly pointed out, to experiment a new kind of freedom. Few writers have celebrated in such an enthusiastic way the fact of sharing different languages, different geographical spaces and, as a result, different cultural identities. His interest in Scotland, as part of Gaelic culture, must be emphasised: as German poet and radio broadcaster Michael Augustin, one of his best friends, declared in 2012,

> Pearse showed great interest in poets writing in Scottish Gaelic. He met and knew the greatest contemporaries and I remember him talking about them on the radio as well. One of his classic poems, 'Achnasheen', is set in Scotland, with references to Ireland and Barcelona.[3]

Undoubtedly, Hutchinson is a perfect example of so-called cultural blending or cultural hybridisation, and, in more ways than one, a perfect representative of cultural internationalism. As a result, he always tried to keep identities and minor languages alive in terms of equality with dominant ones. For this reason one cannot speak of Hutchinson's work without talking about translation. As Peter Sirr (2011) wrote in *The Irish Times*,

> The languages and cultures he encounters – medieval Galicio-Portuguese [sic], contemporary Catalan, Galician, Portuguese and Castilian as well as Irish – are not simply external associations but form part of a single creative continuum, a world view and a soundscape where 'cicada, chameleon, lagarto' can rub shoulders, where Catalan, Irish and English can occupy the same poem and not seem strange to each other.[4]

And in the volume Sirr was reviewing, *Reading Pearse Hutchinson: From Findrum to Fisterra*,[5] Robert Welch concludes that 'the act of poetry, for Pearse Hutchinson, is an act of translation, whereby things shift in relation to each other'.[6] The many years he spent studying and experiencing Spanish, particularly Catalan and Galician, cultures certainly deserve detailed analysis. Hutchinson, also deeply influenced by music, represents in an extraordinary way the spirit of creativity in a multilingual and multicultural Europe, an authentic and unbeatable passion for diversity. His poetry is built on foundations of tolerance and friendship, and his translations of poets from Iberia, among others, exemplify this well. As Vincent Woods expresses it,

> Hutchinson has always written as one aware of boundaries – cultural, political, linguistic, sexual, national – and who has sought, through his work, to question the legitimacy of those boundaries, to examine and interrogate their origins and structure, to suggest ways of crossing them, or ways, indeed, of breaking them down altogether. We see that time and again in his poetry of Spain: the recognition of separate languages and cultures, the expression of anger at simplistic centralism, the need to seek and tell the truth from the past, the importance of the proper naming and acknowledging of things and people.[7]

A fascinating author, Hutchinson's rich cultural work and life deserve closer study.

One of the most repeated quotations from Hutchinson's writing is not a line from one of his poems, but a phrase, a sentence he wrote on a postcard he sent to his mother at the age of seven. This is, for example, the first sentence which appears in the introduction to Philip Coleman and Maria Johnston's *Reading Pearse Hutchinson: From Findrum to Fisterra*, already cited, published after the poet's death. As Hutchinson states in his own introduction to the celebrated volume of translations *Done into English*,[8] he wrote to his mother on a postcard: 'When I grow up, I'll take you to sunny Spain […]' (15). This expression of a childhood desire undoubtedly marked the rest of his life, and was already pointing at the dreams and passions of the future poet. He never took his mother to Spain, but at the heart of this sentence beats the origin of everything, the initial moment marking Hutchinson's construction as a transnational poet, as a great creator of a free poetic atmosphere, a semantic magma, which could be read in several languages, and understood as music must be understood, with a sense of both the local and the universal. Music, incidentally, was another of Hutchinson's great passions.[9]

Of course, Pearse, as his friends usually called him, even in formal contexts, resists the labels or classifications literary criticism so typically proliferates. To start with, Hutchinson always focused on words' infinite possibilities, but was also aware that language is a weird and wonderful material with which to work. For him, language was a precious substance containing virtues not entirely understood, malleable, transformable, able to change even the nature and composition of the poem during the writing process, capable of resulting in one poetic piece or another, depending on circumstances. Hutchinson considered a poem could not be understood as a solid and stable entity, even in its final form, but rather as a dynamic compound open to many possibilities. His attitude towards literature recalls the postmodern idea of blurring boundaries. For him, poetry – and literature, in general – should be regarded as human manifestations that, in order to be complete, must go beyond local experience, although he was very much aware of the national, or even nationalistic, backgrounds in which many of those manifestations were produced. Despite the fact local cultures take place in specific contexts, very much attached to their ancestral heritage, Hutchinson wanted culture to become a liquid element, to flow from one place to another, to be shaped and reshaped according to circumstances and transmitted as fully as possible, often by means of translation and, as a result, generating new forms of culture and new complexities. For Hutchinson, translation should be considered as a complex literary act in which the language could reach its highest potential: but, as he 'regarded himself as "a man of languages rather than nations"',[10] his emphasis was always on his undisputed linguistic abilities to help the reader to celebrate and enjoy any kind of cultural manifestation. He could speak several languages, but had learnt most of them as part of an ideological and cultural liturgy. In almost any circumstance, he wanted to experiment, and, in order to achieve this, he considered it was necessary to experiment with foreign cultures in their original sound and form. All in all, he explores the construction of identity from life experience, from the constant movement and permanently changing interrelationships within diversity.

Identity for Hutchinson may be tied to a single place at first: it might be the place of birth or the individual's workplace. But, for him, the creation of identity is more a process of systematic reconstructions, a perpetual evolution which demands new cultural material be incorporated from different experiences, something that occurs mostly while moving geographically from one place to another. This idea of dynamic or permeable identity can be compared to the central idea of Hutchinson's poetics, which he emphasised early in the 1960s as the importance of cultural empathy. This is, it might be argued, the appropriate term, the celebration of the otherness as a vehicle to express new knowledge and enjoyment, the manifestation of the multiple and manifold nature of identity. This is not only based on the traditional and often stereotypical energy derived from the foundational place (and the real and metaphorical landscape), but also on the emotional attachment to numerous local experiences, in different countries and with very different people. These result in an emotional and intellectual fluidity more in line with Hutchinson's transnational concept of culture. He built his own evolving identity from his empathy with minority cultures, continuously challenging the intellectual and political domination of the centre, and his poetry constantly celebrates difference. This can be observed in his first poetry collection, *Tongue without Hands* (1963), in which languages are shown as permeable entities, which can be combined and mixed in an almost unpredictable way – and seemingly without limits – to produce a new cultural element. This maintains the original properties of its individual components, but simultaneously offers a new dynamic entity, sometimes by using apparently unimportant materials, often taken from minority or marginal areas of cultures and languages.

It must be pointed out, however, that Hutchinson, though resistant to any form of chauvinism, defends robust local cultural structures. He does so even though he always operates in an almost fluid and organic system, resulting, as has been noted earlier, in the exchange, celebration and promotion of otherness and rejecting any kind of domination or linguistic colonisation. He believed in the importance of minorities, simply because he thought that they were not influential enough in history, because they had been unfairly deprived of respect and consideration. From the very beginning of his career, Hutchinson consciously left the well-trodden path of domination and often canonical interpretations of literature deployed by major cultures to settle in the margins, on the liminal border, where nuances and flavours seemed to play completely new and unexpected roles.[11] He was aware, in short, as Philip Coleman has said,[12] citing Ramazani,[13] that 'the poetics of transnationalism can help us understand and imagine a world where cultural boundaries are fluid, transient, and permeable'. Although the fluid state of matter has been partly linked, in the contemporary world, to the development of new technologies, Hutchinson, from the 1950s onwards, always worked on the ground, being aware, sometimes to very detailed and specific extremes, of local cultures and artistic minority. For this, he used two of his greatest, indeed almost only, tools: conversation and the telephone. He was very proud of having looked for new territories and new languages, and always said he had never felt comfortable with accepting his original cultural context. As such, he had decided to look for new ones. He sought new experiences of life, language and culture, because he always considered all these must be regarded as a unity. Languages were his real territories, more real than a physical place in which to live. He believed above all in the value of the spoken word, in the richness of verbal communication, and in the unstable, fluid and dynamic nature of the written artefact.

Hutchinson's contacts with southern Europe started during his holiday in Spain and Portugal in 1950. They would be intensified later, when he lived in Barcelona (from 1954), but at that time the poet was already very interested in discovering new cultures and new landscapes. In fact, his interest in discovering other identities and other worlds and, of course, in interpreting other languages, can be acknowledged when he registered to study Italian and Spanish (Castilian, as he often said) at University College Dublin in 1947. Hutchinson explained in detail in a radio interview, and especially in the above-mentioned introduction to *Done into English*, how much he wanted to cross borders and imbibe other lights and other flavours. Galicia would remain forever in his memory, and also Portugal, a lesser-known, though an extremely powerful and rich geographical connection he cultivated, which Vincent Woods has researched.[14] Catalonia is a constant presence in the work of Hutchinson, to the point that the Catalan flag was always on the wall of his bedroom at Findrum (together with a map of Galicia). This chapter, however, does not address his many links with Catalonia: his relationship with Catalonia has been studied extensively and disseminated in some detail by numerous translators, poets and other cultural figures with whom he had dealt. And, of course, it was disseminated, directly or indirectly, by Hutchinson himself.

Hutchinson and Scotland

It may be that Hutchinson's connections with his native country, Scotland, have not been so widely examined so far: perhaps they have been considered too obvious, given it was where he was born.[15] He was a man who could not understand poetry without friendship, and developed important relationships with Scottish poets, especially Iain Crichton Smith. His Scottish background can be detected not just in his writings or his opinions about a great variety of issues, but in very minute and particular aspects, throughout his work, particularly with regard to the vernacular language: undoubtedly Scotland permanently seeped into his expressions, language and references.

Among the different Scottish elements often present in his writings, his evocative sound of Scottish Gaelic terms and the music behind his words emerge as the most significant ones. Of course, at different times of his life, Hutchinson tried to keep in touch with his literary counterparts in Scotland. Hugh MacDiarmid was one of those prominent figures he was profoundly interested in.[16] According to Wes Davis,[17] Maurice Lindsay, the poet and broadcaster, gave him, while still a young man, MacDiarmid's Glasgow address and he became influenced by the man widely seen as responsible for the revival of Scottish vernacular poetry. Besides MacDiarmid, he had some kind of relationship with other Scottish writers, such as the Gaelic poet Sorley MacLean and the folklorist and poet Hamish Henderson. Eiléan Ní Chuilleanáin, who co-edited *Cyphers* with Hutchinson, confirms his permanent interest in the language and culture of his native Scotland: 'Scottish writing in both Scots Gaelic and the Lowland dialect of English was most important to Pearse. I would point to various references, for example the poem 'Pibroch' about the Highland clearances',[18] writes Ni Chuilleanàin. 'Pibroch', the last poem from the collection *The Frost is All Over* (1975), is a well-known and moving poem about a Scottish coffin-ship[19] and a piper who has no money to pay for his passage.

The importance of names is always current in Hutchinson's work. The sense of place (often defined as the need to preserve the name of places in their original language in order to transmit authenticity) is a constant also in modern Irish literature, from Brian Friel to Seamus Heaney. The replacement of original place-names has been considered a common colonial practice, a symbol of cultural domination, which contributed to the depersonalisation of local geographies, eliminating memories and sense of place, often provided by the original language. Such a deprivation he considered painful indeed, because geographical names include many elements, both linguistic and emotional, contributing to the construction of local identity. Hutchinson summed this idea up in just one famous line of poetry from *The Frost is All Over*: 'To kill a language is to kill a people'.[20] Seán Hutton also talks about the cultural domination exerted by linguistic imposition, and about the impact of original place names in Hutchinson:[21]

> Cultural and linguistic oppression also find a place in his poetry. The enforced changing of personal and place names inspire 'She

Made her False Name Real' – based on the forced conversions of Jews in Majorca, under the Inquisition – and 'Affection' – in which an Irish place name complains that 'the ignorant invaders [call] me out of my name / their tongues bloated with conquest' and that 'the hands of music | [are] cut off in sport'. His splendid poem 'Achnasheen' reflects on a Scottish place-name:

> How could there be any Gaelic 'for' Achnasheen?
> It isn't Gaelic any more. It could never be English.
>   Despite the murderous maps,
>   despite the bereft roadsigns,
>   despite the casual distortions of illiterate scribes,
>   the name remains beautiful. A maimed beauty.
>   Hiding behind it somewhere
>   its real name [...]
> and on the possibility of,
>   a heaven of freedom to give
>   things back
>   their true names ...
>   Like streets in Barcelona,
>   like Achnasheen,
>   Belfast.

Unquestionably, the word 'Achnasheen' encapsulates a fascinating ancestral sound and an original Gaelic place-name. As a result, we might conclude that it operates here as a kind of identity icon in Pearse Hutchinson's poetry. This is not least the case if we consider what Benjamin Keatinge (2011: 156) writes about the poem:

> You cannot separate language and name from the cultural specifics and regional traditions they are imbued with [...]. Language, landscape and nationhood are intertwined. These questions of identity are, of course, widespread in Irish literature. Hutchinson's poem 'Achnasheen' (from *The Frost is All Over*, 1975) expresses the same

> sentiments as Seamus Heaney's more famous poem 'Anahorish' [...] where the fascination of place names is foregrounded [...]. Hutchinson appeals, like Heaney, for 'a heaven of freedom to give | things back | their true names' [...]. But in many cases the old names survive, if not on maps then in the cultural memory of local people [...].[22]

Eiléan Ní Chuilleanáin also mentions this poem on different occasions, most notably when referring to Hutchinson's defence of so-called minority languages. She describes 'Achnasheen' as a poem containing 'language trapped in history, mangled and silenced'.[23] For the poet Michael O'Dea ('Achnasheen' indeed, a corruption of the Gaelic) is 'a pleasing connection with [Hutchinson's] poetry'.[24]

On 23 August 2000, in one of several unpublished conversations Hutchinson had with the Galician writer and researcher Emilio Araúxo,[25] there are some revealing moments about when the Scottish world enters directly into his poetry, usually encapsulated in particular expressions or even unexpected words. Hutchinson was always very interested in Celso Emilio Ferreiro, the celebrated Galician poet included in Hutchinson's translation anthology, *Done into English*. Referring to his poem 'Galician Folk Songs' from the collection *The Frost is all Over*, a poem dedicated to Celso Emilio Ferreiro, Hutchinson observes that, in failing to find sufficiently appropriate rhyming vocabulary in English, he turned to Scots and wrote the third part of the poem in Scots ('Scottish from the south', he says) 'The rhyme I refer to', transcribes Emilio Araúxo, 'is among *eat* and *greet*, which is *cry* in Scots'. Hutchinson moved from one language to another as if all of them were parts of the same whole.

> Ma mither is sae puir
> We hae nae breid tae eat:
> She staps ma face wi kisses,
> And syne she starts tae greet.[26]

Something similar happens in the 'Connemara' poem, from *Watching the Morning Grow* (p. 36). Humorously enough, Hutchinson explained to Araúxo that in line thirty-three he used the Scottish word *rumplefyke* (anal itching) to make fun of himself (followed by a line containing the commercial name of three drugs). Hutchinson argues that laughing at oneself is always very healthy, especially for a poet.

If Scotland was a constant presence in Hutchinson's poetry throughout his life, Wales was also given some prominence. As an enthusiastic promoter and defender of all languages which had been restricted to their domestic boundaries by historical circumstances (or simply political reasons), Hutchinson considered Welsh ideal territory for his permanent linguistic vindication of minorities. Menna Elfyn, one of the most prominent figures in Welsh letters, was in close contact with Hutchinson during the last years of his life. When I questioned her about Hutchinson's interests in Welsh literature and about how they had met up for the first time, she responded in a particular emotional way:

> Oh, whenever the name Pearse is mentioned my heart beats a little faster – and also I have a twinge of feeling so utterly useless as a friend. We first met in Edinburgh when as you rightly mentioned we took part in a Celtic braiding of Ian Crichton Smith, Pearse and myself. He and I hit it off immediately and spent the rest of the evening discussing politics and language (he was very enthusiastic about my activist past as I'd twice been imprisoned for non-violent language campaigns for the Welsh language).[27]

Undoubtedly, Hutchinson was unable to conceive poetry, or literature, without taking into account friendship and cultural commitment.

Far from being only a poet, Hutchinson was most active in disseminating the cultures with which he was deeply involved in many different ways. For many years, he was related to professionals of the media (namely, from RTÉ), and could be considered a journalist himself for more than, perhaps, forty-five years (mostly as a radio broadcaster and a newspaper columnist). As is well-known, he presented an excellent cultural programme, *Óró Domhnaigh*,[28] on RTÉ for a couple of seasons (1977–78) of which unfortunately only two complete recordings survive on file.[29] Vincent Woods has written in detail about this experience which, of course, he shared, in an essay included in *Reading Pearse Hutchinson: From Findrum to Fisterra*. One achieves, after reading several of the programme's scripts provided by Woods (who also reproduces some excerpts in his essay), a remarkable perspective on Hutchinson's musical and literary interests. The programme comprises a fascinating journey through Hutchinson's artistic preferences, and an impressive way to learn more about his personality. One instance, for example, is an excerpt from the script where Hutchinson refers to Scots Gaelic songs and makes a brief commentary to illustrate the beautiful song 'Eleanor Plunkett', performed by Clannad:

> Here Clannad sing a lively song in Scots Gaelic, to which their own Donegal Irish is perhaps closer than any other brand of Irish. The tune inspires an adventurous insertion of a rock passage, unusual in Irish traditional groups. Eleanor Plunkett is a beautiful, wistful tune, authentic Ceol na nUasal, and it is superbly played here on the harp and tin-whistle.[30]

Though Pearse Hutchinson celebrated traditional Irish music all his life, and, for example, loved Sean O'Riada's early performances at the Gaiety, and met him personally, he was also very fond of the Scottish musical tradition. It was a common thing for him to play *sean-nós* music from Scotland and Wales on his radio show, *Óró Domhnaigh*. According to Woods, 'There was a Scottish singer, Jeannie Robertson, Pearse loved her singing [...] and another wonderful Scottish singer-woman called Jean Redpath, he would play over and over and over once when he found her voice [...]'[31] For Eiléan Ní Chuilleanáin, there is also a very interesting and significant social element in Hutchinson's musical preferences, namely when he refers to traditional music:

> In Ireland traditional music has often been preserved by poor people, in poor areas of the country, where it has been closely associated with the Gaelic language. The great singer Darach Ó Catháin whom he knew in Leeds had emigrated and worked as a labourer.

And in Scotland *whose history was so important to him* [my emphasis] the Gaelic language and music belonged to the defeated Jacobites.[32]

Hutchinson and Iberia

Though always friendly, familiar and affectionate, Hutchinson was said not to be particularly fond of interviews. Or, at least, he was not very fond of formal interviews, so to speak. (Apparently, he didn't like his photograph to be taken either).[33] But he loved conversation. No doubt, his literature goes far beyond the printed letter: his is also oral literature and, unfortunately, ephemeral. Extraordinarily keen on cultural exchange and political analysis, he, above all, practiced with great skill the art of establishing fascinating linguistic connections between the different cultures he was so committed to. According to friends and colleagues, when he was invited to talk, Hutchinson always preferred to follow an adventurous meandering conversational track, consisting mostly of long monologues, a combination of ideas, anecdotes and memories crossing from one place to another in a rather chaotic movement. The exception, of course, was when he was translating poetry: then he could not stand lack of precision. There are several interviews, long or short, published in different journals and newspapers that constitute good research material. Among them, the most interesting and comprehensive is the long conversation with Philip Coleman included in *Reading Pearse Hutchinson: From Findrum to Fisterra*.[34] There are more written interviews besides this (together with his well-known radio appearances), most of them brief, fragmentary, but always interesting: Hutchinson's discourse was manifold, and used to talking in a very spontaneous and natural way about almost everything.[35] He could spend hours at home or in a pub, talking with friends, researchers or translators, and even with people he had not met before. The only condition, one might say, was maintaining a natural communicative process, if possible over some drink. He also became famous with those who experienced his long telephone conversations: it is interesting to know that the telephone has a major presence in Hutchinson's poems, because he used it as a powerful tool to keep constantly in touch with his many friends in different countries, and also as a means to correct and improve his translations, working in conversation with the authors themselves over the phone.

After Hutchinson's death on 14 January 2012, my research moved towards the more personal and intimate side of the poet's life in Iberia, fundamental to understanding his literary work, almost from the beginning of his adult life. It is not easy, however, to keep detailed track of Hutchinson's life in Spain. Paradoxically, more than the written word, the spoken word was his favourite territory, the context in which he made things happen. Undoubtedly, Hutchinson, in the most difficult years of his life in Dublin, found in other languages new possibilities of expression. We can read some of his ideas about the relevance he attributed to minority languages in the brief introduction he wrote for *Done into English*, a seminal book which, as already mentioned, includes a wide selection of his translations from different languages and dialects into English. He later observed that he had found liberation in Irish:

> As I wrote in the poem 'Leathfhírinne' (Half-Truth),
>
>> Clear to me – sudden miracle –
>> our forebears didn't eat stars;
>> nor were they the saints those false apostles fancied,
>> nor the madmen you'd think from feigned madness.
>
> In other words, Gaelic too was the real world, a liberating world, mine.[36]

He had found he could express in Irish part of his spirit, which he had been unable to express in English for years. Castilian, as he preferred to call it, instead of Spanish, together with Catalan, Galician and Portuguese, are also fundamental languages to understanding Hutchinson's poetry, because he used language not just from the technical point of view, as part of his profession of translator, but also as a sentimental access to the nature of minority cultures. For him everything was contained in the essence of words, and he was conscious that it was necessary for a poet, and also for a translator, to understand poetry in the original language, to hear the original music and to convey this music to the reader in a foreign language. For him there were several translations for a single poem, and all of these could be correct. Not only was he a brilliant translator from all those languages, but also these languages tinged and gave flavour and colour to his own verse.

At this stage, despite the publication of *Reading Pearse Hutchinson: From Findrum to Fisterra*, it is clear that Hutchinson has not received the close and enthusiastic attention he deserves. This is an idea consistently expressed by many of his colleagues and friends, among them the Galician poet and lecturer at University College Cork, Martin Veiga. Maybe the nature of Hutchinson's work and poetic production makes him somewhat elusive on occasions. Fortunately, the Pearse Hutchinson Archive at NUI Maynooth will shortly reveal new and interesting materials and will become a fundamental resource for future research.[37]

The fact that Hutchinson deserved more attention in Iberia, made me look for his literary connections, specifically in Galicia. All those I contacted were delighted and enthusiastic to talk about him. In their remembering him, it was easy to detect a kind of spiritual communion among the people who knew him well. Many of those intellectuals who produced some kind of criticism on Hutchinson, or translated part of his poetry in the latter years of his life, met him in Dublin, at Findrum, a house which became a kind of a mystic place. There, he used to greet visitors from anywhere and sustain long conversations with them.[38]

Hutchinson discovered Galicia during his first trip to Lisbon in 1950, aged 23, and later continued towards Andalusia, accompanied by Bert Achong. There is a broad description of these first impressions, unsurprisingly fragmentary, collected by Vincent Woods in an essay, mentioned above, about the experience of Hutchinson in Lisbon and his relationship with Portuguese literature and culture. Also in the introduction of *Done into English*, as previously noted, the poet speaks of his first voyage to Vigo, aboard the *Highland Mail*, where he discovered many Galician emigrants preparing to embark for South America. This Hutchinson found very similar to an American wake and seems in particular to be one of those moments of epiphany, so to speak, that marked the beginning of the idyll between

Hutchinson and Galicia. Vincent Woods reflects on the contents of a letter Hutchinson sent to his mother, written when leaving Vigo in 1950, and is very pleased that such letters have been preserved and can be found among the legacy of the poet:

> Hutchinson and Bert Achong spent just two days in Lisbon before travelling on to Andalusia. We may thank his mother, Caitlin Hutchinson (or MacElhinney as she was before she married Pearse's father, Henry Warren Hutchinson) for preserving so many, (perhaps all) of the letters he sent back to the family in Dublin from his travels abroad. In this instance one letter give us some small insight into that first journey to Portugal in April 1950. This letter I found about three months ago among Pearse Hutchinson's papers while compiling what will in time be a remarkable family archive, and national treasure – the Hutchinson archive of literary and political material:
>
> Leaving Vigo,
Tuesday, 29 August 1950
>
> A athair 's a mháitrín díl,
> I hope you weren't too alarmed by the sudden idea I took in London of going to Lisbon instead of Paris. It all happened very suddenly. […] I saw a big poster advertising a very cheap trip by ship from Tilbury dock – leaving that (Sat) morning at 11 o' clock – to Rio de Janeiro, via Vigo, Lisbon, Las Palmas, Buenos Aires, and Montevideo. It occurred to me then that to boat as far as Portugal, and to go by bus or train from there into Spain would be an original and wonderful idea […][39]

In the same essay, Woods points out that what we know about the experience of Hutchinson in Lisbon is mainly reflected in the different recordings he made in the last three years of his life, which mostly included memories of his trips.[40]

While the influence of the Iberian landscape is decisive in his poetry, as Martín Veiga puts it, 'His fascination with Iberia starts with a genuine love for the place and a close identification with the landscape'.[41] Galicia enters Hutchinson's literary life through a Portuguese edition of the so-called *Cantigas de amigo*, particularly, according to Vincent Woods, the poems by Martin Códax included in this volume.[42] Hutchinson speaks of his first literary relationship with Galicia through medieval literature in an important and revealing interview with David McLoghlin (focused almost exclusively on his vision of Galician culture and political position), published in 2013 in *Cyphers*.[43] Then, the poet discovered some revealing figures of Galician culture in whom he immediately became interested. This is the case of Uxío Novoneyra, a Galician poet from the Courel Mountains (on the border between León and Lugo) a poet very much linked to his native land. Pearse came across him because he happened to read one of his poems, 'Moucho' ('The Owl', which, of course, he translated), in *Claraboya*, a local magazine published in León at the time.

Catalonia has been, so far, better represented than Galicia in Hutchinson's biography, most probably because he lived there for some time, and because it had important literary and personal connections for the poet. Of course, he was very much aware of Galician culture from his own readings. He knew about the most relevant local writers, about local politics, about Galician history. He accumulated a wide knowledge of Galicia, but he always wanted to know more. This is the reason I find the conversations he sustained with Emilio Araúxo so revealing. While the current representation of Hutchinson's work translated into Castilian may be considered inferior to what the writer deserves, Araúxo placed Hutchinson on the map with regard to poetry translated into Galician. Similarly, Hutchinson contributed extraordinarily towards improving an understanding of the Galician world abroad. For example, thanks to Hutchinson's efforts, Galician poetry, including work by Araúxo and other contemporary poets, began to appear in English, especially in *Cyphers*. Later, in 2003, as has been highlighted, Hutchinson published an anthology of poetry from different European cultures and 'minor' languages, *Done into English*, where the names of Curros Enríquez, Celso Emilio Ferreiro and Uxío Novoneyra, among others, appeared. Emilio Araúxo, who became a close friend of Hutchinson, introduced the poet through his various publications on these themes. Notably, these include the aforementioned *Lenda*, a small publication from 2004, now out of print, and, of course, the outstanding issue number 11 of *Amastra-n-gallar*, devoted almost entirely to the poet. There are other occasions in which Hutchinson's work appears briefly in Araúxo's publications (e.g. *Amastra-n-gallar*, no. 9), where the Galician translation of 'From one lover to another', a poem from *Expansions*, is included.

However, perhaps the most important part of the intense literary relationship between Araúxo and Hutchinson still remains unpublished. Through long conversations, Araúxo collected many handwritten notes which would eventually contribute to complete the picture of Hutchinson's cultural, political and, above all, literary affinities and interests. Arguably, it is impossible fully to understand Hutchinson's poetry without taking into account the poet's relevant commentaries collected *viva voce* by Araúxo, who met Hutchinson for the first time in 1987, when he was looking for an Irish poet to be included in his book *Do lado dos ollos* (see note 33). There he interviewed seventy-nine poets from around the world, translated, of course, into Galician. This first conversation, the prelude of a long and deep friendship, took place, as was often the case with Hutchinson, over the phone. The content of this brief interview, referred to earlier, provides some of Hutchinson's poetics' key themes. From the beginning, Araúxo was astonished at the vast range of knowledge Pearse Hutchinson displayed about almost every aspect concerning Spain, not only in the literary field, but, perhaps even more, in the political sphere. Evidently, his years in Catalonia had contributed to this knowledge, but the incredible thing, on which Araúxo insists, was the impressive amount of information he had of even the most contemporary issues. In his almost daily conversations with Araúxo, Hutchinson displayed passion for Galicia and for many Galician poets. In 2000, for example, there are several observations of Hutchinson around Castelao, one of his Galician favourites:

> Then, he tells me about his emotional reading of Castelao's letter 'To The Irish Patriots', especially when referring to the Mayor of Cork.

He was unable to stop his tears when reading the letter. For Pearse, Cork is a city with a 'Mediterranean' environment, with 'extraordinary' people. Then, he talks about the visit he made these days to an old friend, a poet and publisher who lives in Northern Ireland, Robert Welch. During the meeting between the two friends, Pearse showed him the paintings of the famous album by Castelao, *Nós*, and Robert Welch had to dry his glasses several times, because his tears fell with emotion. 'He's a very sensitive man'. Above all, they become much excited about the picture that mentions Ireland: 'Irlanda, levántate y anda'. […] He pointed out, moreover, that as Robert Welch has a small publishing house, he, Pearse, intends to publish in it a 'pamphlet' about Castelao. Finally, he wonders if Galicia always showed attention and affection for Ireland.[44]

Hutchinson often talked about different aspects of Galician culture and history. He was able to name various Galician poets and their respective works in nothing but a few lines, and, from time to time, introduced comments on his well-known passion for finding links or coincidences between languages:

'I like a lot *Os dous de sempre* (Castelao)', he points out. Then, he refers to the [Galician sur]name *Búa*.[45] He tells me that the Irish word '*bua*' means 'victory'. He adds: 'I like these little coincidences of language. Maybe I am, like Joyce, a Dubliner.' He says that Bloomsday is going to be celebrated on the 16th. Pearse is invited to recite poems for the occasion, and he is thinking of reading one by Uxío Novoneyra. He has not decided whether it will be in Irish or in bilingual form. He adds that he agrees with [José Núñez] Búa when he states that 'Castelao is a master of Galician prose'. And he wonders if Castelao looks great in any artistic field. He thinks so. He is amazed that, for example, through the 'masterful polemic prose' he uses in *Sempre en Galiza,* Castelao inserts a lyrical remark, saying: 'Long live lyricism!' Then, he elaborates on the alleged lack of an epic poem in Galicia. 'Pondal is not my style … as Rosalia or Curros.

> I like Curros [Enríquez] very much.' And he ends [the conversation] by reiterating that it is admirable that Castelao makes a 'defense of lyricism in the heart of a book of prose-epic'.[46]

From the conversations with Emilio Araúxo we realise that Hutchinson's knowledge of Galicia (and Spain) was most impressive. He was able to quote the Galician classics in detail, starting from medieval times, but also its contemporaries. He had read Galician prose and poetry extensively, and was able to identify any author's key concepts or political ideas. In these transcriptions, he also talks about Blanco Amor, and, of course, he refers repeatedly to Uxío Novoneyra, absolutely central to his conception of Galicia and the Galician landscape, and, to some extent, the author who was responsible for his attraction to Galician culture. Araúxo sent a copy of *Os Eidos* to Hutchinson who read the book for him that night with great emotion. Many other issues concerning politics, ideology, identity, and literature, both past and present, in relation to Galicia, but also to Ireland, Scotland and Europe in general, appeared in these conversations, and on occasions Hutchinson talks in a very personal and direct way about some of his contemporaries.

To conclude, it is of fundamental importance to recognise the relevance of Hutchinson's knowledge and awareness of a wide variety of European cultures. He is, no doubt, a poet without boundaries, who, at the same time, is highly conscious (and very proud) of local identities. He understands culture as a continuum which is reflected in the fluid and often interchangeable nature of languages, which for him constitute the real tool and the real essence of cultural exchange. Hutchinson believed, above all, in friendship, and he was incapable of understanding literature, or poetry, without the human elements which are essential to its nature. His interests ranged across all aspects of life and were not limited to the strictly artistic. From his writings and direct testimonies from friends and colleagues, we can conclude that Hutchinson considered himself a part of Iberian cultures, mostly from the emotional point of view. Catalonia and Galicia are fundamental to an understanding of his literature, but also of his way of life. He constructed his poetry with very noble materials, such as cultural diversity, freedom, dignity, friendship, love and endearment. And, of course, Scotland was always present, as a fundamental part of his literature, with the sound of her music, the echo of her native words, and the influence of her poets, providing a constant and valuable perspective to his fascinating and seductive interpretation of the world.

Acknowledgements

This chapter has been possible thanks to the Research network *Rede de investigación de Lingua e Literatura inglesa e Identidade II* (E2014/043), funded by the Galician Government. This grant is hereby gratefully acknowledged.

The chapter is, in fact, the first step of a larger project, which aims to investigate in depth the literary, social and cultural relationship Pearse Hutchinson established with some areas of northern Spain, notably Galicia. It also provides an overview of some most remarkable Scottish interests (Pearse Hutchinson, despite his powerful literary and personal ties with Ireland, was born in Glasgow). Hutchinson's work covers so many areas and so many fields that it is hard to deal with it without omitting some relevant issues. Actually, it seems that he was interested in almost everything around him until the end of his life. To write this chapter, and also for the rest of the project on the poet, I have enjoyed the generous contributions of many people who knew him well. I have not used many academic sources, nor many critical studies, among other things because they are not especially abundant, at least not before his death. I want to express my very special gratitude for his great contribution to Emilio Araúxo, for providing me with extremely valuable information derived from his transcripts, unpublished until now, of several conversations he maintained with Pearse Hutchinson. To understand Hutchinson's relationship with Galicia, this material must be regarded, I would argue, as absolutely essential, and will constitute a fundamental tool for our further research about the poet. There are also valuable contributions from Vincent Woods, who knew him deeply and worked with him in Dublin. At the time of writing this chapter Woods was organising and digitising the poet's unpublished writings and the rest of his literary legacy. This will be preserved as the Pearse Hutchinson Archive at

NUI Maynooth. Along with Vincent Woods, I must thank the poet and professor Eiléan Ní Chuilleanáin, joint editor (along with Pearse) of the magazine *Cyphers*, who also helped me understand Pearse Hutchinson's literary and human personality. I shall not forget the poet Michael Augustin, Radio Bremen broadcaster, who was always willing to provide information about the poet, whom he knew very well. Also I want to thank for their feedback, direct or indirect, Coleman and Mary Johnson, editors of *Reading Pearse Hutchinson, From Findrum to Fisterra*, probably the most elaborated and rigorous academic book on Hutchinson published so far. From the very first, the indications and translations provided by Professor Jorge Sagastume revealed quite interesting and groundbreaking information to me. And of course, poet and UCC lecturer in Galician Studies Martin Veiga cleared the way to Hutchinson's Galician influences and sources. Finally, I want to thank José Luis Prieto-Montero, who has completed a brilliant doctoral thesis on the relationship between Hutchinson and music, under my supervision. Prieto-Montero, as a result of his research, provided me with some valuable information about Hutchinson's life and work. Without all of them this research would not have been possible.

Notes

1. Pearse Hutchinson, 'Declaracións', *Lenda*, ed. Emilio Araúxo (Santiago de Compostela: Cadernos Amastra-n-gallar, 2004), p. 21.
2. Hayden Murphy, 'Pearse Hutchinson', *The Herald*, 19 January 2012, www.heraldscotland.com/comment/obituaries/pearse-hutchinson.16504339 [accessed 12 August 2013]
3. Michael Augustin, e-mail to the author, 22 June 2012.
4. Peter Sirr, 'The freshness of what happens', *The Irish Times* (20 August 2011), www.irishtimes.com/culture/books/the-freshness-of-what-happens-1.602841
5. Philip Coleman and Maria Johnston (eds), *Reading Pearse Hutchinson: From Findrum to Fisterra* (Dublin: Irish Academic Press, 2011).
6. Robert A Welch, 'The Solar Energy of Pearse Hutchinson' in ibid., p. 23.
7. Vincent Woods, 'Jasmine and Lagarto: Pearse Hutchinson's Poetry of Spain', *Estudios Irlandeses*, 5 (2010), p. 118.
8. Pearse Hutchinson, *Done into English: Collected Translations* (Oldcastle: The Gallery Press, 2003).
9. Jose Luis Prieto-Montero has been doing extensive research on Hutchinson in the last few years. He has just presented his Dissertation (full text is now available at ruc.udc.es/bitstream/2183/15771/2/PrietoMontero_JoseLuis_TD_2015.pdf) on the relation between Hutchinson and music, entitled *Galicia, Irlanda y el impacto de la música tradicional en la poesía de Pearse Huchinson*. Music was a substantial part of Hutchinson's life. He was

interested in traditional music from Scotland, Ireland and Galicia, among others, as can be detected in many of his poems. Music also influenced his literary style.
10 Murphy, 'Pearse Hutchinson'.
11 'In one of the conversations of Hutchinson and Emilio Araúxo, namely one of 23 August 2000 (conversations that we use as a direct testimony of Hutchinson's interpretation of art and life in the final part of this essay), Hutchinson refers to what he considered 'the ridiculous issue of canonical literature'. (Emilio Araúxo, e-mail to the author, 20 December 2013).
12 Philip Coleman, 'At Ease with Elsewhere', *Dublin Review of Books*, 11 (Autumn, 2009) www.drb.ie/essays/at-ease-with-elsewhere [accessed 12 November 2013].
13 Jahan Ramazani, 'A Transnational Poetics', *American Literary History*, 18.2 (Summer, 2006), p. 355.
14 Paper presented by Vincent Woods, Irish Studies Seminar, University of Porto, September, 2011. This manuscript has been kindly provided by the author.
15 There is, to be sure, plenty of information about Hutchinson's personal ties with Scotland in the documents which constitute his legacy, now under the protection of NUI Maynooth.
16 According to *The Oxford Companion to Modern Poetry in English*, ed. by Jeremy Noel-Tod and Ian Hamilton, 2nd ed. (Oxford: OUP, 2013), p. 285: 'Hugh MacDiarmid was an important exemplar for Hutchinson's writing, which brings socialist and nationalist politics to a concern with language as the site of beauty and violence'.
17 'Pearse Hutchinson remembers Maurice Lindsay's *Modern Scottish Poetry: An Anthology of the Scottish Renaissance, 1920–1945* as one of the first books he ever bought first-hand. [...] [B]ut it was through another scrap of writing that Lindsay may have had greater effect on Hutchinson's life as a poet. In 1948 Lindsay gave the young Hutchinson the Glasgow address of Hugh MacDiarmid. Having worked up his "partly Dutch courage", Hutchinson made a pilgrimage to see the most influential poet in Scotland. What he discovered in MacDiarmid's presence was a form of courage that did not require a bottle: "I was, like others of my generation, in full flight from the far-from-hidden Ireland of sexual repression, with which I mistakenly, though understandably, identified Irish nationalism. [...] Meeting MacDiarmid at that point, listening to his talk of my country and his, was one of the things that helped me to come to terms with Ireland"' (*Leonard L. Milberg Collection of Irish Poetry*, compiled by J. Howard Woolmer, with essays by Wes Davis, ed. by L. Logan and Patricia H. Marks (Princeton: Princeton University Library, 1998). Quoted from *Amastra-n-gallar*, 11 (Winter, 2006), pp. 25–28. This issue was almost entirely devoted to Hutchinson and edited by Emilio Araúxo.
18 Eiléan Ní Chuilleanáin, e-mail to the author. 22 December 2013.
19 Hutchinson often includes in his books explanations and notes about his own poems; about this one in particular, he writes: 'In July, two hundred people of Ross, thirty-three families and twenty-five single men, boarded the Hector at Ullapool on Loch Broom. The ship was so rotten that the emigrants were able to pick away its timbers with their fingernails ... The people left in good spirits, and when the piper was ordered ashore because he had no money to pay for his passage "they pleaded to have him allowed to accompany them, and offered to share their rations with him in exchange for his music... In New Scotia they went ashore behind the piper, wearing the tartan that was still under proscription in Scotland (John Prebble: *The Highland Clearances*, Penguin)".' Cit. by Pearse Hutchinson, *The Frost is All Over* (Dublin: The Gallery Books, 1975), p. 47.

20 *The Frost is All Over*, p. 42.
21 Séan Hutton, 'Parables of Franciscan complexity: Notes on aspects of Pearse Hutchinson's poetry', *Armastra-n-gallar*, 11 (Winter, 2006), p. 56.
22 Benjamin Keatinge, 'The Long-Banned Speech We Talked In: Pearse Hutchinson and Minority Voices', in Coleman and Johnston (eds), *Reading Pearse Hutchinson*, p. 156.
23 Eiléan Ní Chuilleanáin, 'Pearse Hutchinson in five decades', *Amastra-n-gallar*, 11, p. 77.
24 Michael O'Dea, 'As Good as Bread', *Amastra-n-gallar*, 11, p. 82.
25 Some of these unpublished conversations, kindly provided by Emilio Araúxo, are used here for research purposes for the first time. Most of them refer to Hutchinson's ideas about Galicia and Galician poetry, but there are also many reflections of Hutchinson's ideas about politics, minority languages, and literature in general. In my view, the transcriptions of these conversations, when completed, will offer new insights on Hutchinson's human and artistic perspectives, above all those referring to Galicia and Galician culture.
26 'Galician Folk Songs', *The Frost is All Over*, p. 29.
27 Menna Elfyn, e-mail to the author. 3 January 2014. The passage quoted comes from the following longer text:

> Oh, whenever the name Pearse is mentioned my heart beats a little faster – and also I have a twinge of feeling so utterly useless as a friend. We first met in Edinburgh when as you rightly mentioned we took part in a Celtic braiding of Ian Crichton Smith, Pearse and myself. He and I hit it off immediately and spent the rest of the evening discussing politics and language (he was very enthusiastic about my activist past as I'd twice been imprisoned for non-violent language campaigns for the Welsh language). Anyway, I did promise to try and bring him to Wales but at that time I was always 'elsewhere' and not in a position to arrange much of anything – my own life being chaotic as well with the travelling which hasn't really stopped. But we wrote once or twice to one another and now and again people would contact me as Pearse told them if they go to Wales then they would have to meet me! Bless him. It's how I got to meet Michael Augustin although I'd read with Sujatta Bhatt at another literary festival. Well, anyway, the last letter or so I wrote to Pearse and I'm not sure when that would have been – I got no reply and was told that his correspondence was passed on to him in his local pub. Well perhaps he never got it. He did send me a review, a glowing one he had done of one of my books […]. We did meet again around 2002 at a festival in Dublin and once again rekindled our friendship and he was over the moon at my being there and meeting again. Once again I mentioned that perhaps he could come to Wales some time but I could see too that he wasn't in a fit state to travel that far. In fact, I helped to take him to his room that evening. So that's it, I'm afraid. I did start writing a poem full of shame at having done so little to a person who thought of me as a friend and indeed I was and still am. The trouble with poetry is that one spends so much time away now – at readings so that it becomes increasingly difficult to keep in touch to those who mean so much to us. I still dip into his poetry now and again and feel I am back there with this wonderful, delightful man who was so sensitive and yet so bold too. The evening we walked the city in Edinburgh he was

offended by some remarks made to him by a couple of men – so we spent the rest of the evening with me trying to reassure him and untangle his hurt.

28 According to Vincent Woods, 'Óró Domhnaigh: Pearse Hutchinson as Journalist, Broadcaster and Critic', in Coleman and Johnston (eds), *Reading Pearse Hutchinson*, pp. 93–212, this programme, technically elaborated by producer Tony McMahon (and later by some others, such as Harry Bradshaw), basically consisted of a combination of music and selected texts read by Hutchinson. I had the opportunity of reading a small part of the programme scripts: they provide us with a complete picture of this cultural project to which Hutchinson was deeply committed.
29 According to Woods (*op. cit.*, p. 198), 'of some 104 programmes recorded and broadcast in the series it appears that only two of the original recordings have survived intact in the RTÉ radio archive: the first programme of *Óró Domhnaigh*, recorded on 22 December 1976 and transmitted on 2 January 1977, and a programme recorded on 15 April 1978 and transmitted on 16 April 1978'.
30 *Óró Domhnaigh*. Excerpt from the original script. Undated. Provided by Vincent Woods.
31 Vincent Woods: a conversation with José Luis Prieto-Montero. 28 October 2013. This transcription has been provided by Prieto-Montero.
32 Eiléan Ní Chuilleanáin, e-mail to José Luis Prieto-Montero. 17 November 2013.
33 Emilio Araúxo writes about this: 'The only phobia Pearse had, as far as I know, was photography. He did not like being photographed. I don't know why, and I don't think I ever asked him the reasons for this reluctance. I do not think it was, let's say, for "coquetry". There was a resistance that must have unconscious roots. And it was a pity, because of all the poets I knew, he was one of the most, shall we say, "photogenic". But you knew that he felt very uncomfortable when the camera appeared before him. Interestingly, when you sent him the pictures, not only did he reconcile with them, but even experimented a kind of "narcissistic" endearment with the image'. (E-mail to the author, 17 January 2014. My translation).
34 Philip Coleman, 'From Findrum: Pearse Hutchinson in Conversation', in Coleman and Johnston (eds), *Reading Pearse Hutchinson*, pp. 213–236.
35 Hutchinson's loquacity occurred in spontaneous conversation, as Galician writer Emilio Araúxo has often pointed out. In his travels to Ireland, Araúxo took many notes during his informal conversations with Hutchinson. He also interviewed him, briefly, for a Galician publication about poetry from different parts of the world: *Do lado dos ollos, arredor da poesía, entrevistas con 79 poetas do mundo* (Vigo: Ediciáns do Cumio, 2001), pp. 165–66. From time to time, Araúxo also included in the books he edited brief excerpts of his conversations with Hutchinson (see *Lenda*, pp. 21–23).
36 Hutchinson, *The Soul that Kissed the Body* (Oldcastle: The Gallery Press, 1990), p. 15.
37 On 27 March 2014, The Gallery Press published a posthumous collection by Hutchinson, *Listening to Bach*.
38 One of those who visited Hutchinson in Dublin in his last years was Professor Jorge Sagastume, director of the Spanish branch of Dickinson College, who started a very close relation with Hutchinson and talked so often with him that they even maintained a conversation the day before Hutchinson's death. Jorge Sagastume started to translate Hutchinson's poems and published them in an academic journal edited by Johns Hopkins University, *Sirena, Poetry and art and criticism* (Issue 2010:1; it also contains

some academic essays on Hutchinson's poetry, written by Sagastume and others). He then compiled these translations in a book, *Distorsiones: Selección poética*, trans. Jorge Sagastume (Buenos Aires: Ediciones Al Margen, 2010). The other writer and researcher, who emerges as a key figure to understanding Hutchinson's relationship with Galicia, is the aforementioned Emilio Araúxo (born Coles, Galicia, 1946). Araúxo met Hutchinson in Ireland, not Galicia, but put him in contact with Galician poet Xosé Luis Méndez Ferrín, and also provided Hutchison with information about the Galician cultural and political icon, Alfonso R. Castelao (see note below). From the very beginning, Hutchinson was very interested in this outstanding Galician figure. Additionally, Galician popular rebellions in the past, together with the historical impact of the Spanish Civil War in Galicia, were among his major interests. But the most fascinating part of Hutchison's relationship with Araúxo is not that referring to the poet's translations into Galician, but their personal relationship, a friendship which continued through conversations and letters into the final years of Hutchinson's life.

39 Woods, '*Óró Domhnaigh*', pp. 93–212.
40 What we do know about that first visit to Portugal comes from an unpublished, indeed un-transcribed memoir of his travels that Hutchinson recorded in the last three years of his life. I have listened to the opening section of this recording, the first of six hour-long cassette tapes and there are vivid details and recollections of his first time in Portugal. From that tape: 'We disembarked at Lisbon under a blue sky, an utterly clear sky without a single cloud. I convinced myself that it was bluer, and therefore hotter, than any sky I had seen over Ireland or my native Scotland […]' (my transcription).
41 Martín Veiga, 'Travelling South: Representations of Iberia in the Poetry of Pearse Hutchinson', in Coleman and Johnston (eds), *Reading Pearse Hutchinson*, p. 145.
42 Namely, the poem 'In a Church in Vigo once…', included in *Done into English* (2003), p. 35.
43 David McLoghlin, 'An Interview with Pearse Hutchinson', *Cyphers*, 76 (2013), pp. 50–54.
44 Emilio Araúxo, Conversation with Pearse Hutchinson: 13 April 2000, transcription by Araúxo. My translation.
45 José Núñez Búa, who, in 1950, published a biography of Alfonso Rodríguez Castelao.
46 Transcription by Araúxo, emailed to the author, conversation on 22 May 2000. My translation.

13. 'Shall Gaelic Die?': Iain Crichton Smith's bilingualism – entrapment or poetic freedom?

STÉPHANIE NOIRARD

Does choosing a language impinge on your writing? This is a question Iain Crichton Smith, as a bilingual poet, often had occasion to ponder. He was brought up in the Gaelic language until he went to school where he then had to speak English and was confronted solely by an Anglocentric culture. As an author, he thus found himself in a state of what Labov calls 'linguistic insecurity'[1] and this is a feeling which he expresses well when he admits: 'I find myself in an ambiguous position both with regard to language and with regard to the preconceptions of what I do in art, and I must say that it has been at times a nightmarish labyrinth. It has resulted in desperate manoeuvres in order to be true to myself.'[2] This comment emphasises the double nature of the bilingual poet and the artistic barrier it leads to as the language dichotomy may tend to result in annihilation or entrapment rather than strength or freedom.

This chapter will not focus on the poet's state of mind and self-analysis but rather on his English texts to assess the prosodic outcome of his 'desperate manoeuvres'. In other words, does the poet manage to free himself from his linguistic maze? A Gumperzian approach[3] will therefore be adopted, pointing out the main differences between Gaelic and English, and giving concrete examples of how the structures of the latter are modified by the former. This will be followed by a discussion of the interest of these modifications and the Gaelic reading of English verse. Finally, as perhaps Crichton Smith's deepest questioning engaged with, Language in its differential sense, as opposed to tongue, will be examined together with its issue in the poems.

Everyone who has read the plays of John Millington Synge will have noticed the peculiarity of his formulations as the English sentences are symptomatically imitating the Irish Gaelic structures, thus highlighting the poliglossic situation of the islanders. The hybrid language it creates, however, though attested in Ireland, is the fruit of an artistic choice and craft. The craft is perhaps less obvious in the texts of Iain Crichton Smith but awareness of the basic differences between Scottish Gaelic and English is enough to point to oddities and what may cautiously be termed dialectal variations. Grammatically, there are four main differences between the two languages which directly affect English: noun phrase organisation, word order, impersonal structures and the auxiliary or verb 'be'.

Unlike English, Gaelic is deeply rooted in noun phrases and paratactic chains of nouns following particular declension dependency often occur. In this case, William Gillies notes that there may be either a purely genitival construction such as 'mullach taigh a' mhinisteir' (*'roof house the minister i.e. the roof of the minister's house'*), or compound nouns in which the dependent noun in the genitive case has truly become an adjective such as 'taigh samhraidh' (*'house of summer i.e. summer house'*).[4] These deep Gaelic structures are much represented in the poems of Iain Crichton Smith and it is possible to quote examples such as 'winters of pervasive snow' (p. 1),[5] 'setting of sun' (p. 2), 'Sunday of wrangling bells' (p. 24), 'veer of yacht' (p. 145), 'hunters of golf balls' (p. 156), or 'hulk of the humming dead' (p. 246). The proportion of nouns, whether simple or compound, moreover, is much higher in Gaelic than in English, which accounts for Crichton Smith's nominalisation impulse, notably his constant use of the -ing form.

A second feature is the syntax, English being a subject-verb-object (SVO) language while Gaelic is a verb-subject-object-adverbial (VSOAdv) one. Yet, though the verb always comes first in Gaelic sentences, the other elements are quite flexible and may take up second position if topicalised. When this happens, it often results in a doubling of the subject. For instance, 'tha iad beag' (*'they are small'*) may become 'is ann beag a tha iad' (*'it is small that they are'*). A phrase such as 'here there is the Land of the Straight Lines' (p. 153) or 'they all come in, / the villager' (p. 202) are perfect illustrations of the underlying mother tongue. Adjectives are also almost systematically placed after the noun in Gaelic and so in Crichton Smith's poems, but this is arguably a more common feature of English poetry *per se*. Still, the high proportion of postponed adjectives and even compound adjectives in Crichton Smith's translations gives them a characteristically Gaelic flavour which may then be retraced in his English poems. The comparison of his translation of Duncan Bàn MacIntyre's 'Ben Dorain' with 'Deer on the High Hills' is, in that sense, illuminating. The fifth stanza of the second movement of 'Ben Dorain', for instance, reads: 'It's the stag, the proud roarer, / white-rumped and ferocious, / branch-antlered and noble, / would walk in the shaded / retreats of Ben Dorain, / so haughtily-headed' (p. 76) while section IX of 'Deer on the High Hills' describes 'heads like yours, so scrutinous and still, / yet venomed too with the helpless thrust of spring, / so magisterial, violent, yet composed' (p. 41).

A more uncommon feature in English poetry, and in English generally speaking, however, is the use of the indefinite pronoun 'one', which is very common in Gaelic. Douglas Dunn remarks about Iain Crichton Smith that he 'uses the English indefinite pronoun with a frequency which most Scottish writers usually seek to avoid. One doesn't say 'one' very often, in prose. Does one? One was brought up to say "you" or "we" or to take a chance on "I".'[6] Yet he relates this frequency to the absence of class consciousness in Lewis society and, although he may not entirely be wrong, there is no denying that the influence of the native Gaelic is here as well. As a result, lines such as 'nevertheless one should not so return / till soldier of the practical or doer / one wholly learns to learn' (p. 36) sound slightly constrained in English, thus revealing an underlying Gaelic structure.

Finally, just like Spanish, Gaelic has two verbs to mean 'be': 'tha' and 'is'. The difference between the two has started to become blurred, but as William Gillies puts it, 'tha' was originally associated to 'transient, superficial characteristics', while 'is' suggests 'permanent, inherent attributes'.[7] These differences, of course, leave no visible trace on the surface structure of the English sentence but when turning to the prosodic interest of an English influenced by Gaelic, it will be found that it does cross-fertilise meaning as a whole.

First, however, it is necessary to focus on whether the Gaelic structures contribute to an entrapment in the sense that they lead to a loss of meaning or oddities that may defeat the readers' expectation of what a poetic contents should be. A poem such as 'Some Days were Running Legs', which retraces a childhood on the island of Lewis, provides one answer to the question. This is evident in the first two stanzas:

> Some days were running legs and joy
> and old men telling tomorrow would be
> a fine day surely: for sky was red
> at setting of sun between the hills.
>
> Some nights were parting at the gates
> with day's companions: and dew falling
> on heads clear of ambition except light
> returning and throwing stones at sticks. (p. 2)

The sentences are not valid in English and require a rewriting process which would result in: 'Some days our legs would be running and joy was in the air / when old men said tomorrow would certainly be a fine day: for the sky was red where the sun set between the hills. // Some nights we parted at the gates / with day's companions: and dew fell on heads clear of ambition except for light / then we'd return and throw stones at sticks.' The only other way to give grammatical sense to the sentences is to read '-ing' forms as strict nouns. And even then, the poem remains strikingly unusual, perhaps illustrating what Crichton Smith described as his 'desperate manoeuvres'. The instability this creates, however, reflects the state of linguistic insecurity Gaelic-speaking children may have felt when confronting the world of education and English. For not only may bilingualism be experienced as a source of guilt and linguistic instability, it is also sometimes regarded as a limit to self-expression and self-definition. As Michelle MacLeod puts it in her analysis of 'What is Wrong' (p. 179), 'linguistic dichotomy [is] an illness'[8] to which a poetic cure must then be found. Thus, what the reader loses in terms of meaning or reading flow may be gained in terms of experience; this is perhaps one way of addressing negative aspects of bilingualism.

To find a real innovation in terms of prosodic structures, one must, however, turn not to grammar but to verse proper and the Gaelic techniques that are transferred into the English poem. These consist more particularly in a greater range of assonances and alliterations or rhymes, not at line ends but internally. In 'Some Days were Running Legs', the gerundive mark is part of it in as much as it creates a *homoioteleuton* – similar sounding endings to words, phrases, or sentences – hence a sense of internal rhymes, as in 'running, returning, flooding, turning', which, besides, bear similar vowel sounds. Other such sound-patterns include 'red-setting', 'back-black', or linked verse such as 'Some nights were shawling mirrors lest the li<u>gh</u>tning / <u>st</u>rike with the eel's speed out of the storm' (my underlining), and systematic alliteration or assonance, most visible in the line 'bare smooth backs. The toothed rocks rising'. This gives the otherwise unrhymed poem a new dimension at the crossroads of two different poetic systems, a frontier area of prosodic experimentation. This is all the more so as they demand a different scanning of the lines, which is still accentual but requires a more syllabic awareness as sound patterns are repeated and attract focus.

Form is foregrounded further as English words are used with their Gaelic meaning in Crichton Smith's poetic work. This is the case of colours, for instance, which, as Derrick McClure points out, often relate to a state of mind or particular emotion rather than to a visual characteristic.[9] 'Glas', for instance, which is perceived as either 'green' or 'grey', expresses melancholy while 'dearg', meaning 'bright red', stands for violence or madness, and 'donn', which means 'brown' in English, refers to 'gloom'. Although their use in English does not necessarily imply a symbolic change, it nonetheless allows the poet to play on translinguistic polysemy so that associations like 'sad and brown landscapes' (p. 30) or 'dull / acres of brown paint' (p. 65) sound less incongruous than immediately perceptible, so with 'brown words' (p. 103) or 'brown ending' (p. 368). In other cases Gaelic images or metaphors are directly projected into the English text, thus considerably enriching it. This is the case in phrases like 'a primrose in [our] mouth' (p. 103) or 'leaves gape open' (p. 4), where 'mouth' or related 'gape' may refer to the Gaelic 'beul', meaning of course 'mouth', but also 'beginning', thus leading from the conventional image of the poet with a flower in his mouth to the flower at the beginning, the onset of the poem, and from wide open leaves to leaves newly opening in spring. Conversely an expression such as 'the terrible mouth of the gale' (pp. 2-3), though metaphoric in English, actually refers to the beginning of a storm when read with a Gaelic perception of the word 'mouth'. Further on, a metaphor like the thunder's 'tacky' or 'tacketty boots' which is recurrent in the poems has no double meaning but is directly borrowed from the Gaelic, which is also the case for the 'dog's tooth' or rainbow, the salmon as a symbol of the knowledge of past and future events, or the cat and horse as symbols of death. These cultural borrowings again expend meaning and creativity in English while offering a different perception and reflection on the world.

Metaphor is a crucial craft as it enables the poet not only to play with the two languages, but also to extend their possibilities through mutual influence. It also pertains to a way of trying to contact the world, a world which may be felt as fading or lost for a bilingual poet who has not truly come to terms with his two languages. In that light, the fact that the Gaelic language possesses two verbs to express existence, the being of what is described, is fundamental. William Gillies notes that in the case where either 'tha' or 'is' is possible in a given structure, poetic texts usually prefer 'is'.[10] It could, therefore, be argued that there is, on the part of poets, a move towards the essence of things rather than a simple description of transient characteristics, because 'is' tends to equate the tenor to the vehicle, hence tending towards what Paul Ricoeur calls 'identification' rather than simple 'resemblance', as opposed to comparisons which only focus on likeness and not definition.[11] Hence in the first section of 'Oban 1955-1982', the sea is not compared to but literally becomes 'sheaves of endless blue on blue', a definition and identification all the more powerful as it appears just after a most realistic description, 'the very stones are green' (p. 262) so that metaphoric and realistic truth are made to coincide as the world is slowly revealed to the poet. Moreover, the identification process soon comes to be applied to self-definition and self-representation in the world. A sentence such as 'half of this world I am' (p. 240), with its Gaelic topicalisation on the predication, thus takes up a denser meaning as inner life and the outside meet and as subject and world are made to merge.

It is however certainly difficult to assess exactly to what extent bilingual authors, sensitive though they may be to the question of language, are aware of all these processes. As Crichton Smith himself has it, 'I cannot tell how my English sounds or reads to an Englishman,'[12] thus pointing to the difficulty of self-judgement. Yet one thing is certain, his reflection on his bilingualism leads him to thoughts on language generally speaking and how it may be worked on to gain poetic freedom.

There is no denying that the poet is aware of his language being '*in extremis*'[13] as he himself says and yet he refuses to remain entrapped in the illusive vision of an edenic, pure language. On the contrary, he refuses to endorse a romantic vision of the Highlands. This is clearly demonstrated in a poem like 'Ceilidh', especially in the first stanza which reads:

> Some ragged tartans hang above the stage.
> There are wooden trestles and they all come in,
> the villagers, to listen to their past.
> Some finished passion has removed all haste
> and granted courtesy instead of rage.
> The years have taught them how to lose not win. (p. 202–03)

The word 'ceilidh' means 'to pay a visit' and alludes to the community feeling within a Gaelic society. The festivity or ball it refers to nowadays however, has become slightly debased and Iain Crichton Smith turns it into a parody of identity no one believes in any longer. This is made obvious in the first three lines. The first perfectly iambic pentameter is quite ironic as it emphasises how meticulously everything is planned and decorated in order to recreate an all too hackneyed identity. Yet this is a shabby, ragged, soulless ballroom as the lexicon of dereliction and the determiner 'some', which points to unspecified qualities, highlight. The rhythm used for the description soon deteriorates as does the syntax, to such an extent that, for one moment, the ghostly villagers who come in are dehumanised and it is almost as if the trestles had taken their place in the sentence 'There are wooden trestles and they all come in, / the villagers', where the syntactic break is sustained by the enjambment. Looking closely at the sentence, however, it is possible to detect, behind the apparent oddity, a form of topicalisation involving the doubling of the subject, which is typical of the Gaelic language.

The impingement on the English meaning it engenders shows that, contrary to the backward-looking culture which is described in the poem and epitomised in clichés or relic-Gaelic words such as 'tartan', 'ceilidh', or 'glen', the native language is still alive and strong enough to permeate through the learned tongue and change, intensify, extend its meaning. It acquires strength by becoming a means of criticism, irony and subversion while the linguistic space takes on a new dimension. A kind of interlect is thus created as English and Gaelic merge in what Prudent would define as a 'continuum' in which they both add to each other while no longer individually corresponding to the new system their fusion creates.[14] Perhaps this is what Iain Crichton Smith called a 'higher language like a hawk in the sky, that can see the roads, that can see their end, like God who built the roads' (p. 105), in other words, a more modern language which may be renewed and experimented upon. But is it, really? To what extent can this new idiom solve the question of the possible conformity or at least closeness of the language to the world, of the signifier to the signified? Can it find a way out of mimesis?

The question is reflected upon in 'Shall Gaelic Die?'

> I came with a 'sobhrach' in my mouth. He came with a 'primrose'.
> 'A primrose by the river's brim.' Between the two languages, the
>   word 'sobhrach' turned to 'primrose.'
> Behind the two words a Roman said 'prima rosa'.
> The 'sobhrach' or the 'primrose' was in our hands. Its reasons
>   belonged to us. (pp. 103–04)

To take up the exact measure of this poem, it is necessary to remember that it was originally written in Gaelic and then translated into English. Iain Crichton Smith is indeed a poet-translator and has thus acquired an intimate knowledge of and concern for linguistic stakes. His self-translations are, more often than not, actual rewritings that imply much structural change, and, as for the translations he makes of other poets, they are attempts to liberate poetry from a word-for-word stasis and let the meaning unfold through concentrating work on structure, pattern and sound instead of remaining entrapped in a dictionary. Perhaps one of the best instances of such translations is his rendering of Duncan Bàn MacIntyre's 'Praise of Ben Dorain', in which he relies on both the musicality and stress pattern of English and Gaelic deeper structures and prosodic rules to bring his text closer to the musical pattern of the pibroch on which the original poem is based. In so doing, Crichton Smith reinvents a prosody for the English language in order to let Gaelic ring through the new text. The result is not awkward but dynamic and powerful. Behind such free translation lies the poet's wish to help the reader experience the text and not the pragmatic, academic search for exact meaning and what is expressed is a profound and liberating love of language almost for language's sake.

The stanza from 'Shall Gaelic Die' just quoted directly addresses the gap between signifier and signified. It is expressed through a hyper-determination of the flower, 'sobhrach', 'primrose', *'prima rosa'*, which highlights the uselessness of words, their inability to reach the essence of the object – *'la primevère est l'absente de tout bouquet'* as Mallarmé would say. This is reinforced by the fact that, in the line 'I came with a "sobhrach" in my mouth. He came with a "primrose",' the words 'sobhrach' and 'primrose' may refer either to the flower or to the words themselves. Finally, in the English version, 'sobhrach', when first encountered, defeats meaning hence embodying the complete disappearance of both word and thing. So, shall Gaelic die and English with it and poetry with them because it is locked in a prison of words? Iain Crichton Smith's answer is 'no'. The poetic space becomes a place where he freely plays, not only with linguistic codes but also with cultural, stylistic or musical norms. It becomes a pluridimensionnal, polyphonic locus where English and Gaelic are not subordinated to each other but complementary. That is why in 'Shall Gaelic Die?' he argues: 'A million colours are better than one colour if they are different. / A million men are better than one man if they are different. Keep out of the factory, O man, you are not a robot. It wasn't a factory that made your language, it made you.' The parallel constructions which contradict the meaning in their uniformity highlight the monotony of similarity and uniqueness. Similarly the ambiguous third person neutral pronoun – which may refer either to the language or the factory – shows how important the native tongue is, while criticising what could be termed an oedipal relationship between man and his mother-tongue, a relationship which prevents him from improving as he constantly hopes for an ideal, pure language. It must be remembered at this point that Iain Crichton Smith was an innovative writer who did not hesitate to break away from traditional Gaelic themes and to use the language to explore topics as wide-ranging as rock music, linguistics, the economic situation of the 1970s or the conquest of space. Desacralising Gaelic, confronting it with new themes, the modern world and even English is thus a way of freeing the language from deathly conventions and traditions, keeping it alive and moving.

The awareness of Language and languages in fact, and the use of their ambiguities, double meaning, cross-references or abstractions first leads to a necessary questioning of poetry, its role and stakes, and then to creation, based on words, of language, as material to be shaped again and again. In that light, the last line of 'Shall Gaelic Die?' acts as a plea for language unification and freedom: 'The "sobhrach" or the "primrose" was in our hands. Its reasons belonged to us.' 'I' and 'he' have become 'us', that is, they are no longer separated subjects speaking different languages but united hands working on a similar matter. This union is reminiscent of the wedding described in poem eighteen of 'An t-Eilean is An Cànan' ('*The Island and the Language*') where the 'sense of home coming' and 'symbolic marriage' described by Michelle MacLeod[15] is not an acknowledgement of the supremacy of Gaelic over English, but the coming to terms with bilingualism as a possible stable and fair union. For it is the poet's duty to make poetry resonant and free. It thus becomes evident that, although bilingualism is a tormenting issue for Iain Crichton Smith and although it sometimes affects his poetry both in terms of meaning and theme, the poet manages to turn it into an asset. Rather than remaining entrapped in tautology or meaninglessness, he uses it as a powerful tool to question language at large, criticise poetry, experiment and create. And while language may be a barrier or a limit, it seems it is here to be crossed and to serve as a landmark to freedom.

Notes

1. As exemplified in W. Labov, *The Social Stratification of English in New York City* (Cambridge: Cambridge University Press, 2006).
2. Iain Crichton Smith, 'Structure in my Poetry', *The Poet's Voice and Craft,* ed. by C. B. McCully (Manchester: Carcanet, 1994), pp. 104–22 (p. 104).
3. Cf. J. Gumperz, *Language and Social Identity (Studies in Interactional Sociolinguistics)* (Cambridge: Cambridge University Press, 1983).
4. William Gillies, 'Scottish Gaelic', in *The Celtic Languages*, ed. Martin Ball (London and New York: Routledge, 2000), pp. 145–223 (pp. 198–99).
5. Page references are to the collection, Iain Crichton Smith, *Collected Poems* (Manchester: Carcanet, 1995).
6. Douglas Dunn, 'The Wireless behind the Curtain', in *Iain Crichton Smith: Critical Essays,* ed. Colin Nicholson (Edinburgh: Edinburgh University Press, 1992), pp. 51–72 (p. 59).
7. Gillies, p. 210.
8. Michelle Macleod, 'Language and Bilingualism in the Gaelic Poetry of Iain Crichton Smith', *Scottish Studies Review,* 2:2 (Autumn 2001), pp. 105–12 (p. 106).
9. J. Derrick McCLure, 'Douglas Young and Sorley MacLean', in *Gaelic and Scots in Harmony,* ed. Derick Thomson (Glasgow: Glasgow University Press, 1988), pp. 136–48 (pp. 141–43).
10. Gillies, p. 210.
11. Cf. P. Ricoeur, *La Métaphore vive* (Paris: seuil, 1975).
12. Iain Crichton Smith, 'The Highland Element in my English Work', *Scottish Literary Journal,* 4:1 (1997), pp. 47–60 (p. 58).
13. Ibid., p. 57.
14. For further discussion on interlect see L. F. Prudent, 'Diglossie et Interlecte', *Langages,* 15:61 (1981), pp. 13–38.
15. Macleod, p. 112.

14. Henry Adam's *Among Unbroken Hearts* (2000): Mankind's desperate quest for freedom

DANIÈLE BERTON-CHARRIÈRE

In Henry Adam's *Among Unbroken Hearts* (2000)[1] four characters, covering a wide age-range, meet in a village in a wild, deserted rural area of northern Scotland, represented as a dead-end open space which paradoxically offers little opportunity to free oneself from alienating factors. The place appears lonely, cut off from the rest of the world (or at least from any urban centre). Three men – Ray, Neil and Chaimig – and a young girl – Amanda – look lost in the midst of this forsaken *locus*. Ray has just inherited his grandmother's home after her death. He is back in the village in which he was brought up, having travelled there in the company of Neil, his friend. He thinks it will take only a matter of a couple of days to sort things out. In fact, their visit turns into a much longer stay, one forever as far as Ray is concerned. He meets the only inhabitants apparently still there, whom he has not seen for ages. These are Chaimig, now very old, blind and somewhat senile, needing taken care of, who used to look after Ray when he was a child, and his granddaughter, Amanda, who would like to leave to study in Glasgow.

Stranded and confined in this lonely place, the four of them recreate, in effect, a tense and stifling dramatic and symbolic *huis-clos*. They feel entrapped in an oppressive deadlock. The locked door is that of their alienated minds: the idea of the absence of literal escape keeps haunting them. These individuals find no figurative escape from one another either. In this play, the *topos* turns into a literary and dramatic exploration of mental alienation as well as a desperate quest for liberation. Introspection somehow combines with Sartre's echoed philosophical ideas of objectification and competitive subjectivity. Each character looks at another (the Other) and at him/herself (his/her own Self turned into an/Other) made object under scrutiny in the process, themselves being the subject *doing* the action the others (sometimes including themselves) are *enduring*. Because there is no break from others, each person is faced with the incapacitating horror of being turned into an object under constant surveillance. Unfortunately, within this frame, there is no possible escape from the hell of objectification, and each character is also competing to be subject, to be the observer, and not the person under observation. Introspection makes things both more complex and more painful. All the characters feel ensnared, and, for the very first time, have to face their actual present selves, what they have become owing to age, addiction, guilt, love and wrong choices of all sorts. The concepts of in/determinism and origination intrude upon their reflection, puzzling and disturbing their psychological balance. Imprisonment, escapism and related topics are examined through this quartet of very different *personae*. Yet, despite the pessimistic turn of the play, hope somehow helps the characters fight against the deep disappointment of their past dreams for the future.

In his work in general, Adam explores the deep longings and failings of humankind, revisiting a certain number of 'myths' – whether Scottish or not – through a transtextual network. His playtext here is rich and its subtext philosophical and metadiscursive. He uses a mixture of Scots, Scottish dialect, sociolect, geolect and even the junkies' idiolect or jargon – very little Standard English – to verbalise, articulate and reverberate the characters' desires to liberate themselves from bonds, from alienating others, from addictions, and, even worse, from their painful selves.

Quest for freedom

Ray has stayed away from the Scottish hamlet of his childhood, and from his roots (at least, those he knows), for a very long time. His grandmother's death and her choice of him as heir have made him go back to where he should belong, although he has felt separate for years. No one has forced him to do this; no violence has been used to make him change his mind and to allow links and feelings to resurface. As a free individual in a free society, he has chosen to accept the situation and be the new owner of a '*farmhouse in the far north of Scotland*' as the first stage directions indicate (p. 7). His decision-making corresponds to one of the many definitions of liberty, supposedly no subject of dispute, in David Hume's words,

> By liberty, then, we can only mean *a power of acting or not acting, according to the determinations of the will;* that is, if we choose to remain at rest, we may; if we choose to move, we also may. Now this hypothetical liberty is universally allowed to belong to everyone who is not a prisoner and in chains.[2]

Ray, then, has moved up north, and in the very first scene, he and his mate, Neil, arrive with travel bags. Ironic about the state of the place – it is full of cobwebs and dust – Neil jokingly exclaims 'home sweet home', and then bombards Ray with questions about his broken family, including an absent father. They all seem to have tried their luck unsuccessfully under various skies (including Australia), and then had to return to the starting point: 'Ma granny went til make her fortune. She made a baby instead' (p. 8). These unfortunate travellers are what Ray calls his history, his identity: 'At's ma history, ye know? At's who I am.' Being identified through one's lineage (whatever it may be) sounds like an encroachment on individual freedom and, so, is why Neil teasingly asserts: 'Nobody has roots any more Ray. It was on the news. Did nobody tell ye? [...] You're an individual [...] a free man in a free land' (p. 8). Apparently, however, neither exterior limiting factors nor obstacles prevented Ray from willingly undergoing what he thinks is his last journey to the village of his ancestry, the only remaining branch of an elliptic family tree. He thinks he will never go back, once the sale of the property completed. The cord finally severed, he will be completely free from his unsatisfactory past. Ray remembers that, in his quest for independence and self-determination, he once fled a probable marriage and a stable life with Marion (Amanda's sister) to lead what was anticipated as an ideal existence, one deprived of any bonds, whether of marriage or of social rules and constraints.

Unexpectedly for Ray, on his return, memories pave his way and become hindrances, obstacles which make his certainties fade away. Remorse, guilt and nostalgia overcome him: past summers are recalled as 'blissfully idyllic' (p. 13) and his granny's belongings – Neil thinks them 'old shit' – he just cannot dump (p. 24). Interior pressure prevents him from getting rid of material things which happen to be laden with reminiscences of his/THE past, pregnant with part of his identity, of his Self. Although, for Thomas Hobbes, 'Liberty is the absence of all the impediments to action that are not contained in the nature and intrinsical quality of the agent',[3] Ray finds in himself the need to change and an incapacity to throw this place up: something powerful is attaching and fixing him to it all, putting an end to his useless utopian wanderings.

Ray had sworn he would never return, and yet he is back. Exterior causation (I mean the cause and effect process) and necessity may be advocated to explain his paradoxical attitude. In fact, his granny's will (including her actual will and testament) attracted him back to the village. Necessity made him dream of better days, at the prospect of selling the unexpectedly inherited farmhouse and of making some money out of it:

NEIL: Ever thought aboot sellin iss place?
RAY: Selling it?
NEIL: Yeah. Taking the money and running like hell. (p. 25)

But this reasoning disregarded the emotional reactions human beings are sometimes unable to control: as Thomas Nagel explains,

> From the inside, when we act, alternative possibilities seem to lie open before us [...]. The same applies to our internal consideration of the actions of others. But from an external perspective, things look different. That perspective takes in not only the circumstances of action as they present themselves to the agent, but also the conditions and influences lying behind the action, including the complete nature of the agent himself.[4]

Ray's returning to the village revives and stirs up sentiments and memories. Although old Chaimig has always taken him for a strong man and a fine poet, Ray's vision of himself is less laudatory. He is weak and immature; he has submitted to a tormented mind and to all sorts of addictions to soothe the alienating pain. In his case, internal and external perspectives seem at odds. Ray is given to doubts; he doesn't know what to do and when to leave. His mind has to undergo the struggle between autonomy (one's own freedom) and responsibility (related to the freedom of others), and it threatens his equilibrium. In Nagel's words,

> Just as the basic problem of epistemology is not whether we can be *said to know* things, but lies rather in the loss of belief and the invasion of doubt, so the problem of free will lies in the erosion of interpersonal attitudes and of the sense of autonomy. Questions about what we are to say about action and responsibility merely attempt after the fact to express those feelings – feelings of impotence, of imbalance, and of affective detachment from other people.[5]

Ray is hoping that, maybe, time will tell. But, in the village of his childhood, the past engulfs the present and the future. Dust covers everything in his granny's lodging; old Chaimig finally binds Ray and Amanda through their love to him; and both Ray and Neil seem to suffer from the Peter Pan syndrome. Time has stopped somehow, or clocks have become slow. Chaimig praises Ray's poetry as able to control time: 'Aye. Aye. Ye captured it. Ye captured it see. Ye put oot yur han and took time by e mane. Ye whispered in his ear an calmed him. At moment, it's yurs now. Forever. Ye made time stan still. Is at noh a wonderful thng?' (p. 38). Ray rediscovers his past as though nothing had changed, from the framing landscape to people's feelings within it. Yet, everyone *has* changed: Chaimig is blind and losing his mind, and Amanda wishes to fly from the bird-trap nest to go to Glasgow University. She is no longer the cheeky schoolgirl peeping on flirtatious teenagers from the top of the cliffs. She has matured too soon.

The surrounding wild Scottish landscape, with its cliffs, raging winds and seas enhanced by unlimited skies, is breathtaking. Yet, it seems, paradoxically, both boundless and stifling. Inside its vastness with no limits to the eye, Amanda, Neil and Ray feel imprisoned. Such experience of the surrounding landscape is personal, as is the sense of freedom upon which Dana Nelkin[6] comments in her paper, 'The Sense of Freedom':

> We appear to have an inescapable sense that we are free, a sense that we cannot abandon even in the face of powerful arguments that this sense is illusory. It has often been suggested, perhaps most notably by Kant, that we have such a sense of freedom in virtue of being rational deliberators. More precisely, rational deliberators, in virtue of their nature as rational deliberators, necessarily have a sense that they are free. This claim has a great deal of intuitive plausibility: it is when we engage in rational deliberation about what to do that we are most likely to become aware that we have a sense of ourselves as free. Even skeptics about free will, who are convinced that they are not free, often admit to a sense that they are free when they deliberate about what to do.[7]

The sense of freedom Chaimig relies on, despite his incapacitating handicaps and age, the young ones, in contrast, cannot experience. They feel entrapped in a sublime but lifeless painting with no visible frame. Ray's poetic mind and eye expand the virtues of beauty and ignore the realities of earthly things when he verbalises his memories of what surrounds him: the landscape is enclosed in his head. He amplifies the aesthetic dimension of his creative dreamer's perspective:

> RAY: [...] I used til love it though. Bein here. I remember one time, playin up in e woods – I came til e edge o e trees. I looked down on e land, e green o e fallow, beyond at e hoose, beyond at e field ye were ploughin ... all e way doon til e edge o e cliff ... an above ye there wiz at huge blue sky, an e sea below ye, stretchin all e way oot til Norway, an e sun in e sky, burning lek a pot o molten gold, white gold, burnin ... times lek at ... ye wish ye could live forever. (p. 35)

Though the natural environment has not changed since his departure, his mental vision has. The sense of eternity provided by the beauties of the landscape has disappeared. Now, even when on top of the cliffs, with his head touching the sky, and with the sea way down below, he cannot be elated. He is subdued and tempted to jump off like a lemming, but he is under Amanda's surveillance. Neil has a theory about these emblematic and exemplary rodents, that they illustrate the determinism all post-lapsarian beings have to face:

> NEIL: Goes back to the time before the continental shift. They're heading for their old breeding grounds. It's wired into their blood. Hard drive. Couldna stop even if they wanted to. Just keep on going. (*Illustrates the trajectory of lemmings.*) (p. 10)[8]

Neil himself, however, thinks differently:

> NEIL: 'What? Jump off a fucking cliff? Just because you did it? Fucking crazy?' It was like somebody has actually sat down and planned out your whole fucking life for you. Take the first job they offer you, marry the first girl lets you fuck her, on and on, your whole fucking life. Fucking suicide, eh? (pp. 24–25)

One wonders if there is here for the young men a hint of Harold Pinter's *Ashes to Ashes*, while Chaimig, at the end of his life, seems to reflect Beckett's Hamm in *Endgame*, patiently waiting for death. Yet, he can still enjoy a form of communion with nature and rare moments of happiness with a genuine, pantheist capacity to transcend his failing senses:

> CHAIMIG: Aye, id's a long time since a felt e sea on ma feet. Id wis good o ye til take me. They think cause a'm blin it means niything til me, boot id's something, ken, chaist til feel e salt in e air, chaist til hear it. A spent a lot o time oot ere, wan way or anither. (p. 35)

Neil's rebellious vision of life simplistically and sarcastically goes against traditional norms. Ray used to share it. But their junkie friend Christie's suicidal drowning – as the only way out he found possible – has redefined and readjusted his viewpoint. Compromise and sacrifice can also be understood as part of the individual's exercise of liberty and of the common wealth. Syringes and heroin, egotistic day-to-day living, all forms of illusory escapism abuse young minds eager to remain free from all sorts of constraints. At the other extreme, even with Highers successfully passed with A's, and university acceptance, serious and loving Amanda cannot detach herself from her grandfather, bound to him by a sense of moral responsibility and duty.

Henry Adam's quartet offers a summary of the positive and negative sides of the concept of freedom in a pessimistic representation of life and, while the topic of freedom is open to interpretation, in *Among Unbroken Hearts* pessimism prevails. Hoping seems to provide no way out, but a dead end. The atmosphere is bleak, and expectations constantly dashed. Who believes Ray and Neil will finally be treated, detoxified and reliable enough for Amanda to leave and live her life? Will Ray liberate her? Neil, who is attached to Ray, but who remains an outsider throughout the play, finally feels free to escape in the last scene, sensing the danger the very place and his mate represent for him. Is he making the right decision himself? The end is open and the spectators can imagine what may happen. Will Ray's hoping to be cured and detoxified remain wishful thinking? Can Ray's quest for identity and identification be resolved? So many questions derive from the clash between internal and external perspectives, as Thomas Nagel explains:

> While we cannot fully occupy this perspective toward ourselves while acting, it seems possible that many of the alternatives that appear to lie open when viewed from an internal perspective would seem closed from this outer point of view, if we could take it up. And even if some of them are left open, given a complete specification of the condition of the agent and the circumstances of action, it is not clear how this would leave anything further for the agent to contribute to the outcome – anything that he could contribute as source, rather

than merely as the scene of the outcome – the person whose act it is. If they are left open, given everything about him, what does he have to do with the result? [...] In either case we cease to face the world and instead become parts of it; we and our lives are seen as products and manifestations of the world as a whole.⁹

Growing up and emancipation versus the Peter Pan syndrome

All the characters, whether present onstage or mentioned in the course of action, must cope with problems related to dependence and interdependence. Being weaned and severed from past ties and influences is but one part of the curing process. Ray and Neil would like to quit heroin addiction, Chaimig would like to depart his life at home (and not in a nursing home) as soon as possible, and Amanda would like to study in town. But none of the young ones can resolve to act, even when an alternative solution is offered to them. Neil cannot convince Ray to start the anti-addiction programme he has chosen for himself, and Amanda shows no enthusiasm when Ray offers to take care of Chaimig: 'AMANDA. A canna chaist leave him lek everybody else did.' (p. 71) [...] 'RAY. A'm coming back, Amanda. A'm kicking junk an coming back for good. A'll look after him' (p. 71). Is he so unreliable to her mind that she does not trust his intentions as more than 'chaist words' (p. 38), as Ray calls his poems? Ray's problem is to face change, growing up, or growing old, and to envisage breaking free from ties, whether physical or mental as the stage direction stresses: '*Transition. Time passing. Music.* RAY *paces the room, breathing heavily, the sickness kicking in. He reacts physically against the pain and mental turmoil. Whatever he does he can't get free*' (p. 72).

The *Peter Pan* book Neil and Ray find in the farmhouse, and keep reading throughout the play, symbolises the difficulty they have in becoming adults and making mature decisions. In the final scene, Ray admits that he regrets the silly choices he made when younger, and avows his difficulty in acquiring any maturity:

RAY: Ye know e stupidest thing? E stupidest thing o all? All at stuff we used til laugh at, all e stuff we thought we were

> rebelling against, that's all I want now. I want a wife. I want kids. I want to grow up and be a man. Is at noh e stupidest thing ye've ever heard in your entire fucking life? (p. 67)

He realises it is high time he should stop escaping through artificial devices and 'be a man', leading a 'normal' life and facing responsibilities. But is it not too late? Is it possible to do so with his degree of immaturity and constant escapism? Marion, his former girlfriend, is a married woman and a mother now, whereas he is still wavering between teenage and adulthood. The spectator gets the impression that, like Peter Pan, he will never grow up. Through their reading J. M. Barrie's novel, Ray and Neil reverberate and voice the incapacitating 'Peter Pan syndrome' that restraints their lives to a minimised dimension, or to a maximised dreamlike escapist version. Henceforth, Ray's proposal to stay with Chaimig and look after him sounds ambiguous. Is it to assist the old man or to stick to the father-figure, the parent substitute, who looked after him when he was a child, and to recreate this quasi-father/son link that would maintain him in perpetual childhood? Who is going to protect whom in such a relationship? His choice may be more selfish than it seems.

The 'Peter Pan syndrome' is defined as a reluctance to accept the responsibilities of maturity and adulthood, and derived from the book by J. M. Barrie. The reference is both quasi-medical[10] and literary, thus widening the transtextual scope. Although the myth of the *puer aeternus* is archetypal, the source revealed by the name of this tendency is Barrie's novel. Mixing the fictitious character and story embedded in a child's universe and an immaturity syndrome renders the complexity of a reality refusing reality itself, and taking refuge in the illusion of the supposedly protective world of childhood. Yet, when sickly Ray is read the story of Wendy and Peter by Neil, it grows, distorted and perverted, into a nightmarish vision.

Conclusion

In *Among Unbroken Hearts*, death appears as the definite and eternal escape resolving the eternal child's (*puer aeternus*) quest for freedom. The anecdote recalling Christie's suicide by drowning shows how the young man fled the inevitable death by overdose that was his predictable lot. Well-named, allegorised Christie knew his hell on earth was 'never going to be over' (p. 72). The metaphor of the wall used by Henry Adam to depict Humankind's determinism, objectification and weakness also renders these young people's lost sense of freedom:

> RAY: He used to say to me ye know… he used to say – 'Look oot ere, see what they're doing? They're building a wall'. And he was right. One by one they were taking everybody we knew and moulding them into bricks for their wall. But noh us, ye know? They could never get us. Well they got him. As soon as he walked into the water they got him. Now he's just another brick. Another brick walling me in. Maybe that's all he ever wiz. (p. 67)

Among Unbroken Hearts can also be read as a celebration of the somehow therapeutic power of poetry writing, a creative form of retention of memories and of liberation from alienating haunting thoughts:

> RAY: Ye wish ye could live forever.
> CHAIMIG: Aye min, at's e poet in ye. (p. 35)
> […]
> RAY: And sometimes I could hear myself dreaming
> And I'm sure you could hear too
> As we lay in that room
> Full of obituaries to dead men
> We both had gently slept with
> When our ideas
> Seemed clear
> And solid (p. 37)
>
> Vague memories of that time
> Flood me with desire
> Then float away

> Lazy dreaming
> Without retention
> With you
> I forget
> To think. ('Marion', p. 38)

Henry Adam's playtext is a metadiscursive pretext whose characters' experience perhaps exposes its author's seeking to set himself free from his own ghosts, from literary, dramatic and theatrical models. The subtext reveals a process of creative identification and emancipation. It represents the personal deliverance and recognition of the Self of a man, and of an author. To what extent this play is autobiographical is impossible to say, but what is obvious is the dramatist's paying tribute to his roots, and exposing how he is breaking free of them. Choosing the Scots of his native Caithness as the normal mode of expression of his characters who rarely speak standard English, and referring to Neil Gunn, Caithness-born like Adam, by name and to Peter Pan cannot be regarded as chance. Through transtextuality, commentary takes place, and difference is asserted. The character's quest for freedom remains simultaneously fulfilled and yet unfulfilled as each person's break for freedom can be only partially achieved, and longing and frustration intermingle in what I called in the opening paragraph 'a dead-end open space which paradoxically offers little opportunity to free oneself from alienating factors'.

Notes
1. Henry Adam, *Among Unbroken Hearts* (London: Nick Hern Books, 2001). The play was premièred at the Traverse Theatre on 13 October 2000.
2. David Hume, cited at *Our Freedom Reconciled with Determinism*, ed. Ted Honderich, www.ucl.ac.uk/~uctytho/dfwCompatHume.htm.
3. Thomas Hobbes, Excerpt 1, *From Liberty and Necessity* in *The Determinism and Free Will Philosophy Website*, ed. Ted Honderich, www.ucl.ac.uk/~uctytho/dfwVariousHobbes.htm.
4. Thomas Nagel, *Freedom and the View from Nowhere* in Ted Honderich (ed.) www.ucl.ac.uk/~uctytho/dfwVariousNagel.htm.
5. Thomas Nagel, ibid.
6. Dana Nelkin, 'The Sense of Freedom' in *The Determinism and Freedom Philosophy Website*, ed. Ted Honderich, www.ucl.ac.uk/~uctytho/dfwNelkin.html.

7   Dana Nelkin, 'Introduction', 'The Sense of Freedom', ibid.
8   See *Harold Pinter: Plays* (London: Faber, 1993), vol. 4, p. 416.
9   Thomas Nagel, 'Freedom and the View from Nowhere' in *The Determinism and Freedom Philosophy Website*; ed. Ted Honderich www.ucl.ac.uk/~uctytho/dfwVariousNagel.htm.
10 'The syndrome is not currently considered a psychopathology, given the World Health Organization has not recognized it as a psychological disorder. However, an increasingly larger number of adults are presenting emotionally immature behaviours in Western society. They are unable to grow up and take on adult responsibilities, and even dress up and enjoy themselves as teenagers when they are over 30 years old.': www.sciencedaily.com/releases/2007/05/070501112023.htm. Dan Kiley popularised the term, 'the Peter Pan Syndrome', in *The Peter Pan Syndrome: Men Who Have Never Grown Up* (London: Corgi, 1983).

Notes on Contributors

José Miguel Alonso-Giráldez, Senior Lecturer of English Language and Literature and staff member of the Research Centre for Irish Studies 'Amergin' at the University of A Coruña, has published widely on his main interests, Irish and Scottish literature, especially Yeats, Joyce, Heaney and Bernard O'Donoghue. Writing for the regional press, he broadcasts a weekly one-hour radio programme on contemporary literature and literary criticism.

Marion Amblard, a researcher in British studies, teaches at Grenoble Alpes University. Her research mainly focuses on Scottish painting from the eighteenth century onwards. Having published several articles on Scottish art, the representation of Scottish identity in the visual arts and Jacobite painters, she is a regular contributor to *Scottish Art News*.

Jean Berton is Professor of Scottish Studies at Université Jean Jaures, Toulouse, and current President of the French Society for Scottish Studies. Extensively published on Scottish culture – particularly twentieth and twenty-first century literature and theatre of the Highlands – his research includes the indigenous languages of Scotland.

Danièle Berton-Charrière, Professor Emerita, Université Blaise Pascal, Clermont-Ferrand II, France, has written on Cyril Tourneur and on computer assisted analysis, published on the Renaissance, drama and theatre of all periods, intersemioticity, and computer assisted lexicometry and stylostatistics. She has translated plays, including contemporary Scottish writing, for the stage.

Ian Brown, Professor Emeritus at Kingston University, London, playwright and poet, has been ASLS President and Saltire Society Convener. Published widely on theatre history, cultural praxis and Scottish literature and culture, his most recent volume is *History as Theatrical Metaphor: History, Myth* *and National Identities in Modern Scottish Drama* (2016) and poetry collection, *Collyshangles in the Canopy* (2015).

David Clark is Head of English at the University of A Coruña. Published widely on Scottish and Irish Literature, he is a founding member of the 'Amergin' Research Institute for Irish Studies. He has translated poetry and prose from and into Spanish, Galician, English and Scots. He is a board member of the European Irish Studies Federation (EFACIS) and the International Committee of ASLS.

Margarita Estévez Saá is Senior Lecturer in English and American Literature at the University of Santiago de Compostela. She has published essays on James Joyce, Muriel Spark, Doris Lessing, P. D. James, Janet Frame, Deirdre Madden, modern and post-colonial literature, contemporary Irish literature, and feminist criticism.

Lesley Graham is a Senior Lecturer at the University of Bordeaux. Her research interests centre on nineteenth-century Scottish literature, her publications including several articles related to Robert Louis Stevenson, his entourage and legacy. She is currently editing a volume of Stevenson's essays for the forthcoming New Edinburgh Edition of the Collected Works of Robert Louis Stevenson.

Rubén Jarazo-Álvarez is Senior Lecturer at the University of the Balearic Islands. A board member of the Spanish Society for the Study of Popular Culture, his research focuses on Cultural Studies and Anglophone cultures' influence in Spain. Recent co-edited volumes include *In the Wake of the Tiger: Irish Studies in the Twenty-First Century* (2010) and *Press, Propaganda and Politics: Cultural Periodicals in Francoist Spain and Communist Romania* (2013).

Philippe Laplace lectures at the University of Franche-Comté, Besançon. Author of a monograph on Gunn, *Les Hautes-Terres, l'histoire et la mémoire* (2006) and publishing director of the online review *e-crit3224* and deputy director of the *Annales Littéraires de Franche-Comté*, he has edited or co-edited various books including *Environmental & Ecological Readings. Nature, Human & Posthuman Dimensions in Scottish Literature & Arts* (2015).

María Jesús Lorenzo Modia is Professor of English Literature at Universidade da Coruña and Dean of the Faculty of Philology. Her main research interests are modern and contemporary literature by women, translation, reception and cultural studies. Published widely, she has edited several collections on language and literature, including *Ex-sistere: Women's Mobility in Contemporary Irish, Welsh and Galician Literatures* (2016).

Andrew Monnickendam is Professor of English at the Universitat Autònoma de Barcelona. Recent publications include, with Aránzazu Usandizaga (eds), *Back to Peace: Reconciliation and Retribution in the Postwar Period* (2007) and *The Novels of Walter Scott* (2013).

Stéphanie Noirard is a Senior Lecturer in English literature at the University of Poitiers. Her research focuses on Scottish contemporary poetry. She has published articles on the subject in various journals including *Études Anglaises* and *Civilisation* as well as chapters in *Mountains Figured and Disfigured in the English-Speaking World* (2010) and *Brittany/Ireland: What Relations?* (2015).

Alan Riach, Professor of Scottish Literature at Glasgow University, is author of *Representing Scotland in Literature, Popular Culture and Iconography* (2005), co-wrote *Arts of Independence* (2014), co-edited *The Edinburgh Companion to Twentieth-Century Scottish Literature* (2009) and edited *The International Companion to Edwin Morgan* (2015). His most recent books of poems are *Homecoming* (2009) and *Wild Blue: Selected Poems* (2014).

Gilles Robel, Senior Lecturer in British Studies at the Université Paris-Est, LISAA (EA 4120), Marne-la-Vallée, France, has written widely on David Hume's political thought, in particular *Lumières et conservatisme dans la* *pensée politique de David Hume* (1999) and is author of a translation and critical edition in French of Hume's *Essays (Essais moraux, politiques et littéraires et autres essais*, 2001*)*.

Pilar Somacarrera is Associate Professor of English and Postcolonial Literatures at the Autonomous University of Madrid. Her main research fields are Scottish Literature and Canadian Literature in English. In 2015, she was a visiting fellow at Edinburgh University's Institute for Advanced Studies in the Humanities with a project, 'A Postcolonial and Transatlantic Approach to Scottish-Canadian Women Writers'.

www.ingramcontent.com/pod-product-compliance
Lightning Source LLC
Chambersburg PA
CBHW050242170426
43202CB00015B/2889